T0277088

The New York Times

RED-EYE CROSSWORDS

The New York Times

RED-EYE CROSSWORDS
150 Challenging Puzzles

Edited by Will Shortz

ST. MARTIN'S GRIFFIN ❧ NEW YORK

The New York Times

RED-EYE CROSSWORDS

ACROSS

1 Bite-size sweet
10 Complains loudly
15 Locomotive
16 1946 University of Pennsylvania invention
17 1950s–'60s sitcom headliner
18 Instagram filter
19 What many cats play
20 It's snowy in Florida
22 Left
23 Oxygen tent locale, briefly
24 Home of Harpers Ferry: Abbr.
25 Flock member
27 Literary adverb
28 Dundee denial
29 Nikkei unit
30 Salmagundi
32 Prefix with phobia
33 Basilica honoree
34 Former silkworms
36 Time indicator, of sorts
37 Media giant that owns the Detroit Free Press
39 4-Down inventory
40 Gedda or Ghiaurov of opera fame
41 "Cap'n ___" (Joseph C. Lincoln novel)
42 "Phooey!"
45 Singer who said "People make music to get a reaction"
46 "Tastes terrific!"
47 Actress Gardner
48 Oriole rival
49 Junior senator from Texas
51 Food whose name means "feathers"
53 Eatery
54 Nuclei
56 Profession for Laura Bush before the White House
58 Rushed
59 "Cinderella" stepsister
60 Perfect
61 Type-A types

DOWN

1 Linguistic 30-Across
2 Record glimpsed on Norman Bates's Victrola
3 1-Down, e.g.
4 Michelin Guide recommendations
5 Lun ___ (Tuptim's beloved in "The King and I")
6 Certain rate-hike circumvention
7 Pizzeria supply
8 One logging in
9 Cashes in
10 "___ on Prop . . ." (campaign sign)
11 Over
12 Many "Jackass" stunts
13 In a state of nirvana
14 Not stay together
21 Online realm since 2006
24 Common British Isles shader
26 "Where you book matters" sloganeer
31 Some Olympic coups
32 It's 8 for O
34 Artery
35 Not going astray
37 Trattoria dish
38 Delay
39 Midway missile
42 Cook, as Swiss steak
43 Erle Stanley Gardner pseudonym
44 Shenzi, Banzai and Ed, in "The Lion King"
50 Fraternity letter
52 Hombre, once
53 Techno- tack-on
55 Dict. demarcation
57 Sidebar requester: Abbr.

by Barry C. Silk and Brad Wilber

ACROSS

1 Like cork trees and flying lizards
6 "Jersey Shore" housemate's music-biz name
14 Jersey Shore vacation option
15 Big Dipper's setting
16 One offering help in passing?
17 Take up enthusiastically
18 See 34-Down
19 Where Lee Harvey Oswald was a lathe operator
20 City where some believe Cain and Abel are buried
21 Warden in drab clothes
23 Take down with a charge
24 Spring event in the Summer Olympics?
25 Setting that makes things right?
27 Less agreeable
30 Be a lush
35 Chicken à la rey?
36 Buzzes, say
38 Tiny amount
39 Was revolting
41 Was a rocker?
43 Tie __
45 Up
46 Hyperbola parts
50 House meeting place
54 Theoretical
55 Predictor of fame
56 Elasticity
57 School meeting places
59 Photometry unit
60 Be an unhelpful interrogee
61 Luck life
62 Life or death
63 Leaf part

DOWN

1 Go on the fritz
2 Monty Python theme composer
3 Gaps
4 Like cute nerds, in slang
5 "__ did you nothing hear?": Hamlet
6 Stress, to Strauss
7 First-class regulars
8 Keeping buff?
9 Jock: Abbr.
10 Raider in the battle of the St. Lawrence
11 "__ Paw" (Oscar-winning Disney short)
12 "Eyewitness" director Peter
13 Hurdy-gurdy sound
15 Flashed
19 Tuareg rebellion locale of 2012

22 Erase
26 Three-ring setting
27 Some rescue work
28 Neighbor of Rabbit
29 Bunk
31 Foreshadow
32 One not getting benefits, say
33 Make baloney?
34 With 18-Across, software developer's concern
37 Constituent of molding sand
40 Touching scene at an airport?
42 Animation
44 European president who attended Harvard
46 Bank
47 Path

48 One of 64 in a genetic table
49 Piece of work
51 Napoleon, notably
52 Where things may be heating up
53 Molto adagio
58 Bit of sportswear
59 Head

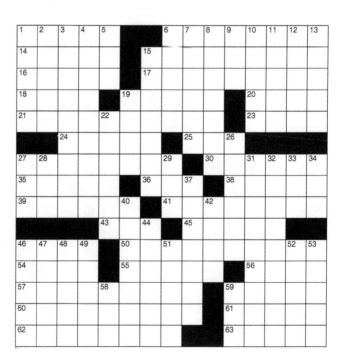

by Kyle Dolan

ACROSS

1 Attaché feature?
7 Lawrence who co-wrote "The Empire Strikes Back" and "Return of the Jedi"
13 Seat of Ireland's County Kerry
14 One of the former Barbary States
15 Pride : lions :: ___ : crows
16 "Don't get so worked up!"
17 Ordered pair?
19 ___ running
20 Moving briskly
21 Public record?
23 Not down with anything
24 Deadeye
27 Surprised expression
28 Many old B films
29 Constant critic
31 Leery of being noticed, maybe
32 Decides on
33 Symbol of liberty in the French Revolution
34 Last course, often
35 Domineering men
36 Gridiron cry
37 They deliver on Sunday
39 Ideal world?
40 Sulking peevishly
41 Underattended, say
42 Grocery staple
45 Tub accessory for the head
48 Old-fashioned promotions
50 La to la, e.g.
51 Common gathering in a public square
52 Bet
53 Menelaus' kingdom
54 Menorah inserts

DOWN

1 Bread boxes?
2 Common casino locale
3 One who wants in on the deal
4 Aged
5 Emotionally demanding
6 Dean's "Lois & Clark" co-star
7 Word puzzle popular since the 1930s
8 Bother
9 Unspecific recipe quantity
10 "If opportunity doesn't knock, build a ___": Milton Berle
11 Diploma holder, for short
12 Tiny criticisms
14 Ever since that time
16 Cribs
18 Brainstorming session aids
22 Anti-Ballistic Missile Treaty signatory, briefly
23 Flimsy lock
24 1978 disco hit featuring the warning "Don't fall in love"
25 Body of water belatedly added to the course of the Erie Canal
26 Discussed
30 Mafioso foes
32 Bahla Fort site
36 Clicker, of a sort
38 Michael who once led Disney
41 Decrees
42 Omar of TV and film
43 Clutch
44 Memory unit prefix
46 Diplomatic assignment
47 Joins
49 Unsteady walker, maybe

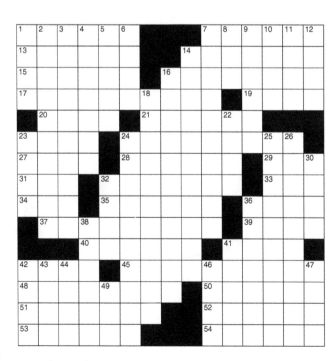

by Patrick Berry

4

ACROSS

1 It has a close "Kentucky" cousin
16 Tax deferral options
17 Water gun fight?
18 Tumblers
19 Nonprofessional
20 "Thus weary of the world, away she ___": Shak.
21 Burnable medium, briefly
23 Slender runner
25 One may remove grease with elbow grease
30 SC Johnson brand
32 Does a Ludacris impersonation
34 Grid great Greasy
35 Not the least bit
37 "That's expensive!"
39 Sum symbol
40 Rice alternative
42 Stop on Amtrak's California Zephyr
43 Dead player?
45 Key contraction
46 ___ ed
47 Larry of the original "West Side Story"
49 Went nowhere
51 They're usually pixelated on TV
59 Kelp is a natural source of it
60 One who orders trunks to be moved?
61 Member of a drill team?

8 Sawmill supplier
9 Fish in a dragon roll
10 They have bills and appear on bills
11 Renowned boxing gym in Brooklyn
12 Outer limits
13 Diomedes speared him
14 Having good balance
15 They were retired in '03
21 Like new notes
22 Freshwater aquarium favorite
23 Many a dama: Abbr.
24 Deck
26 Brand
27 Renaissance composer of "Missa Papae Marcelli"
28 How troglodytes live
29 Clean out

31 DiMaggio and others
33 Fitting decision
36 Wisconsin county or its seat
38 A.L. East team, on scoreboards
41 Really cheap shots?
44 Monthly
48 Spanish royal
49 Attic promenades
50 Book review?
51 Weigh-in section?
52 Woody trunk
53 Korean War weapon
54 Abbr. by Hook or by Cook
55 Drs. often take over for them
56 iPhone talker
57 Fall scene
58 Fundació Joan Miró designer

DOWN

1 U.P.S. deliveries: Abbr.
2 Poor as ___ (destitute)
3 Belly dancers' bands?
4 Native of Caprica on "Battlestar Galactica"
5 Corker
6 Done to ___
7 Alternatives to racks

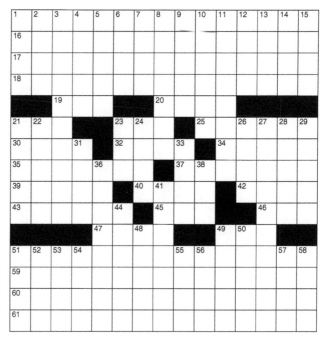

by Martin Ashwood-Smith

ACROSS

1 Vacation destination
6 Spots for thirsty travelers
15 Scooter
16 It's rendered in the kitchen
17 Group studying torts and procedures, typically
18 Psychiatric hospitals
19 Hardly a free spirit?
20 "Thinking back . . ."
21 They often precede showers
23 German port on the Baltic
24 Large bill holder
25 Historical role in Spielberg's "Munich"
26 Mrs. Lincoln's family
27 Cry of surprise
28 Camp accouterments
29 Dandy
30 Stage, as a historical scene
32 Like a ballerina
36 Fox tribe neighbor
37 Operates, as a booth
38 Be useful
39 Cars whose only color until 1952 was bottle green
42 One of the 12 tribes of Israel
43 Just dandy
44 Oscar-winning film based partly on the book "The Master of Disguise"
45 Bowling splits in which the 5 and 10 pins remain
47 Big name in classical education?
49 1969 role for Dustin Hoffman
50 Recovering

51 It's written with a minus sign
52 Freebie often containing alcohol
53 "To conclude . . ."
54 Extra protection from the elements
55 Source of morning stimulation, maybe

DOWN

1 Harder to see through, say
2 Queen or her subject?
3 Opportunity for a singer or comedian
4 The Shroud of Turin and others
5 Car that offered Polar Air air-conditioning
6 Disobeys standing orders?

7 New York's ___ Cultural Center, promoter of Hellenic civilization
8 Requiring greater magnification
9 Some world leaders
10 Pregnant, maybe
11 Some C.I.A. doings
12 Yellow
13 Inveighed (against)
14 Changing places
22 Bygone station name
26 Put to waste?
28 Some Quidditch equipment
29 End of story?
31 "Don't worry about it"
32 Herb whose name is derived from the Latin for "to wash"
33 One employing trompe l'oeil effects

34 Pets
35 "Now, look here!"
37 It serves as a reminder
39 Footwear similar to klompen
40 Childish retort
41 Terrible time?
42 Reach, in a way
43 ___ Gleason, Tony winner for "Into the Woods"
45 Like wigwams and igloos
46 Have some catching up to do
48 Captain's place

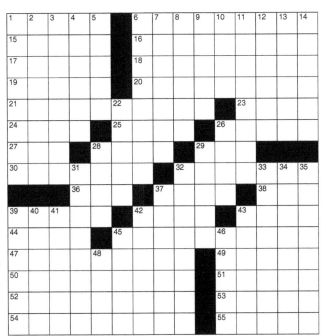

by Kevin G. Der

ACROSS

1 Fast-paced alternative to Scrabble
12 Lance cpl.'s org.
15 It has a Page Navigation menu option
16 100 sawbucks
17 Cop car, to a CBer
18 Inhibiter of free speech
19 Exchange some words?
20 Follower of Bush or Clinton
21 Many an Israeli
23 Part of some bargain store names
24 Do-or-die situation
27 ___-to-be
28 Green on a screen
30 Texas' ___ Duro Canyon
31 High style of the 1700s
32 Oppenheimer's agcy.
34 Vocal trio
36 1983 song with the lyric "Let's leave Chicago to the Eskimos"
40 Women, poetically, with "the"
41 Nonverbal equivalent of "You have got to be kidding me!"
43 Cannes neighbors?
44 Financier Kreuger called the Match King
45 Start another tour
47 "Man!"
50 Alternative to nuts?
51 Like 36 of this puzzle's answers
53 Grease monkey's pocket item
55 Formal identification
57 Mix for a mixer
58 Draw to an end
59 Spanish gentleman

60 Professional organizers?
64 Fidelity offering, briefly
65 Feature of 007's car
66 Cornerback Law and others
67 Beyoncé alter ego

DOWN

1 Katharine Lee ___, "America the Beautiful" lyricist
2 Court wear, maybe
3 "I swear, man!"
4 Have an edge against
5 Its website has lesson plans, briefly
6 Vintage fabric
7 Get set
8 Sharp knock
9 Org. whose members look down in the mouth?
10 Its flag has an eagle in the center: Abbr.
11 Some foreign misters
12 Wear that was one of "Oprah's Favorite Things" four times
13 Circumnavigator's way
14 "Transformers" actress, 2007
22 Impugn
24 Call from a tree
25 Tenor ___
26 Trio in Greek myth
29 Round houses?
33 Bow no longer shot
35 Hits with wit
36 2007 book subtitled "Confessions of the Killer"
37 John's place
38 Simple winds
39 "The Twilight Saga" vampire

42 "A Severed Head" novelist, 1961
46 Itinerary start
48 Thing taken to a slip
49 Ulcer treater
52 Mad bit
54 Beau chaser?
56 Endings of rock names
58 One way to crack
61 1977 Steely Dan title track
62 One side in some chalk talks
63 One might show muscles, in brief

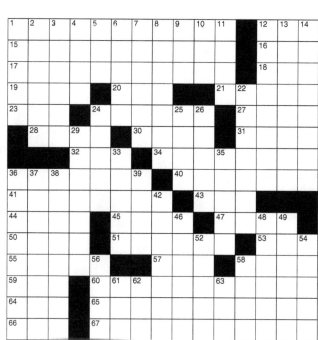

by David Steinberg

ACROSS

1 Frigid
7 Question at the door
15 Miss out on a board
16 "'Sup?"
17 Subject for a golf lesson
18 Emphatic approval
19 Petition
20 51-Down and others: Abbr.
21 Nighttime
22 Hunky-dory
23 Clobbered
25 Birds in a clutch
26 Group that no one on earth has ever joined
29 Sun disk wearer, in myth
30 Petition
31 "That's quite enough!"
35 Abridged
37 "What's it gonna be?"
38 Feature of a certain bandit
39 20-Down, e.g.
40 Nut
41 What a nonconformist ignores
44 "___ magnifique!"
46 Big employer in Hartford, Conn.
47 Canal checker?: Abbr.
48 One who's trustworthy?
49 Doesn't just grab
50 Green shade
52 Public, as views
54 Instruments played with mizraabs
56 "I'd like you to leave"
57 Nips in the bud
58 Bank guards?
59 Ambush locale in Episode 1 of "The Lone Ranger"

DOWN

1 "Cute" remarks
2 Thallium sulfate, e.g.
3 Figure out on the street?
4 Stick with it
5 One way to pay
6 Civic leader?
7 "Beg pardon?!"
8 Shop alternative
9 Takes credit?
10 Gabriel or Giorgio
11 Basic library stock
12 Iron-pumper
13 Australia's ___ Rock
14 Lose a lot?
20 Nissan ___
22 Italian friend
24 Question in a long-distance relationship
25 Humble dwellings
27 Civil engineering safety feature

28 Square, in old slang, as indicated by forming a square with one's hands
32 1969 hit with the repeated lyric "Big wheel keep on turnin'"
33 So that one can
34 Takes some hits
36 Red states
37 Humble dwellings
39 Short trunks
42 Possible protein shake ingredient
43 Sample in a swab test
44 Weber per square meter
45 Turn red, say
48 Drill bits?
49 Away from port
51 Christopher Columbus Transcontinental Hwy.

53 Kind of port
54 Pouch
55 Frequent form request: Abbr.

by Ian Livengood

ACROSS

1 Body that doesn't remain at rest?
7 Having way too much on one's plate
14 It's not normal
16 Dismissive confession follower
17 Start liking a lot
18 Rare electee
19 ___ B
20 Ingredient in an Americano
22 Like Fabergé eggs
23 Repeated battle cry
25 Megadyne fractions
27 Chef DiSpirito
29 Dog it
30 Texts, e.g.: Abbr.
34 "The Valley of Amazement" novelist, 2013
36 Org. for female shooters
38 Inuit knife
39 Writer of the ethnography "Germania"
41 Get out of the blasted state?
43 What isn't the small print?: Abbr.
44 Suffocating blanket
46 Get off the drive, say
47 Food factory stock
49 Ninny
51 Utter
52 20th-century treaty topic
55 Priceline possibilities
56 Release
59 2012 Pro Bowl player Chris
61 Once-common "commonly"
62 Game that can't be played
64 She wrote "The Proper Care and Feeding of Husbands"

66 "Spread the happy" sloganeer
67 Queen's weapon
68 Producing zip
69 Strips at a pageant

DOWN

1 Given a 20 for food, say
2 Drink that often makes a person sick
3 Road hog
4 Record label abbr.
5 Johns of Britain
6 John of Britain
7 Recife-to-Rio dir.
8 Bible
9 Like Huns
10 Refusal to speak
11 Flatten, as a rivet
12 Throw out
13 Keep from

15 Demonstrate a wide range on a range?
21 Gone private?
24 Early CliffsNotes subheading
26 Restin' piece?
28 Energy bar ingredients
31 "You guessed it . . ."
32 Like some diets that avoid pasta
33 People people
35 Ninny
37 Lincoln and others
40 Diesel discharge
42 Primary and secondary, briefly
45 Bunches
48 Habitual high achiever?
50 Label stable
53 C.D.C. concern
54 "Phooey!"

56 Some heavy planters
57 Like some flags: Abbr.
58 Not full-bodied
60 "Modern Gallantry" pen name
63 Swimming gold medalist Park ___-hwan
65 Key component: Abbr.

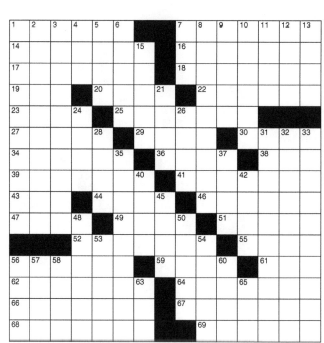

by James Mulhern

ACROSS

1 "No more wasting time!"
16 Pixar, e.g.
17 Was just getting started
18 Some foreign friends
19 Union ___: Abbr.
20 Breathers
21 "Dawson's Creek" star James Van Der ___
22 It's a state
24 Unduplicated
25 ___ Toy Barn ("Toy Story 2" setting)
26 Parked cars
28 A Kennedy
29 Fix
31 Makes a fuss over, with "on"
33 What Sports Illustrated's annual Swimsuit Issue has a lot of
35 Marker's mark maker
39 Bottom line?
41 Cruise
42 Professional org. with a "healthy" balance sheet
45 Musical instrument for a geisha
47 MASH unit
48 Pioneering map publisher William
50 1998 film in which Donny Osmond has a singing role
51 One on the staff?
52 Thin as ___
54 Romanian capital
55 Albert's sitcom co-star
56 Numbats
59 Washington report starter
60 Charm

DOWN

1 Caribbean capital, to locals
2 Cloisonné, e.g.
3 Sets things straight
4 Trash talk
5 "Dream Caused by the Flight of a Bee Around a Pomegranate a Second Before Awakening" artist
6 Tribe of Chief Shaumonekusse
7 It hangs around trees
8 Immobilized
9 Needing
10 Grp. that's got your number?
11 Texting ta-ta
12 Many Rwandans
13 Defensive reply
14 Nitpick
15 Gave a boost
22 Practice test?
23 Square things
26 Setting for "Ocean's 11"
27 Actor Alain
30 Strain
32 Home for E. B. White's Wilbur
34 Pose as
36 "Live más" sloganeer
37 Classic song that begins "When my baby / When my baby smiles at me"
38 "CSI" star William
40 Few of them were made after 1929
42 Source of the word "admiral"
43 One of two in a rumba
44 Pineapples: Sp.
46 Prepares, as some mushrooms
49 "If I ___ Have You" (2001 Best Original Song Oscar winner)
51 Kind of star
53 "Leading With My Chin" memoirist
55 Air force?
57 Slip into
58 Grp. with the 1971 gold album "Pictures at an Exhibition"

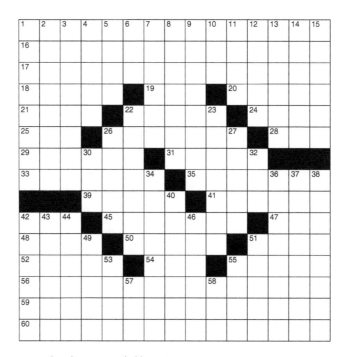

by Chris A. McGlothlin

10

ACROSS

1 Her 1994 memoir has the chapter "Desert Storm"
12 Plant visitor
15 What watts and volt-amperes have
16 Elementary education, briefly
17 High interest?
18 Choice for a portrait
19 U.K. honours
20 What you may open the door for
21 Aftermath
22 Fun time
23 Toddler coddler
24 Display options, briefly
25 Serpent with a Zulu name
26 Zany
28 On track to win
31 Use pumice on, perhaps
33 He wrote of a "vorpal blade"
35 Gets to a seat, say
36 Member of the German Expressionist group Die Brücke
38 Sky boxes?
39 Exhibit explainer
40 Strawberry, for one
42 Tom Clancy's "Every ___ Tiger"
43 Polaris or Procyon
44 Persian language unit?
47 "The Wizard of Oz" farmhand
48 Psychoanalyst Melanie
49 Hometown of the mathematician Fibonacci
50 Much like
51 Words accompanying a low bow
53 X or Y lead-in
54 Uno's alternative

55 Suzanne, e.g.: Abbr.
56 Light insufficiently

DOWN

1 Muddle
2 Great Rift Valley port
3 Dodges
4 Some 27-Down
5 Prefix with culture
6 Like some inspections
7 Danger dinger
8 Old Sony format
9 Come together
10 Cock-a-leekie eater
11 Incubator
12 Sent out in waves?
13 Composer of several "Gnossiennes"
14 Man's name that sounds noble
21 Cooperation exclamation

23 "___ With the Long Neck" (Parmigianino painting)
24 Pro athlete in purple and gold
25 Cary's "Blonde Venus" co-star
26 Dispenser of Duff Beer
27 Desk set
28 Made no mistakes on
29 No breakfast for a vegan
30 TV antiheroine for 41 years
32 One whose shifts shift
34 Development site
37 Warrant
41 Handle
43 Subject to change
44 Screw up
45 Business fraudster Billie Sol ___

46 General who won 1794's Battle of Fallen Timbers
47 Navigates a switchback, in part
48 Severinsbrücke's city
49 One may be fingered
51 "Revolution" or "Hound Dog" starter
52 Port named after a U.S. president, informally

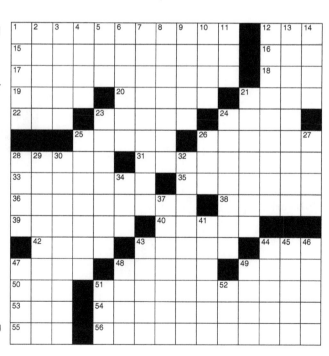

by Will Nediger

ACROSS

1 Drill command to rifle carriers
12 Bit of nonsense famously replacing "strangers in the night"
14 1979 ABBA single
16 Emblem of a pharaoh
17 Hooey
18 Show with an early episode titled "Crate 'n Burial"
19 Dragon roll ingredient
20 Like grade skippers
22 N.Y.C.-based grp. with its own police department
24 Potential fire hazard
26 Philatelic collectible
27 Littermates compete for them
29 Not had by
30 Sty chore
32 Like Lesbos and Lemnos
34 Patriotic chant
36 Synthetic fiber used in bicycle tires and bulletproof vests
39 Fourth-brightest star in the sky
43 Big Green rivals
44 John P. Marquand's "The Late George ___"
46 Family name in "Look Homeward, Angel"
47 Part of a U.S. president's name that's Dutch for "neighbors"
49 Something one might hang in a street
50 Davis of the screen
51 Nabokov heroine
52 Throughout, in verse
54 Suffix of saccharides
56 Prefix with saccharides
57 Is guilty of petitio principii
61 Got a +2 on
62 500m or 5,000m competitor, say

DOWN

1 Florida food fish
2 Permanent data storer
3 "Your Movie Sucks" author
4 One of Utah's state symbols
5 Paste holder?
6 Passeport detail
7 It helps produce a kitty
8 Fivers
9 Longtime first name in TV talk
10 Century-starting year
11 Nobody's opposite
12 Wretched
13 Code broken by some singers
14 Startled reactions
15 John with an Oscar and a Tony
21 Turn off a lot
23 Solution for toys in the attic?
25 Common standard for model railroads
27 Twinkling topper
28 Flip
31 Spot that may be on the environment, briefly
33 Fig. that's in the neighborhood
35 Query after a wipeout
36 Food stuck in preparation
37 Lost
38 Witchy women
40 Worse for wear?
41 Not printed up?
42 Container for a round
45 Like much baby food
48 "I would ___ surprised"
50 Plague
53 Actress Jennifer of "Pride and Prejudice"
55 Sonic creator
58 More than nibble
59 Snap targets, for short
60 Mooring rope

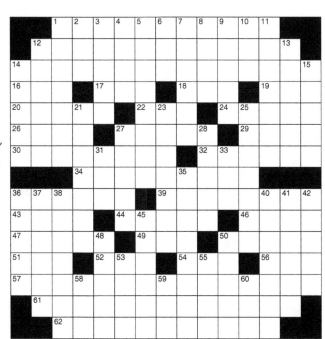

by Ned White

12

ACROSS

1 Things millions of people have received in history?: Abbr.
4 Snap
15 Dieter's beef?
16 Foreigner hit in the musical film "Rock of Ages"
17 ___ poco (soon: It.)
18 Western way
19 Guy
21 Golfer who turned pro at age 15
22 ≠
23 Ticket number?
24 Lock combinations?
25 Jewish community org.
26 Running back's target
27 Five minutes in a campaign itinerary, maybe
29 Physics class subj.
30 Chestnut, say
31 2013 Spike Jonze love story
34 Piece in a fianchetto opening
36 Squalid
38 Yo-yo
39 Play with someone else's toy?
43 "Check it out!," in Chihuahua
44 Induces a shudder in
45 Hominy makers extract it
46 One attached to a handle
48 Decks
49 Something a baton carrier might pick up
50 ___ passu (on equal footing)
51 Head, for short
52 This point forward
53 Sri Lankan export
56 Day of the week of the great stock market crash, Oct. 29, 1929

57 It once had many satellites in its orbit
58 Prefix with gram
59 Prized cuts
60 Nutritional inits.

DOWN

1 Biblical figure famously painted nude by Rembrandt
2 Certain temple locale
3 Not likely to blush
4 Steep-sided inlet
5 It may be on the line
6 Nickname on old political buttons
7 Watchmaker's cleaning tool
8 Threesome needed in Wagner's "Ring" cycle
9 Bar ___
10 Call routing abbr.
11 Peewee

12 Useful item if you 39-Across
13 "Three Sisters" sister
14 Fool
20 Tree with burs
24 Shipping choice
25 Protest vehemently
27 Low-priced American vodka known affectionately (and ironically) as "Russia's finest"
28 Brewers' hot spots
31 Music genre of Poison and Guns N' Roses
32 Poet arrested for treason in 1945
33 Golden Globes nominee who was a Golden Gloves boxer
35 River through Silesia
37 Reddish remnant
40 Quit working

41 Austrian neighbor
42 "___ alive!"
44 Curb
46 Health store snack ingredient
47 "Inside the Actors Studio" channel
49 Nancy Drew never left hers behind
50 Honeycomb maker
51 "I'm game"
52 Left or right, say
54 "No kiddin'!"
55 "The Power to Surprise" sloganeer

by Doug Peterson and Brad Wilber

ACROSS

1 Bivouac, maybe
9 Presses
14 Classic parental advice to bored children
16 Needle
17 Line of suits?
18 1970s NBC courtroom drama
19 Tacoma-to-Spokane dir.
20 Lupin of fiction
22 Scheming
23 ___ finger
26 Bond phrase
27 20-Across, e.g., informally
28 Gramps, to Günter
30 Wise
31 Standard offspring
32 Wordsworth or Coleridge
35 String bean's opposite
36 Phrase from Virgil appropriate for Valentine's Day
38 Favorites
39 Handy work in a theater?
40 Gifts of flowers
41 Carly ___ Jepsen, singer with the 2012 album "Kiss"
42 Yamaguchi's 1992 Olympics rival
43 Agent of psychedelic therapy
44 Unhinged
46 Pig leader?
50 Spanish name suffix
51 Dr. Seuss title character
53 Liquor letters
54 ___ Vedra Beach, Fla.
56 Entrepreneur who's well-supplied?
59 Full-length
60 Going nowhere
61 Cold forecast
62 "Clever thinking!"

DOWN

1 Adrien of cosmetics
2 Valuable chess piece, to Juan Carlos
3 Like horses
4 P.G.A. stat
5 Cool ___
6 Magical opener
7 Fate personified, in mythology
8 Delivers a romantic Valentine's Day surprise, maybe
9 Total
10 Root word?
11 TV listings info
12 Forever
13 Informal goodbye
15 "Don't stop now!"
21 Quiet break
24 Sticks figures?
25 Building materials?
29 Base letters
31 Home of Lafayette College
32 It was used to make the first compass
33 Dodger's talent
34 Policing an area
35 Broods
36 Fictional island with a small population
37 Prefix with -graph
41 Paris's ___ La Fayette
44 Some U.N. votes
45 Skateboarding trick used to leap over obstacles
47 Like Humpty Dumpty
48 Me.-to-Fla. route
49 The Friendly Islands
52 First name in blues
55 Wine container
57 "All the same . . ."
58 ___ de guerre

by Bruce Haight

14

ACROSS

1. Position papers?
10. Joneses
15. Vanity case?
16. When Epifanía is celebrated
17. Picayune
18. Not barred
19. Low prime, in Paris
20. Newfoundland, in Naples and Nogales
22. Grp. that suspended Honduras from 2009 to '11
24. Messages using Stickies, say
25. Certain guy "ISO" someone
28. Emmy-nominated show every year from 2006 to '09
32. Suffix with 18-Across
33. Just-once link
35. Beta testers, e.g.
36. Steely Dan's title liar
37. One blowing up a lottery machine?
38. Prozac alternative
39. Winnebago relative
40. Odds and ends
41. Clan female
42. Mexican president Enrique ___ Nieto
43. Clear
44. Crane settings
46. Van follower, often
47. Japanese guitar brand
49. Toy type, for short
51. Flippers, e.g.
55. Members of a joint task force?
59. "It's ___ wind . . ."
60. Dole
62. Green with five Grammys
63. Writer of the graphic novel "Watchmen"
64. Home to the Villa Hügel
65. Outdoor contemplation location

DOWN

1. Didn't spoil
2. Sun or stress
3. MSG ingredient?
4. Certain DNA test
5. Follows a physical request?
6. ___ vez más (over again: Sp.)
7. Photoshop addition
8. Mention on Yelp, say
9. Aspire PC maker
10. Tycoon Stanford
11. Bridge opening option, briefly
12. Managed to get through
13. Where to read a plot summary?
14. Totally out
21. Overnight activity
23. Iconic "Seinfeld" role
25. Eighth-century Apostle of Germany
26. Old collar stiffeners
27. Engagement parties?
29. Company that added four letters to its name in 1997
30. Sides in a classic battle
31. Longtime Cincinnati Pops conductor Kunzel
34. Pavement caution
36. One of a silent force?
44. Longtime name in banking
45. Its seat is Santa Rosa
48. Lawyer on "Ally McBeal"
50. No modest abode
52. 2009 Grammy winner for "Make It Mine"
53. Farm block
54. "Mr. Mom" director Dragoti
56. Cross
57. Purpose of many a shot
58. Old carbine
61. End to end?

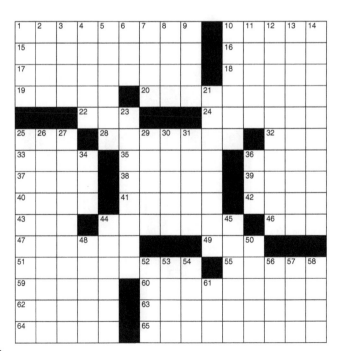

by Julian Lim

ACROSS

1 Freight hopper
6 Much-hailed group
10 Pretreater target
14 Slab strengthener
15 Days long gone
16 End of an Asian capital's name
17 Queen's Chapel designer ___ Jones
18 Stamp act?
20 Like some unhealthy relationships
22 Not so normal
23 Be cognizant of
24 Lamebrain
26 Certain letter attachment
27 Unpleasantly surprised
29 ___ Altos, Calif.
30 Provider of early projections
34 Catchphrase that encourages extravagance
35 Sky hooks?
36 "___ fly through the air with the greatest of ease"
37 DQ offerings
38 Worker who handles your case?
42 Originate
43 With this, you'll probably manage
46 Squared away
48 Panhandler, of a sort?
50 They run out of clothing
52 Stand
53 Fill-in
54 Make cuts, say
55 It would "make other cars seem ordinary," per ads
56 Brewery apparatus
57 Breaks down
58 Teammate of Robinson

DOWN

1 Many folk bands
2 Girl's name that means "born again"
3 Stand
4 Holiday travelers?
5 One with a thing for laughter?
6 Spiral-shaped particle accelerators
7 1998 purchaser of Netscape
8 Head piece?
9 Bob in the Songwriters Hall of Fame
10 Bandies words
11 Swingers
12 Another time
13 18th-century Hapsburg monarch Maria ___
19 Las Vegas block?
21 Put forward
25 Needs
27 Snarky comments
28 Overbearing types
30 Buildings often segregated by floor
31 Reserved
32 Worker also known as a cordwainer
33 Scams
34 Leaves from the Orient
35 Big name in outdoor art
39 Made slow progress
40 Nabokov's longest novel
41 Furry toys
43 Canadian ranger
44 Rounded items?
45 Tarsus location
47 Change
49 Get behind something?
51 Lightly tease

by Patrick Berry

16

ACROSS

1 Ones who think things are good as gold?
11 Like metals used by 1-Across
15 Feared sight on the Spanish Main
16 Obama's favorite character on "The Wire"
17 Like some parents
18 Big long-distance carrier?
19 Coastal fish consumers
20 Much may follow it
21 Composer of the opera "Rusalka"
23 Deal with
25 People might pass for them, for short
27 High line in the Middle East
28 Small cell
30 Brand of body washes
32 Grp. with the Office of Iraq Analysis
33 Art that uses curse words?
37 Volt-ampere
38 Takes the plunge
39 Peak transmission setting of old?
41 Declines, with "out"
42 Fall apart
44 Score abbr.
45 First name of Woodstock's last performer
46 Split second?
47 Golden, in Granada
49 Hit with skits, for short
51 Get off the drive, say
55 No-gooder
57 2012 baseball All-Star Kinsler
59 Some plans for the future, briefly
60 Rackets
61 High spirits?

64 Land capturer, in literature
65 "Bummer"
66 Tied
67 Whip wielder

DOWN

1 Vaulted areas
2 Tall order at a British pub
3 Big picker-upper?
4 Frequent Monet subjects
5 Projection in the air, for short
6 Kind of bust
7 "___ a man in Reno" ("Folsom Prison Blues" lyric)
8 Well-trained boxer, maybe
9 Punk rocker Armstrong with a 2012 Grammy

10 Reached 100, say
11 Near to one's heart
12 First drink ever ordered by James Bond
13 Do-gooder
14 Composer called a "gymnopédiste"
22 Woe, in Yiddish
24 Symbols of might
26 Scuzz
29 Facebook connections in Florence?
31 Start sputtering, say
33 Aid in fast networking
34 One getting messages by word of mouth?
35 Site of the 1992 Republican National Convention
36 Very small (and very important) matter
37 Like some missed field goals

40 Weapon in "The Mikado"
43 Telejournalist's item
45 Part of many a training regimen
48 Plant in subsequent seasons
50 "Swing Shift" Oscar nominee
52 In the back
53 Game stew
54 Locale of London Stansted Airport
56 "Good ___ A'mighty!"
58 Side in an Indian restaurant
62 Certain sorority chapter
63 Tapping grp.

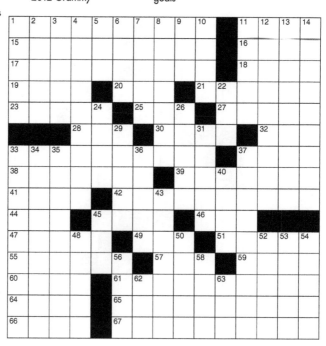

by Evan Birnholz

17

ACROSS

1 Modern-day locale of ancient Nineveh
5 People down under?
11 Exceeds the speed limit?
14 Exceed the speed limit, maybe
15 Company with an Energy Boost line
16 Minim
17 Terse admission
18 It'll keep a roof over your head
20 Fall, in a way
21 Like a good lookout
22 Bouillabaisse seasoning
23 They soar at the opera
25 When to do a pressing job
26 Mitochondrion-made material, briefly
27 Back, to a shellback
29 Investments since 1975
38 What a tropical tourist definitely doesn't want to bring home
39 It helps you let go
40 Many of them play at the Olympics
41 Some Windows systems
42 Shakespeare sonnet mentioning Philomel's mournful hymns
43 Title for Liszt
46 Gigantic
52 Text with Numbers
54 Patent
55 Carlito's way
56 Street view
58 First name in popular shorts
59 Bond bit
60 Coors Field player
61 Almost never
62 Really dirty
63 Try again
64 Salk Institute architect Louis

DOWN

1 From Galway, say
2 Cuts into a pizza, often
3 Sailing through
4 Last thing seen by a proof reader?
5 Some Wall Street contracts
6 Go on __
7 Exist abroad?
8 Applies polish to?
9 Flew
10 Squad cmdr.
11 R&B group with the 1972 hit "Back Stabbers," with "the"
12 Proselytizers push it
13 Pickle, e.g.
19 Finder's query
21 Like some helmets and shields
24 Couldn't hit pitches
27 Singer who's a Backstreet Boy's brother
28 Sir James Galway, e.g.
29 Dodgers' foes
30 Hindu hero
31 Legions
32 Suffix with Edward
33 It's around 6 on the Mohs scale
34 "The Lion King" lion
35 Get to
36 "Let me __!"
37 Philatelic goals
43 When the first dogwatch ends
44 It's not a cheap shot
45 Bombers' locale
46 Spelunker's aid
47 Conjure
48 City with major avenues named Cincinnati and Columbus
49 First name among socialites
50 It means nothing
51 All gone
53 Mann's man
57 Ill-wisher
58 Thai pan

by Martin Ashwood-Smith

18

ACROSS

1. 1987 #1 hit with the line "Yo no soy marinero, soy capitán"
8. Throwback
15. Samsung Galaxy Note rival
16. Go-ahead for un hombre
17. Forward to some followers
18. Curt chat closing
19. Where Melville's Billy Budd went
20. Hubble sighting
22. Jesse Jackson, for one: Abbr.
24. Like some double-deckers
28. One's own worst critic?
32. Put off
34. Dayton-to-Toledo dir.
35. Subjected to venomous attacks?
38. Four roods
40. Pawnbroker, in slang
41. Travel safety grp.
42. Modern device seen on a bridge
45. L.A. law figure
46. Take a little hair off, maybe
47. To date
49. Den delivery
52. Beats by ___ (brand of audio equipment)
53. One picking up speed, say?
55. They're game
59. Sack dress?
63. Dish often served with a tamarind sauce
65. Disc protector
66. Carrier with a pink logo
67. Like some stockings
68. If it's repeated, it's nothing new

DOWN

1. Turkey tip?
2. Burlesques
3. Moderate
4. Norton Antivirus target
5. Tina Turner's real middle name
6. Welcome message to international travelers
7. Danza, e.g.
8. Invite to one's penthouse
9. Proof of purchase
10. Ghanaian region known for gold and cocoa
11. Needle or nettle
12. Having five sharps
13. ___ milk
14. III, in Rome
21. Novel groups?
23. They make quick admissions decisions, for short
25. Ink
26. Come by
27. Openly admitted, as in court
28. They sometimes lead to runs
29. Straighten out
30. Italian brewer since 1846
31. Blood members, e.g.
33. Fund
36. Spirit
37. Emmy category, informally
39. Food brand originally called Froffles
43. Photog
44. Cry with a salute
48. Ignored
50. Fade out
51. Like loose stones
54. Decides
56. ___ Drive, thoroughfare by the Lincoln Memorial in Washington
57. Modern posting locale
58. Produced stories
59. .doc alternative
60. Bird: Prefix
61. The Clintons' degs.
62. Cousin of "verdammt"
64. Suffix with official or fan

by Ian Livengood and J.A.S.A. Crossword Class

19

ACROSS

1 Cause for squirming
9 Container for Rip Van Winkle
15 TV show that debuted on 11/3/93 (and start of a parent's distressed cry?)
16 Furnishing in many a tearoom
17 Officer's "gift"
18 Lemony, for example
19 Roles, metaphorically
20 ___' Pea
22 "The king of terrors," per Job 18
23 Anklebones
25 In the company of
27 Guilty pleasure?
31 Poetic member of a Greek nonet
32 Having a gaping hole, say
33 Org. in "Breaking Bad"
36 Setting for "The Shining"
37 Bogart role
39 TV show that debuted on 9/22/04 (middle of the cry)
40 Corporate giant co-founded by Thomas Watson
41 Jackie with acting chops
42 Sit on it
43 TV show that debuted on 1/5/70 (end of the cry)
47 Greek hunter trained by Chiron
49 Language that gave us "slogan," originally meaning "battle cry"
50 Dreaded sort?
51 Outside: Prefix
53 Noted septet
57 Trojan rivals
59 Transfer, as wine
61 Merino, Suffolk and Dorset
62 Like Christmas candles, typically
63 "Says who?," e.g.
64 So-so

DOWN

1 It may come with a bite
2 Pet project?
3 "Etta ___" (old comic strip)
4 Worked up
5 Turner of pages in history
6 Put on a key?
7 Isolate, somehow
8 Burnsian "ago"
9 Govt. agency that supports competition
10 Presented
11 See (to)
12 Thing often controlled by a remote
13 Drops
14 Not in Germany?
21 Ending with dog or jug
24 Flurry
26 Word on a biblical wall
27 Certain playoff game
28 Zodiac symbol
29 Requirement for special handling?
30 Swiss standard
34 To be in ancient times?
35 Subj. line alert
37 Chucklehead
38 Alexander who directed "Nebraska"
39 Guiding light
41 Pledge, e.g.
42 Literary inits.
44 Marco Rubio, for one
45 Straight
46 Will Smith flick of 2004
47 Subject of a celebration on the last Friday in April
48 Chisel
52 Lead-in to Apple
54 Trix alternative?
55 Inter ___
56 Ending with inter-
58 Retired boomer
60 Texter's "No way!"

by Matt Ginsberg

ACROSS

1 Cooler idea?
10 Home to the Great Mosque
15 It included a moonwalk
16 Spirit of St. Petersburg?
17 One stocking bars
18 West African capital
19 Old sitcom sot
20 Pimienta's partner
21 Many instant message recipients
22 "Sketches" pseudonym
23 Bad-tempered
25 Compress, as a file
26 Turn the air blue
28 Where many games can be viewed
29 Prefix with data
30 Motor problems
32 Fat-derived
34 Havana highball
37 Recite mechanically
38 Swank
40 Word before red
41 Beech house?
42 Quarter of zwölf
44 Tables in western scenes
48 Word after red
49 Like time, inexorably
51 "___ I forsook the crowded solitude": Wordsworth
52 Walters portrayer on "S.N.L."
54 Dance piece?
55 Thé addition
56 Produce sentimental notes?
57 Big-name web crawler
59 "The Asphalt Jungle" revolves around one
60 Like Francisco Goya
61 "Breaking Away" director
62 She "made a fool of everyone," in song

DOWN

1 A. J. ___, author of the best seller "The Know-It-All: One Man's Humble Quest to Become the Smartest Person in the World"
2 Director of "The 40-Year-Old Virgin" and "This Is 40"
3 Turn positive, say
4 Some Yale degs.
5 Nellie who wrote "Ten Days in a Mad-House"
6 Martini accompanier?
7 Uses a drunkometer, e.g.
8 Provençal spreads
9 100-at currency unit
10 It was run in the 1980s–'90s
11 Abbr. for the listless?
12 Tab alternative
13 Big name in allergy relief
14 It's flown in
21 ___ Anne's (pretzel maker)
23 Ultra ___
24 Quick missions?
27 Slightly biased?
29 Like some finishes
31 Hole in one on a par 5 hole
33 "No ___ is worse than bad advice": Sophocles
34 Bahrain, Bhutan or Brunei
35 Clearing
36 Popular line of footwear?
39 Endurance race, briefly
40 Cardiff Giant, e.g.
43 Cry for another piece
45 Starfish setting
46 Some opera passages
47 Parlor piece
49 Word on a restroom door
50 Loose
53 Thing twitched on "Bewitched"
55 River known for the goldfields in its basin
57 Sign on an interstate
58 "___ Tarantos" (1963 film)

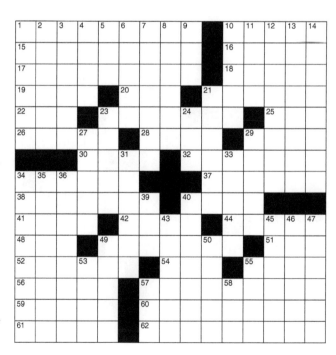

by David Steinberg

ACROSS

1 Did some above-average work
6 Doesn't just tear up
10 One way to get the beat going?
13 Master, in Mysore
14 Hostiles
16 "Well, well, well!"
17 He may be trying to unload crates
20 "Am ___ France?": King Lear
21 Jeans reinforcer
22 They're easily fleeced
23 Chinese dish eponym
24 See 39-Across
25 Magazine industry's equivalent of a Pulitzer
27 Not nixed
29 Composition of some wreaths
31 Living or dead follower
32 Yom Kippur War setting
34 Dam designer: Abbr.
35 Vet
36 Mutating, highly resistant microbe
39 Lang. in which "friends" is 24-Across
40 Start of an intermission?
41 Boo Boo Bear's co-creator
42 "___ name I love" ("America" lyric)
43 Shop spinner
44 Campus letter
45 Fence alternative
47 Old paper parts
49 Monitor option, for short
52 "___ back!"
53 Kind of training done by music majors
54 The shorter you are?
55 Tend to work without a net
58 He proclaimed "I shook up the world"
59 Gervasi who directed 2012's "Hitchcock"
60 Shake in an opera house
61 Year Charles IX was born
62 Rectangular paving stone
63 Unlikely bruiser

DOWN

1 Test pilot's protection
2 Mecca or Medina
3 1985 Ralph McInerny novel
4 Support
5 Longtime airer of "Any Questions?"
6 Place for a delivery
7 Withdrawing words
8 Withdrawing
9 Range of sizes, briefly
10 Mathematics branch associated with fractals
11 Establishing by degrees
12 Jockey Turcotte
15 Many nods
18 Biathlon need
19 Cádiz condiment
26 Twin Cities suburb
28 Jazz player Malone
30 Places for quick operations, briefly
32 Speaks to Shakespeare?
33 Not domestically
35 "In principio ___ Verbum"
37 "Tell ___ story"
38 Things to play with matches?
43 Its natives are called Loiners
46 Master's seeker's hurdle, briefly
48 Shell accessory
50 Holders of many selfies
51 With no sparkle
55 Flight for someone 8-Down
56 Small power sources
57 The Rams of the A-10 Conf.

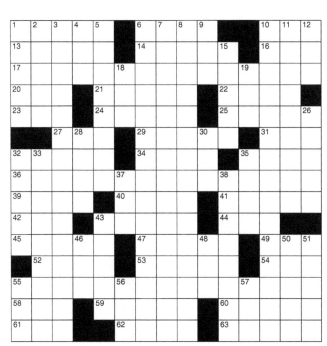

by Alan Olschwang

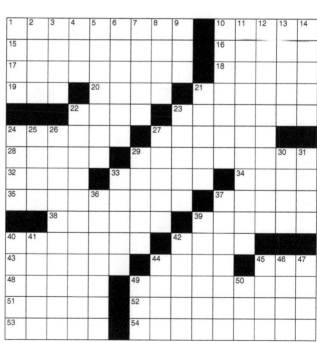

22

ACROSS
1. Like some methods of detection
10. Winter athletes' pull-ups?
15. Without requiring scrutiny
16. Last name in the skin care industry
17. Indication that one wants to get smacked
18. Producer of "whirlybirds"
19. How the descriptions of most things usually end?
20. Cast
21. Like many taxis
22. Bathhouse square
23. N.B.A. team starting in 1988
24. A line, e.g.
27. A lines, e.g.
28. "Essays in Love" writer ___ de Botton
29. People everywhere
32. Since 2010 it's had a shield on its back
33. Buckles
34. Jack for Jacques?
35. Two or three in a row, say
37. Texas state tree
38. Prevent from having anything?
39. What cookies are often baked in
40. Stung
42. Swiss bank depositor?
43. Spare change collector
44. Spare change collectors
45. Vineyard, in Vichy
48. Song of exultation
49. Sexy
51. Failed in a big way
52. Seaweed used in home brewing
53. Some men's sizes
54. One controlling drones

DOWN
1. Relative of a haddock
2. Uplifting company?
3. Bad way to finish
4. Classic two-seaters
5. Blissful
6. Without incident, say
7. Lacking a point
8. A teller might update it: Abbr.
9. Connection between Obama and Robinson?
10. Member of the marmoset family
11. Cold discomfort, of sorts
12. Poppycock
13. Found new tenants for
14. Polar bearers?
21. They're often accompanied by "Hava Nagila"
22. Penalty for some overly prolific posters
23. Rope and dope sources
24. Body bags?
25. Title 54-Across of film
26. Skin behind a slip, perhaps
27. Less likely to have waffles
29. Like supervillains
30. Grape, Cherry or Strawberry lead-in
31. A lot of the time?
33. Need for life
36. Staples of Marvel Comics
37. Cayenne producer
39. Velvety pink
40. Annual winter honoree, briefly
41. Modern two-seater
42. Murphy of "To Hell and Back"
44. "Zzz" inducer
45. Something to buy into
46. Device
47. Miracle on Ice loser of '80
49. Crab house accessory
50. "___ Wed" (2007 Erica Durance movie)

by Ed Sessa

ACROSS

1 Spa supplies
7 Sir Henry ___, pioneer in steelmaking
15 Sulky
16 Getting-off point
17 Household
18 Drink made with tequila, rum, vodka, gin, bourbon, triple sec, sweet-and-sour mix and Coke
19 Contractor's fig.
20 Edward who was dubbed "The Dark Prophet" by Time magazine
22 Invoice nos.
23 Actor/director Schreiber
25 Standouts
26 2014's "The ___ Movie"
27 Contribute
29 Mauna ___
30 Figure skater Kadavy
31 Breaks away from a defender
33 Feature of many a Duchamp work
34 Follow every rule
38 N.B.A.'s Gibson
39 Became tiresome
41 Formal dress option
44 Bush beast, briefly
45 "A Midsummer Night's Scream" author
46 What can help you toward a peak performance?
47 Barbed spears for fishing
49 Classic work in Old Norse
50 Many Ph.D. candidates
51 Assesses
53 End: Abbr.
54 One learning how to refine oils?
56 ___ Mouse
58 Renaissance woodwind
59 Fasts, perhaps
60 Nonviable
61 Engage in horseplay

DOWN

1 Skype annoyance
2 Very unbalanced
3 Had the itch
4 Sustainable practices grp.
5 Durability
6 Anagram of "notes," appropriately
7 Funny or Die web series hosted by Zach Galifianakis
8 Semicircular recess in Roman architecture
9 High rolls
10 Pollster Greenberg
11 High rollers
12 Big name in colonial Massachusetts
13 Cabinet department
14 "The natural organ of truth": C. S. Lewis
21 Well-pitched
24 Tourist
26 1961 Michelangelo Antonioni drama
28 Away from
30 High rollers' rollers
32 Popular sandwich, informally
33 ___ usual
35 Dances onstage
36 "Hmm, ya got me"
37 More sympathetic
40 Most smart
41 Paper-clip, say
42 Pizza chain since 1956
43 Raise by digging
44 Some T.S.A. confiscations
47 Enemy of Cobra
48 Shrub that produces a crimson-colored spice
51 Comic Mort
52 Kind of bread
55 Abbr. on a letter to Paris, maybe
57 National Adoption Mo.

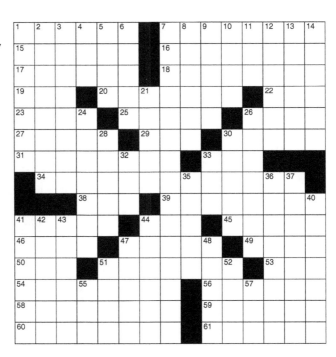

by Brendan Emmett Quigley

24

ACROSS

1 Passed in a blur, say
7 Develops gradually
15 Smoking
16 Change-making
17 Where to look for self-growth
18 Obsolescent storage device
19 Historic first name in W.W. II
20 Locale of three presidential libraries
21 Fried
22 One often behind bars
24 Ditch
25 Doesn't carry on
26 Oxygen's lack
27 Rescuer of Princess Peach
28 Near: Fr.
29 Churchyard gravedigger
30 Signs of things to come
34 Truckloads
35 Hard to grasp
36 Remains after the aging process
37 Opposite of 28-Down
38 Santa's reindeer, e.g.
39 Some sharp words
43 Lou's "La Bamba" co-star
44 Concord concoction
46 Many a "Meet the Press" guest, informally
47 Swindler's moola
48 Hiked
49 Former panelist on "The View" in 2007
51 Many a worker at Union Pacific headquarters
52 Like Enterprise vehicles
53 Fired up?

54 Best, as friends
55 One of Leakey's "Trimates"

DOWN

1 Decorated band along a wall
2 "Reality leaves a lot to the imagination" speaker
3 He directed Bela Lugosi in "Bride of the Monster"
4 High rollers, in casino lingo
5 Cheap, shoddy merchandise
6 Financial statement abbr.
7 Outdoor wedding settings
8 Alchemist's offering
9 Green party V.I.P.?
10 Three Stooges creator Healy and others
11 Concourse abbr.
12 Personalize for
13 Picture
14 Troopers' toppers
20 Almanac info
23 Large pack
24 Get set to take off
27 What an 18-Across's capacity is measured in, briefly
28 Opposite of 37-Across
29 Message sometimes written below "F"
30 Regular embarkation location
31 Series starter
32 Left
33 "___ se habla español"
34 Did an entrechat
36 Flier

38 Voice lesson subjects
39 Protection for flowers in bud
40 Socially dominant sorts
41 Dirty rat
42 Biggest city on the smallest continent
44 Diving bird
45 Mammoth
47 Cookout irritant
50 ___ root (math quantity)
51 Bungler

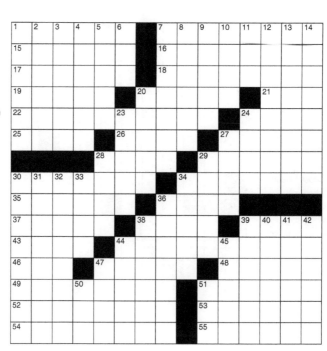

by Greg Johnson

25

ACROSS

1 Those who respond to pickup lines?
8 Drags
15 Central Florida daily
17 Part-time jobs for college students, say
18 Disbelieving, maybe
19 Major-leaguer from Osaka who threw two no-hitters
20 Trap
21 Haddock relatives
23 Constellation described by Ptolemy
25 Part of 56-Across: Abbr.
26 Conductor with a star on the Hollywood Walk of Fame
28 "A Chorus Line" lyricist Ed
31 Iran's Ayatollah __ Khamenei
32 Year the Angels won the World Series
34 Brit's cry of surprise
38 See 16-Down
41 Standard
42 Extreme piques
43 "I'll __"
44 Old letter opener: Abbr.
46 Upper regions of space
48 Org. of which Tom Hanks is a member
51 Mauna __
52 Shaving brand
53 Slip preventer
56 Terminal announcements, for short
58 Writer William
61 Mobile creator
64 Go mad
65 Demanded immediate action from
66 Superlatively bouncy

DOWN

1 __ Nostra
2 Aligned, after "in"
3 Relatively low-risk investments
4 Actress for whom a neckline is named
5 __ 500
6 Unspoiled places
7 Meh
8 First of two pictures
9 Start to color?
10 Range parts: Abbr.
11 Symbols of timidity
12 Modern message
13 Fictional teller of tales
14 Wasn't alert
16 Hijackers who captured 38-Across
22 "What's the __?"
24 First name in '60s radicalism
26 Old club
27 Flourish
28 Connected people
29 Ready
30 Nothing
33 Eastern European capital of 2 million
35 Screw up
36 Sport with automated scoring
37 River of W.W. I
39 Dickens boy
40 Ballpark dingers: Abbr.
45 Positioned well
47 English hat similar to a fedora
48 Where flakes may build up
49 __ nothing
50 Simple sorts
52 Musical grp.
54 Fires
55 Western setting for artisans
57 They may be heavy or open
59 Bee __
60 Formerly, old-style
62 Nautical heading: Abbr.
63 Part of 56-Across: Abbr.

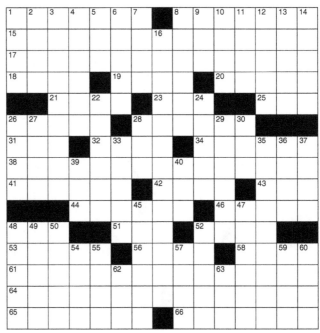

by David J. Kahn

ACROSS

1 It's made from an ear and put in the mouth
12 Highlander's accessory
15 1967 hit by the Hollies
16 One may have a full body
17 Copied the page?
18 They often land next to queens: Abbr.
19 Prefix with flop
20 They often land next to queens
22 Cross quality
23 Move a whole lot
25 Backward
26 Fame
29 Spice stores?
31 Enigmatic
34 Nanny, in Nanjing
35 Question after a surprising claim
36 Party bowlful
37 Supply one's moving address?
38 Network point
39 Now whole
41 Orphaned lion of literature
42 Knit at a social function?
43 Brownie alternative
45 "Veep" airer
46 Pinch-hitter
49 Smallest member of the Council of Europe
52 See 7-Down
53 Withdraw
54 It's between Buda and Pest
57 After
58 Forum setting
59 180
60 Target of a spy

DOWN

1 Herder from Wales
2 Live warning?
3 Voice lesson topic
4 Bulldogs play in it: Abbr.
5 86
6 Rush target

7 With 52-Across, something in a gray area
8 Himalayan production
9 Golfer Aoki
10 Ayn Rand, e.g.
11 Higher-up?
12 Target
13 Every second
14 Jam
21 Product of some decay
23 O's is one more than N's
24 Comb composition
26 Like some pitches
27 Orders
28 Locals call it the "Big O"
30 Where spades may be laid down
31 End of a song often sung by inebriated people
32 Shark's place

33 Polar Bear Provincial Park borders it
37 Minestrone ingredient
39 Repetitive
40 Bunch
44 Self-congratulatory cries
46 Not just wolf down
47 "I'd love to help"
48 Part of Che Guevara's attire
49 Junior in 12 Pro Bowls
50 Highlander of old
51 Period sans soleil
52 Magazine fig.
55 Half of nine?
56 U.S.P.S. assignment

by Barry C. Silk

ACROSS

1 Romania and Bulgaria, once
16 Frank Loesser show tune
17 It might cover an oil spill
18 Doing the rounds?
19 Sporting goods chain with the slogan "Get outside yourself"
20 Potsdam pronoun
21 Peculiar: Prefix
22 Start-up helper: Abbr.
24 Pace at Pompano Park
26 Shoving matches?
29 Relative of une tulipe
31 "Frasier" role
33 Match cry
34 Pooh-pooh
38 "You're probably right"
40 Mojo
41 Sister co. of Virgin
42 Middle square, maybe
43 Sea of ___ (view from Crimea's eastern coast)
45 Chart, in Cádiz
48 Sol mates?
50 Frost-covered
52 Crook's place
54 Many activists' concerns: Abbr.
56 One given up for good?
61 "What a sight for sore eyes!"
62 Its islands are not surrounded by water
63 Unease

DOWN

1 Some defensive weapons, in brief
2 "Love and Death on Long Island" novelist Gilbert
3 Lead-tin alloys
4 Unmarried, say
5 Activist Guinier
6 Some claims
7 "Cool, dude"
8 Many a backpacker, at night
9 62-Across option north of the border
10 Go a couple of rounds
11 Preweighed, in a way
12 Very rarely heard instruments
13 Long shift, perhaps
14 Ending to prefer?
15 Young or old follower
23 Rich person's suffix?
25 Alternative to .net
27 Rural parents
28 Cry of pleased surprise
30 Songwriters Hall of Fame member who wrote "April Love"
32 Get-up-and-go
34 Doo-wop syllable
35 Body part detecting odeurs
36 One getting rid of possessions?
37 "Third Watch" actress Texada
39 Hester Prynne wore one
44 Labor Day arrivals, e.g.
46 Conf. whose membership increased by two in 2011
47 Melodic
49 Not leave the house
51 Prefix with second
53 Sticks in the brig?
55 Utah senator who co-sponsored a tariff act
56 Potential serial material
57 "___ in Full" (Tom Wolfe novel)
58 Security figure: Abbr.
59 Abrupt transition
60 Some picnic supplies

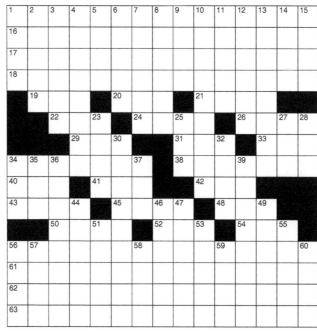

by Martin Ashwood-Smith and Joe Krozel

ACROSS

1 "That's crazy, dude!"
5 Drive to drink, e.g.
15 It's best to stay out of its way
16 Debut Peter Tosh album, and a rallying cry for pot smokers
17 Scheme for the start of a sonnet
18 Opinion leader?
19 Pioneer of New Journalism
21 "r u there?," e.g.
22 Unpolished pro?
23 Stationary
24 Cro-Magnon orphan of literature
25 Head turner
26 Rihanna or Sharon Stone
28 Big name in late-night TV
29 See 25-Down
30 Dandy
31 Ripped
32 U.S. Open champion whose last name is a toy
34 Artist and chess player who said "While all artists are not chess players, all chess players are artists"
38 The end?
39 It takes time to cure
40 McDonald's denial
41 The end
44 It involves hand-to-hand coordination
46 Souls
47 Wish-Bone alternative
48 Lodging portmanteau
49 1967 Calder Trophy winner at age 18
50 ___ Epstein, baseball V.I.P. known as "Boy Wonder"
51 Last name in "Star Wars"

52 Singer with the 1996 triple-platinum album "Tidal"
55 Panache
56 Where Jason Kidd played college hoops
57 Rap's ___ Yang Twins
58 1996 Rhett Akins country hit
59 Store whose shoe department has its own ZIP code (10022-SHOE)

DOWN

1 "Yes?"
2 Certain chili
3 Third degree for a third degree?
4 One may prefer them to blondes
5 Bit of ballet instruction
6 Like Tickle Me Elmo
7 "My treat"
8 Parent company?
9 Internet traffic statistics company
10 Pleasant cadence
11 Strong arm
12 Joint
13 Buckle
14 Forever in the past?
20 Up-to-date
24 Like some seamen
25 With 29-Across, nest egg choice
27 Cockerdoodle, e.g.
28 "Oh goody!"
31 Clipped
33 Young foxes
34 Certain gumdrops
35 It was home to two Wonders of the Ancient World
36 Earn a load of money, in modern lingo

37 Some kitchen detritus
39 Impressive range
41 Tool
42 Fortify
43 Oxygen user
44 Imitated chicks
45 Carnival items served with chili
47 Yellow-brown shade
50 Fictional home five miles from Jonesboro
51 A through G
53 Duck Hunt platform, briefly
54 Historical figure a.k.a. Marse Robert

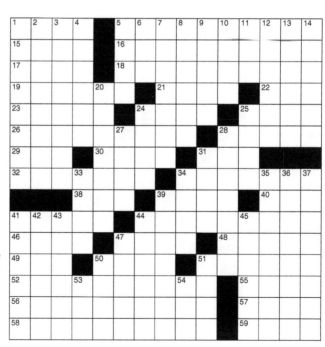

by Ashton Anderson and James Mulhern

ACROSS

1 Retreat
9 "3 O'Clock Blues" hitmaker, 1952
15 "Obviously . . ."
16 Uses, as a chaise
17 Particle ejected from an atom during ionization
18 Home of Bwindi Impenetrable National Park
19 "Star Wars" villain name
20 Identify
21 Celebration of the arrival of spring
22 Blew out
24 Eastern hereditary title
26 Specks
27 Things worn at home?
31 Like some details
32 Maddeningly surreal
33 "Girls" home
34 Some adoption candidates
35 Address found online
36 Ones unlikely to drag their feet
38 ___ Ruess, lead singer of Fun
39 Weep
40 Order of ancient Greeks
41 There might be a battery of them
42 Rid (of)
43 Matt's onetime "Today" co-host
46 Runs the show, for short
47 Like prosciutto
48 Way over the top
50 Head of the Catholic Church when Luther's "95 Theses" was posted
53 Daddy Warbucks's henchman
54 "Gracious me!"
55 Completely safe, as a proposition
56 Lecture series with well over a billion views

DOWN

1 Century starter?
2 Something in that vein?
3 Line outside a club, maybe
4 Erode
5 Leaves of grass
6 Ran
7 High-level appointee
8 It has all the answers
9 Alternative to cords
10 Bowls, e.g.
11 Mauna ___
12 ". . . and who ___?"
13 Network connection
14 Part of a moving cloud
20 Foe of the Vikings
22 Tour parts
23 Bigwig
24 High beams
25 Orders in a restaurant
27 Millionaires and billionaires
28 Theodore Roosevelt's domestic program
29 Rapper ___ Blow
30 Elite
32 Part of a TV archive
34 Model introduced in the 1990s
37 Target of a 1972 ban
38 "Breakfast at Tiffany's," for one
40 Plain-spoken
42 Took in
43 Routing aid: Abbr.
44 Big Apple neighborhood next to the Bowery
45 "Christians Awake," e.g.
47 Semaphore signals, e.g.
49 Asian path
50 Hog roasting locale
51 Planet whose inhabitants age backward
52 Pair of Dos Equis

by Peter Wentz

30

ACROSS

1 Popularity boost due to a certain TV endorsement
12 Rebel in a beret
15 "A thousand pardons"
16 Athlete in a shell
17 Diet, e.g.
18 "Collages" novelist, 1964
19 Arab spring?
20 Mexicans roll them
21 Composers of some rhapsodies
23 Business of 41-Down: Abbr.
24 Wear for Hu Jintao
25 Mythical abode of heroes slain in battle
29 "Each of us bears his own Hell" writer
30 Part of a drag outfit
31 Relatives of black holes
34 Cousin of an agave
35 Dispatch
36 To you, in Toulouse
37 Place for rank-and-filers in the House of Commons
39 Ozone menace
40 Pungent panini ingredient
41 Gets started
42 They often provide illumination in galleries
44 Arm with many vessels, maybe
45 Like angels
46 Palooka
47 Throws for a loop
51 Shakespeare sonnet that begins "So am I as the rich, whose blessed key"
52 Parts of some alarms
55 Fleece
56 White whale's whereabouts

57 Bath setting: Abbr.
58 People sampling mushrooms, say

DOWN

1 Druid, e.g.
2 Spanning
3 Theme of several theme parks
4 Piltdown man, say
5 Dot-dot-dot
6 Casualty of the Battle of Roncesvalles
7 Old dynasts
8 Some spam senders
9 The Negro R. runs through it
10 "Fantasy Island" host
11 Stray mongrels
12 Chancellery settings
13 Where Nord, Nord-Est and Nord-Ouest are departments

14 Arp contemporary
22 "Interesting . . . but museum-worthy?"
23 Org. whose logo has an eagle and scales
24 Opposite of gloom
25 King of Kings
26 1987 Lionel Richie hit
27 21st-century pastime for treasure hunters
28 Leonov who was the first man to walk in space
29 Balboa's first name
31 Alternative to shoots?
32 A cube has one
33 ___-Soviet
35 Like many a purple-tinged moorland
38 "Fur Traders Descending the Missouri" painter, 1845

39 Creator of "30 Rock"
41 Its parent is Liberty Mutual
42 Opposite of agitato
43 Pizza topping
44 Pizza topping
46 Bart and Lisa's bus driver
47 Sacs studied by 58-Across
48 Parts of a sob story
49 Latin 101 word
50 Phishing loot: Abbr.
53 Orange's org.
54 Periodic dairy aisle offering

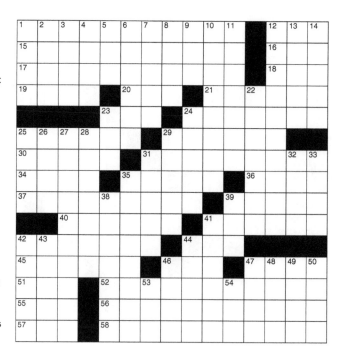

by Mel Rosen

ACROSS

1 "Definitely, dawg!"
10 Art enabled
15 Reading room
16 Timeline segment
17 Reward for knocking 'em dead
18 Moving supply
19 Bare peak
20 Before retitling: Abbr.
21 "It"
22 Drop
24 Name dropper's phrase
26 Cousin of -kin or -let
27 Unpaid babysitters, maybe
29 "Property Virgins" cable channel
30 "Out!"
31 It's often described by horses
33 Regard
34 "And ___ the field the road runs by": Tennyson
35 Common loss after a breakup
37 Rush
39 Clipper feature
41 It can be painful to pick up
43 Radio racket
46 Parentheses, e.g.
47 Slight
49 Subject of the 2011 book "The Rogue"
50 Grp. seeking to improve No Child Left Behind
51 "Pensées" philosopher
53 It might mean "hello" or "goodbye" to a driver
54 Woodchuck, e.g.
56 Bradley with five stars
58 Musician who co-founded Nutopia
59 Popular type option
60 "The Pentagon Papers" Emmy nominee
62 Verbal equivalent of a shrug
63 Something awful
64 A couple of rounds in a toaster?
65 Rain forest, e.g.

DOWN

1 Subtle trick
2 Easy chair accompanier
3 Philanthropic mantra
4 Blue symbol of Delaware
5 Prefix with Germanic
6 The Congolese franc replaced it
7 Crest
8 What's often on wheels in an airport
9 Some punk
10 Parts of many chamber groups
11 Pacific port
12 Visually uninspiring
13 15-Across frequenter, maybe
14 "Add ___ a tiger's chaudron, / For the ingredients of our cauldron": Shak.
21 "No more guesses?"
23 Blots
25 Astronomical distance: Abbr.
28 It's associated with Chris Rock and 30 Rock
30 Occupy
32 Destroys insidiously
36 Pales
38 More than nod
39 Artificial
40 Relative of a throw
42 Country
44 Hero-worship
45 Learn to teach?
48 Capital on the Niger
51 Some preppy wear
52 Left Turn Only and others
55 A leader and follower?
57 A little blue
60 It can make you squiffy
61 Monopoly quartet: Abbr.

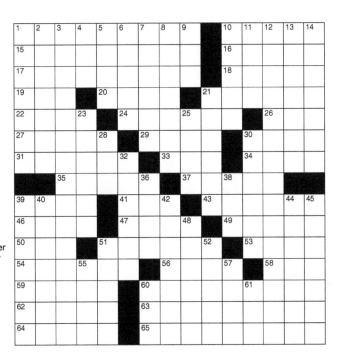

by James Mulhern

ACROSS

1 Simpler
16 Sequential
17 Harry Potter series part
18 Can't take
19 One of a familiar septet
20 Rocks on the Rhein?
21 Gabriel García Márquez's "Cien ___ de Soledad"
22 Weapon in old hand-to-hand combat
23 Figures in "Teutonic Mythology"
25 "Vous êtes ___"
26 Alaska's ___ Fjords National Park
27 Candy pioneer H. B. ___
28 Abbr. in many a military title
29 Small skillet
31 Abbr. before a date
32 Big Chicago-based franchiser
33 1958–'61 political alliance: Abbr.
35 March on Washington grp.
38 Dirgelike
42 20-Across in English
45 Blush
47 Not a good person to entrust with secrets, informally
48 And moreover
49 Answer (for)
50 Goya figure
51 Part of a plowing harness
52 Problem for Poirot
53 Quickly imagine?
55 Swiss city that borders France and Germany
56 Spotless
59 Boos, e.g.
60 "Different strokes for different folks"

DOWN

1 Either of two Holy Roman emperors
2 Better
3 "Get cracking!"
4 White-bearded types
5 Some budget planners, for short
6 Gambling inits.
7 Putting one's cards on the table, in a way
8 Package for sale, say
9 Principal port of Syria
10 "___ out?"
11 Strongbox
12 Raiding grp.
13 Robin Hood and his Merry Men
14 Otherworldly in the extreme
15 Decent
22 "Portraits at the Stock Exchange" artist
24 Look that's not liked
26 ___ party
30 ___ York
32 Seattle's Space Needle or St. Louis's Gateway Arch
34 Something that often follows you
35 Greta of "The Red Violin"
36 Hardly any
37 Immediate, as relatives
39 Seeps
40 Actress in "Ferris Bueller's Day Off"
41 Decorate fancily
42 Bothered
43 Broadway hit with the song "I Wonder What the King Is Doing Tonight"
44 Telescope part
46 Mezzo-soprano Regina
51 Must
54 Blanched
55 Inexpensive writing implements
57 ___ price
58 Bad computer?

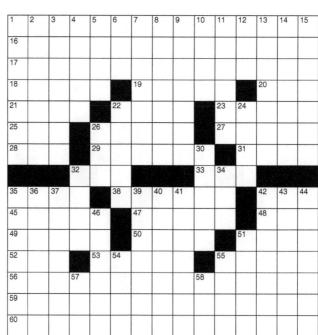

by Stu Ockman

ACROSS

1 Take it easy
8 Vostok 1 passenger
15 Try
16 Supermodel Lima
17 Scale with the highest reading at midday, usually
18 More than startle
19 Show horse
20 Juniors' juniors, briefly
22 Those, to José
23 Organ part
25 Classic Jaguar
26 Latin word in legal briefs
27 Princess Leia was one in "A New Hope"
30 Bamboozled
32 It's nothing new
35 Hot shot?
37 Germany, to Britain
39 It helps you focus
40 Unlocked area?
42 Expenditure
43 T-shirt sizes, for short
44 Allstate subsidiary
46 One who deals with stress well?
48 Hat, slangily
49 Reuben ingredient, informally
53 Completely dry, as a racetrack
54 Rub it in
56 Org. with the New York Liberty
57 BlackBerry routers
59 "This statement is false," e.g.
61 Strong and regal
62 Elvis hit with a spelled-out title
63 Gallery event
64 Sharp-pointed instruments

DOWN

1 Sucker
2 Where French ships dock
3 Like many academic halls
4 Help
5 "Cupid is a knavish ___": "A Midsummer Night's Dream"
6 Biographical data
7 Love letters
8 One foraging
9 Drinks stirred in pitchers
10 [Back off!]
11 Put on
12 Complain loudly
13 Obsessive need to check one's email or Facebook, say
14 Cons
21 U.P.S. cargo: Abbr.
24 Tennis smash?
26 Puzzle solver's complaint
28 Punishment, metaphorically
29 Hypothetical particle in cold dark matter
31 Turn down
32 Five-time U.S. presidential candidate in the early 1900s
33 School handout
34 Colorful party intoxicant
36 Shrill howl
38 "Just wait . . ."
41 Cream, for example
45 Changes for the big screen
47 Short jackets
50 "Watch ___ amazed" (magician's phrase)
51 It takes two nuts
52 Campaign issue
53 Nike rival
54 Mil. bigwig
55 Like sour grapes
58 Long in Hollywood
60 ___ Halladay, two-time Cy Young Award winner

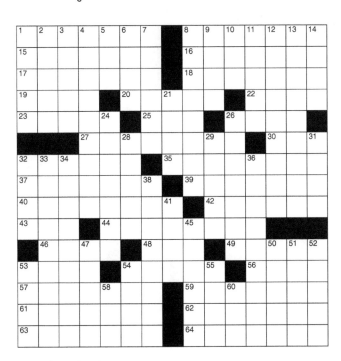

by Joel Fagliano

34

ACROSS

1 "Friday the 13th" setting
5 Cry accompanying a slap
15 Green leader?
16 Office addresses?
17 Tragically heartbroken figure of myth
18 Some cocktail garnishes
19 Noted nominee of 2005
21 Stumped
22 Bit of audio equipment?
23 Controversial thing to play
25 Stats. for new arrivals
27 Base's opposite
29 "That's true — however . . ."
33 Locale for the Zoot Suit Riots of '43
36 Fashion clothes
38 Team unifier
39 They created the Get Rid of Slimy Girls club
42 Brand with a "Wonderfilled" ad campaign
43 Nail
44 Beginning of some tributes
45 Just beginning
47 Longtime rival of 42-Across
49 Midwest terminal?
51 Reality show documenting a two-week trade
55 "A veil, rather than a mirror," per Oscar Wilde
58 Line outside a gala
60 Dreaded message on a returned 32-Down
61 Reverse transcriptase is found in it
64 "To End ___" (1998 Richard Holbrooke best seller)
65 Q&A query
66 Barker in a basket
67 One endlessly smoothing things over?
68 Cross state

DOWN

1 Fencing material
2 Europe's City of Saints and Stones
3 Battlefield cry
4 Abstention alternative
5 "Let ___ Run Wild" (B-side to "California Girls")
6 Physical feature of Herman on "The Simpsons"
7 Home to Main Street, U.S.A.
8 The Hardy Boys and others
9 He called his critics "pusillanimous pussyfooters"
10 With flexibility in tempo
11 Reagan-___
12 Harkness Tower locale
13 Pueblo cooker
14 Red giant that disintegrated?
20 Round windows
24 Brand named after some Iowa villages
26 High (and high-priced) options for spectators
28 Rocker ___ Leo
30 Sci-fi villain ___ Fett
31 They may be made with koa wood, briefly
32 Course obstacle?
33 Elasticity studier's subj.
34 It's canalized at Interlaken
35 Boatload
37 Boatload transfer point
40 Mann's "Man!"
41 Eagle of Delight's tribe
46 Group with the 1963 hit "South Street," with "the"
48 Obsolescence
50 Moisturizer brand
52 Cry accompanying a high-five
53 Treasured strings
54 Politico caricatured by Carvey
55 Start of Egypt's official name
56 ___ Belloq, villain in "Raiders of the Lost Ark"
57 Modern farewell letters
59 Air
62 Wood problem
63 Title for knights on "Game of Thrones"

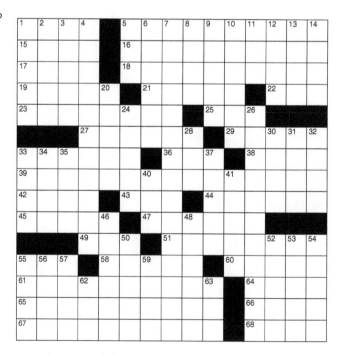

by Evan Birnholz

ACROSS

1 Modern traffic director?
10 Punk theme
15 London's ___ Barnett School
16 News anchor O'Donnell
17 One who's not out all night?
18 Steer
19 T-Pain and Ice-T output
20 Time's 1963 Man of the Year, informally
22 Pick up
23 John or James
26 Fashion designer Marshall
28 Et ___
29 Back
31 Ship captained by Vicente Yáñez Pinzón
32 West of Nashville
34 "Martin Chuzzlewit" villain
35 Silver screen name?
39 "___ Pleasure" (Charlie Chaplin movie)
40 Fixed, as lining
41 Abdominal and lower-back muscles, collectively
42 Embarrassed
43 Unleashes on
47 Writes a Dear John letter, say
49 Novelist Isabel
50 Where one might take a bullet: Abbr.
51 Some seaweeds
54 Actor Franco of "Now You See Me"
55 Skateboard trick named after its originator
57 Not reserved
60 Female lead in "Brigadoon"

61 They'll never hold water
62 Big celebrations
63 Paid a visit

DOWN

1 President beginning in 1995
2 Delaware Valley Indians
3 Hip place
4 Strabismus
5 1901 Kipling book
6 Big ___
7 Words before "to be born" and "to die" in Ecclesiastes
8 Not this type?: Abbr.
9 Change course at sea
10 Physicist ___-Marie Ampère
11 Common conjunction
12 Looking sheepish, say

13 Southern city that's the setting for "Midnight in the Garden of Good and Evil"
14 Beauty's partner
21 Celeb who got the 2,500th star on the Hollywood Walk of Fame in 2013
24 Easy runs
25 Trellis strip
27 Messiah
29 Hung out to dry
30 Groks
33 Kind of pump
34 Beauty
35 Goes head to head
36 "Trust me"
37 "My Big Fat Greek Wedding" writer/star
38 "Go, team, go!," e.g.
42 GPS line: Abbr.

44 Wove (through)
45 Sooner or later
46 Wee
48 U.S. chain stores since 1985
49 Cartoon dog
52 Setback
53 It's by no means a long shot
56 Football stat: Abbr.
58 Scammer's target
59 Mark on a card

by Brendan Emmett Quigley

ACROSS

1 Is guilty of disorderly conduct?
11 Not much
15 Accompaniment for a 17-Across
16 Film featuring Peter Sellers as a matador, with "The"
17 Kid getting into treble
18 Gym request
19 Indication that you get it
20 ___ & Watson (big name in deli meat)
22 Indication that you don't get it
23 Played a club, maybe
24 What to call some femmes: Abbr.
26 Hand-held game device
28 Wedding gown accessory
30 1997 role for Will Smith
31 David, e.g.
34 Fish also known as a blue jack
35 One with long, luscious legs
38 Wagers
39 Trail
40 Geek Squad service
43 Internal development?
44 Many party hacks
46 Word in the titles of six songs by the Beatles
47 TV monitor, for short
50 Quantity that makes another quantity by adding an "m" at the front
51 Intimated
53 Sociologist Mannheim
54 Teriyaki go-with
56 1971 song that was the "CSI: NY" theme
59 Cry that makes children run away
60 Performed hits at a concert?
61 Some home-schoolers get them, briefly
62 1920s scandal

DOWN

1 Brand paired with On the Run convenience stores
2 Strike ___
3 Excited, with "up"
4 Source of the word "trousers"
5 Common word on a Portuguese map
6 Tour tote
7 Organized crime enforcers of the 1930s–'40s
8 Morales of film
9 Power cord?
10 Burns's land, to Burns
11 ___ of steel
12 First place
13 "Since you mentioned it . . ."
14 Cut it
21 Slalom path part
24 What some formulas are based on
25 24-Down producer, informally
27 Large magnets?
28 One hanging by a thread?
29 Want from
31 Boston, Chicago or Kansas
32 Follower of the Sultan of Swat in career homers
33 Email attachment?
35 Warren Buffett's college fraternity, informally
36 Where to find Edam and Gouda: Abbr.
37 Bond film?
41 Tour part
42 Moderator of Tribal Councils on TV
45 Like some humor
47 "Nurse Jackie" star
48 Bygone publication subtitled "America's Only Rock 'n' Roll Magazine"
49 1967 title role for Warren Beatty
52 Rhyme pattern at the end of a villanelle
53 Clement
55 Coneheads, e.g., for short
57 Lead-in to meter
58 Singer

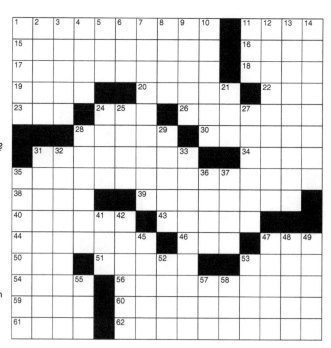

by Sam Ezersky

37

ACROSS

1 Toast often given with Manischewitz
7 Nobel-winning economist who wrote "Fuzzy Math"
14 Precipitate
15 Longtime Tab competitor
16 In the best- or worst-case scenario
17 Like things in "Ripley's Believe It or Not!"
18 Psychobabble, say
20 In the 29-Down, e.g.: Abbr.
21 "___ do, so he shall do": Numbers 15:14
22 Put to work
25 Hell
29 Like players who sweep things
34 Digs in the snow?
35 Olympian in a shell
36 Pitches
38 "Luncheon on the Grass" painter
39 Like much unheeded advice
40 Pick up something common?
43 Line of tugboats?
44 Dye containing indigotin
48 Jackasses, e.g.
51 "It's all good"
53 Actor with the line "Say hello to my little friend!"
56 Take stock of
57 Feature of a Shaw show
58 Ominous final words
59 Accessories purchased just for openers?
60 Big player in the Suez Crisis

DOWN

1 Source of very soft wool
2 Whale constellation
3 Oh-so-dramatic
4 Acrobat producer
5 "___ happens . . ."
6 Perfect expression
7 Pet food in the form of pellets
8 "Luncheon of the Boating Party" painter
9 ___-Aztecan
10 [This is so frustrating!]
11 Storyteller who needs no words
12 ___ impasse
13 Dickens protagonist surnamed Trent
15 Horror film antagonist surnamed Thorn
19 King Arthur's father
23 1971–97 nation name
24 Drove (on)
26 Pat material, maybe
27 Low-class, in Leeds
28 Royals manager Ned
29 Devil dog's outfit: Abbr.
30 Org. affected by Title IX
31 It may be a sacrifice
32 Approve for office installation
33 E'en if
36 Fault, in law
37 "Father Knows Best" family name
39 Like some things you can't handle
41 Shop shelter
42 The Furies, e.g.
44 Timber dressers
45 Nativity numbers
46 Not free
47 Shunned one
48 Be a high-tech criminal
49 Allure or Essence alternative
50 Fix, as a pointer
52 Major star of 2-Down
54 Domain of 38-Across and 8-Down
55 Grp. with many operations

by James Mulhern

ACROSS

1 Prop for Kermit the Frog
6 It's big in the suburbs
15 Kind of acid
16 Something you shouldn't knock?
17 What dots may represent
18 "Stay cool!"
19 ___ mix
20 Ready to play, with "up"
21 N.F.L. stat: Abbr.
22 ___ pants
24 Source of the phrases "cakes and ale" and "milk of human kindness": Abbr.
25 Belize native
26 What "II" or "III" may indicate
28 Profession of Clementine's father in "Oh My Darling, Clementine"
29 R.A.F. award
32 Shrimp
33 Small job for a gardener?
34 Noble one
36 Spelunker's aid
37 High
38 Something cited in a citation
39 Suffix with transcript-
40 Über ___
41 Origin of the word "behemoth"
43 Architect ___ van der Rohe
44 Knockout
45 Where Chekhov lived and Tolstoy summered
49 Big Apple ave.
50 Half of a matched set
51 Inadequate
52 Girl in "The Music Man" with a floral name
55 Nil
56 Desktop item
57 Elite unit
58 Capital on the Raccoon River
59 Something from the oven

DOWN

1 Mangle
2 ___ Tower (Pacific landmark)
3 More green
4 Spelling problems?
5 Brass maker: Abbr.
6 Year that Chaucer died
7 It follows a pattern
8 Stick
9 2001–05 Pontiac made in Mexico
10 Org. in 1950s–'60s TV's "Naked City"
11 Govt. lender
12 Where Syracuse is a port
13 Elderly
14 Relative of ocher
23 Where many accidents occur
24 Lies out
25 Philadelphia tourist attraction
27 Target of a squat, for short
28 1960s dance, with "the"
29 State of sleep
30 Student loan source, familiarly
31 Third-year hurdles, for some
33 2008 Libertarian presidential candidate
35 Lycée breaks
36 Temporal ___
38 It may come with a cookie
41 Kentucky county in a 1976 Oscar-winning documentary
42 Forest ranger?
44 Melvin who was called "The King of Torts"
46 Ruy ___ (chess opening)
47 Relative of ocher
48 Something from the oven
50 Shot deliverer
53 Radiation unit
54 French possessive
55 Use a laser on

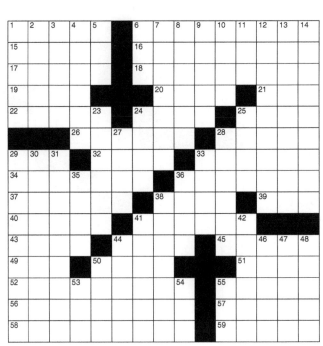

by Barry C. Silk

ACROSS

1 Director in "A Chorus Line"
5 Pistol packer in a 1943 #1 hit
9 Make eyes pop and jaws drop
14 Paradoxical assertion, perhaps
15 Writer of the 644-line poem "Ibis"
16 Stage
17 Seasonal servings
18 1969 Rolling Stones album
20 Like some long flights
22 Part of une fraternité
23 He called the U.S. pres. a "glorified public relations man"
24 Abbr. on some clothing tags
27 Part of a filled-out survey: Abbr.
29 Admiral who bombarded Tahiti in 1914
30 It often results in changes across the board
38 1959 hit with the lyric "One day I feel so happy, next day I feel so sad"
39 At any price
40 Not meant for specialists
41 Some Blu-ray players
42 First of 66 books: Abbr.
43 Fix
44 Couch problem
47 March Madness, with "the"
51 Charges at the door
55 Swan song
58 "Who ___?"
59 Emmy-winning Ed
60 The "O" in F. A. O. Schwarz
61 Looking up

62 Nelson Mandela's mother tongue
63 Sound heard during a heat wave
64 Event with touches

DOWN

1 Corrosion-preventing coating
2 Not very affable
3 With 56-Down, refuse to be cleaned out from a poker game?
4 Literature Nobelist before Gide
5 Stream on the side of a mountain, perhaps
6 Car name that's Latin for "desire"
7 McConnell of the Senate
8 "Peace out"

9 Black-and-white transmissions, briefly?
10 Like most brain neurons
11 Had a beef?
12 Actress Kazan or Kravitz
13 One may get a pass
19 Picture on a chest, for short?
21 They often spot people
25 Withdraw
26 Minor parish officers
28 Jason of "How I Met Your Mother"
29 Five to nine, maybe, but not nine to five
30 Big bass, in fishing lingo
31 Ones remaining
32 Activity that proceeds hand to hand?

33 Heart-to-hearts
34 ___ Jon (fashion label)
35 "Give me ___"
36 Product for young string players?
37 Ones remaining
44 Good name for a worrywart?
45 Achilles' undoing
46 Wayne's pal in "Wayne's World"
48 Extremely excited
49 Ancient master of didacticism
50 Pick up
52 Drag racers' governing grp.
53 ___ Grey, alter ego of Marvel's X-Man
54 Extraocular annoyance
55 Like some oversight
56 See 3-Down
57 ___-cone

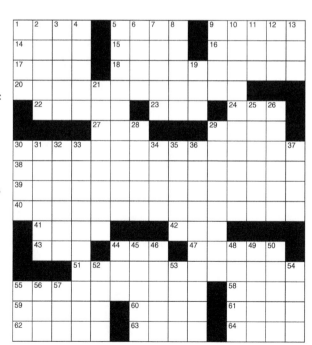

by Martin Ashwood-Smith

ACROSS

1 Gallop
9 "Our Town" family
14 Three- to six-year financial commitment, usually
15 Eponym for a day of the week
16 Livid
17 Where Mozart's "Don Giovanni" premiered
18 Infamous settler on Galveston Island, 1817
19 Fail at stoicism, say
20 Dating inits.
21 Result of pushing too hard?
22 Revlon brand
24 Road sign silhouette
25 Natural barrier
27 Domain name element
28 Tree-dweller that sleeps 20 or so hours a day
29 Recipe for KFC chicken, e.g.
32 Italian artist with the largest painting in the Louvre
35 "Guys and Dolls" number that ends with the rolling of dice
36 Gray ones spark debate
37 Umpire's call
38 "Bonanza" brother
42 Like poodle hair
43 "The Marshall Mathers LP" co-producer
45 Home of Utah Valley University
47 Parlor with simulcasts, briefly
48 Seabiscuit, notably
49 Urge
51 Cousin of a zombie
53 It's often canned

54 Composers Bruckner and Webern
55 Couldn't keep cool
56 Anthem singers at the closing ceremony of the Salt Lake City Olympics
57 Lengthy undertakings

DOWN

1 Denali National Park sits on one
2 One who puts others to sleep?
3 Suppress
4 Show time, in some ads
5 ___ du jour
6 Trunk line
7 Once-common desert fighting force
8 There are three in an inning
9 Not easily taken
10 Air ticket info
11 Sources of chronic annoyance
12 Many watch his movies for kicks
13 Run down
15 Quick
19 Stand for a photo
23 Posed
24 Number of signos del zodiaco
26 Ballistics test units: Abbr.
28 Country whose currency is the shilling
30 Tommy of 1960s pop
31 Stuff sold in rolls
32 Group living at zero latitude?
33 Tartness
34 Allow

35 Classic Doors song in which Jim Morrison refers to himself anagrammatically as "Mr. Mojo Risin'"
39 Exercise in a pool, say
40 Kindle
41 River crossed by a ferry in a 1965 top 10 hit
43 Recitation station
44 It's dangerous to run on
46 Touches
48 French seat
50 "As if that weren't enough . . ."
52 Slew
53 Opposite of hence

by Brad Wilber

ACROSS

1 Tears
9 Philatelist's abbr.
13 Blow up
15 Zero, for one
16 When Winesap apples ripen
18 Genesis source
19 Weapons in Olympic shooting events
20 Actress in a best-selling 1979 swimsuit poster
22 Braves' division, briefly
23 Make less attractive?
24 Mythical hunter
25 Notable buried at the Cathedral of Lima
26 Inside opening?
27 Downs rapidly
28 N.F.L. positions: Abbr.
29 Blew away
30 Ottawa electees, for short
33 Flusters
34 Existed
35 Bungler
36 Soda, at times
37 Tattooed temporarily
38 Red-eye remedy
39 Mitsubishi model whose name means "huntsman" in Spanish
40 Describing an ancient tragedian
41 One of the books in the Book of Mormon
42 Rosalind Russell title role
44 Ball __
45 Lied
46 Filmmaker __ C. Kenton

47 Worker who often takes leaves

DOWN

1 It doesn't hold water
2 Proving beneficial
3 Camp David and others
4 Purple-flowered perennial
5 Patriotic chant
6 Means of attracting publicity
7 Takes courses?
8 World Series of Poker champion __ Ungar
9 Affected sorts
10 Extremely
11 Fulminates
12 Kind of jacket
14 Crooked bank manager, maybe

17 Arizona city across the border from a city of Sonora with the same name
21 Belled the cat
23 Confused
25 Solve
27 Ben of "Run for Your Life"
29 Moon of Saturn
30 Latin America's northernmost city
31 Matthew, Mark, Luke and John
32 Least flustered
33 Life insurance plan
34 Member of a biblical trio
35 Kitchen bulb?
36 Democrat in the Bush cabinet
37 It's a long shot

38 "Casablanca" actor Conrad
39 Emulate Eeyore
40 Capital of France's Manche department
43 Head, in slang

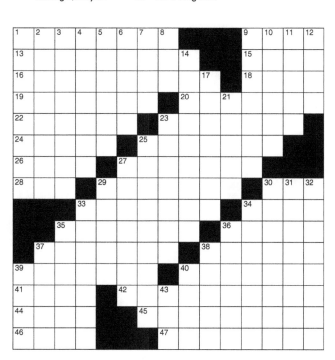

by David Steinberg

42

ACROSS
1 Talk, talk, talk
9 Give stories
14 Basis of comparison
15 National tree of India
16 "Good going!"
17 Words before many a commercial
18 Singer who wrote
19 Battle of Albert setting, 1914
21 United hub, briefly
22 Traditional Christmas gift for a child
24 Accent reduction may be a subj. in it
25 Italian title
26 Unwelcome closet discovery
29 Their sizes are measured in cups
30 1967 album that included "I Can See for Miles"
34 Fiddled
35 "A Study in the Word" host
36 Make a comeback?
37 Old cinema
38 Round stopper, for short
39 Merrie Melodies sheepdog
41 Schoolmarmish sound
46 ___ Brum (car accessory)
47 Having depth
50 Recipient of much 2010s humanitarian aid
51 Giant in test prep
53 Succeeded
55 "Er . . . uh . . ."
56 Boss
57 Largest minority in Croatia
58 "Sounds about right"

DOWN
1 Took downtown
2 Jägermeister ingredient
3 Talking pet
4 Complain
5 Pie-in-the-face scenes, say
6 Sacred thing, to Ayn Rand
7 Sharing word
8 Indie rocker Case
9 Flap of fashion
10 Pub
11 Command to pay attention
12 It may include laundering
13 Down, in a diner
15 They're often seeking change
20 Text, e.g.
23 Loud complaints
27 Life starts in it
28 Certain beach phony
29 Obscure
30 "The King's Speech" director
31 Horace man?
32 Field fungus
33 Subprime mortgagee, to detractors
34 Handle
35 Kawasaki products
39 Doctor's orders
40 Dahlia in Wodehouse novels, e.g.
42 Surrealist known for self-portraits
43 Like many ribbons
44 All-___
45 Bud
48 One who has a hunch
49 Mooring spot
52 Media ___
54 Classic Bogart role, in slang

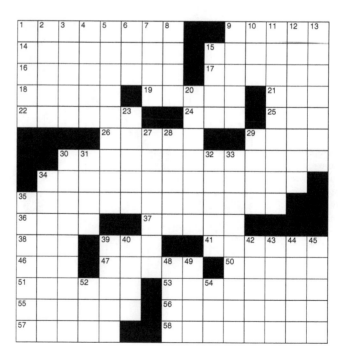

by Peter Wentz

ACROSS

1 Any of the three authors of "Pull My Daisy"
9 They produce minimal distortion
14 He may have many lines memorized
16 Monomer of proteins, informally
17 Elicit a "T.M.I."
18 Like about 30% of 51-Across, belief-wise
19 Head of communications?
20 1,000-pound weight units
21 Suffered a face-plant
22 Rugby-to-Reading dir.
23 Novel title character called "My sin, my soul"
25 Cry of contempt
26 Trip
27 Appeal to
28 Light on TV or Broadway
31 Star of Bombay, e.g.
33 Cousin of cumin and coriander
34 Arrested
35 Riveting piece, perhaps
39 Nickeled-and-dimed?
40 Award with a Best Upset category
41 Its flag includes an image of a nutmeg clove
43 Appeal formally
44 À gogo
45 Prefix with pressure or point
48 "Our Gang" girl
51 Its flag includes an image of a cocoa pod
52 Old Brown Dog and others
53 Old pitcher of milk?
54 Next to
56 Budget alternative

57 Try
58 DuPont development of 1935
59 Subject that includes women's suffrage and the Equal Rights Amendment

DOWN

1 Stains
2 Homebuilders' projections
3 Best New Artist Grammy winner of 2008
4 One needing pressure to perform well
5 Ovid's foot
6 Midwest city named for a Menominee chief
7 Potential virus sources

8 Bone preservation locations
9 Reaction to a card
10 Tag statement
11 Often-overlooked details
12 "Imagine" Grammy winner of 2010
13 County seat on the St. Joseph River
15 Beverage brand portmanteau
23 Engine measure
24 Twitter, Facebook or Instagram
26 Like areas around waterfalls
27 Major cocoa exporter
28 Oscar nominee for playing Cal Trask
29 Very, very
30 Opposite of aggregation

32 What "ruined the angels," per Ralph Waldo Emerson
36 Prod
37 One of Time magazine's cover "Peacemakers"
38 Wily temptress
39 Jason, for one
42 "For real"
45 Co-worker of Kennedy starting in 2006
46 Cigar box material
47 Words before a date
49 Wheels of fortune?
50 Unit in a geology book
52 ___ supt.
55 Juice

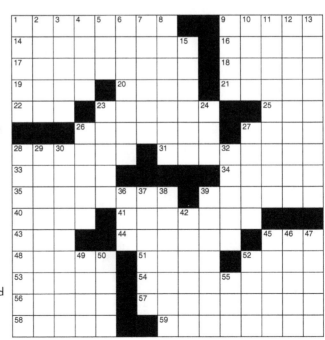

by James Mulhern

ACROSS

1 Cause of an artery blockage
11 Some working parts
15 Foam item at a water park
16 Coming up, to milady
17 Follower of Roosevelt
18 Jordan's Mount ___, from which Jericho can be seen
19 Innards
20 Black hat
22 Sect in ancient Judea
23 Lacking backing
24 E.R. units
25 Protective, in a way
26 Missouri city, informally
29 Knuckle-bruiser
30 "Discreet Music" musician
31 Ludwig ___ van der Rohe
32 "In"
33 Seizure
34 Field of fields?: Abbr.
35 Acoustic units
36 Hunter of a 20-Across
37 Standbys
39 "___ Nibelungenlied"
40 Like hospital patients and much lumber
41 Ephemeral
45 "Saving Fish From Drowning" author
46 Carry on
47 Mom on "Malcolm in the Middle"
48 Free
50 James of jazz
51 Hallmarks of Hallmark
52 Old TV news partner of David
53 Visual expertise

DOWN

1 Tear
2 Pluto and Bluto, e.g.
3 Debacles
4 Some Prado hangings
5 Intensify
6 Conservative side
7 Some candy wrappers
8 Interjects
9 ___ Sainte-Croix
10 Established in a new place, as a shrub
11 Hymn leader
12 They may be thrown out to audiences
13 Flip out
14 One left shaken?
21 Lead role in the film known in France as "L'Or de la Vie"
23 Brokers' goal
25 Some lap dogs
26 Class clown, e.g.
27 A woolly bear becomes one
28 Springsteen, notably
29 Like diamonds and gold
32 Trysting site
33 Dished
35 Overseas deb: Abbr.
36 Hobby
38 Distresses
39 1978 Broadway revue that opens with "Hot August Night"
41 Rialto and others
42 Cuckoo
43 Cuckoo
44 Big V, maybe
46 Veronese's "The Wedding at ___"
49 Bleu body

by John Lampkin

45

ACROSS

1 Decision theory factor
5 Athletic short?
10 Coolers, in brief
13 Indie rock band whose "The Suburbs" was the Grammys' 2010 Album of the Year
15 Jiffy
16 British author of the so-called "London Trilogy"
17 Feature of a Norman Rockwell self-portrait
18 Agitation overseas
19 Hot, spicy brew
21 ___ Records
22 Washboard parts
25 "Sic 'em!"
26 Popular Japanese manga seen on the Cartoon Network
29 "Bonanza" setting
30 Language originally known as Mocha
34 Turkish money
35 Miscellany
36 Tochises
38 Diego Rivera's" ___ Sandías"
39 Ceilings
41 Exotic annual off-road race
43 Dead reckonings?
45 Admits
46 In wait
48 Best-selling food writer ___ Drummond
49 "Bad!"
52 Become dazedly inattentive
54 Ryan of Hollywood
56 One with a password, maybe
57 Writer, director and co-star of the Madea films
61 Master's counterpart
62 Belief in human supremacy

63 Buffoon
64 Goes on and off diets, say
65 ___ Modern

DOWN

1 Pickup line?
2 Furious
3 Rugby formation
4 Subject of Spike Lee's "When the Levees Broke"
5 Reed section?
6 1962 film "___ Man Answers"
7 Energy
8 Actor Stoltz
9 Gaga contemporary
10 Notable Senate testifier of 1991
11 Florida's so-called "Waterfront Wonderland"

12 Password requirer, maybe
14 10-watt, say
15 Old-fashioned shelter along a highway
20 Phone inits.
22 Proceeded like a rocket
23 Time capsule event
24 Tough problem
27 Grayish
28 Downer
30 South African leader beginning in 2009
31 Reanimation after apparent death
32 Insipidity
33 Short
37 Kind of hotel, for short
40 David Ogden ___, actor on "M*A*S*H"

42 Colony unit
44 ___-cone
47 Bold
50 Opera ___
51 Land formation known for its caves
53 Printed slip
54 Unlock, in poetry
55 Old ___, Conn.
58 Willy ___, pioneering writer on rocketry
59 Green start?
60 "___ for rainbow"

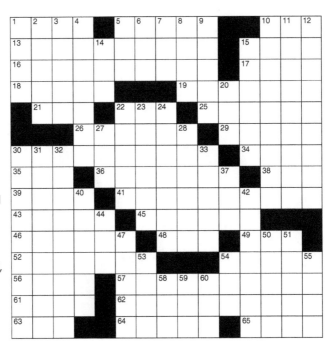

by Kameron Austin Collins

ACROSS

1 Web nuisance
8 With 26-Down, dramatic end to a game
15 Modern-day sanctuary
16 Mostly
17 "The Hurt Locker" setting
18 Jumps all over
19 Place for un bateau
20 Donkey : mule :: ___ : huarizo
22 Admission ticket
23 Cut down to size, maybe
25 Sweet Jazz sound?
27 Meant ___
28 Serape wearer
30 Have ___ at
32 Nick, say
33 Complex data
35 The middle Andrews sister
37 Heartening words
40 Corrupted
41 Show up at dinner?
42 WorkCentre maker
43 Elect
44 Construction material for several theme parks
46 Ruptures
50 Where 24-Down began his managerial career
52 Proverbial battlers
54 Eastern wear
55 Flavorer once labeled a "milk amplifier"
57 Burn to the ground
59 Bunkmates, often
60 Orion's hunting companion
62 #1
64 Jumped all over
65 Professor ___
66 Like some Hmong
67 Solution for storing contacts?

DOWN

1 All ___
2 Flaunt
3 Relief provider since 1916
4 1974 John Wayne title role
5 Not just tear
6 What many racers race on
7 Lightning strike measure
8 River between two Midwestern states
9 Malt finisher?
10 Enrich
11 Reuben ingredient
12 Denouements
13 Plant said to repel bugs
14 Decayed
21 Yearn for
24 See 50-Across
26 See 8-Across
29 Kind of artery
31 Pipe accompanier
34 Las, e.g.
36 People plot things around it
37 Recreation hall staple
38 High
39 Confirm
40 Yellow type?
42 Valentine letters
45 Boards
47 One might get past a bouncer
48 Blue, in Burgundy
49 Moral duty?
51 Get 180 on the LSAT, say
53 Boob
56 Wyndham alternative
58 Elevator at the bottom?
61 Suffix with 28-Across
63 Mate

by John Lieb

ACROSS

1 Family guy
8 Create some ties
15 It often has chips
17 1974 #1 hit written by Bob Marley
18 Almost equaling
19 Brat's place
20 With 24-Across, "The Pianist" star
23 Unlikely donor
24 See 20-Across
25 Common shower garment
29 First name in westerns
30 Conditioning apparatus
34 Family guy, affectionately
35 Once-common commercial fuel
36 Skippered
37 Extremely long string
39 ___ Robles, Calif.
40 Like some symmetry
41 Congolese, e.g.
42 Word menu option?
45 Criminal activity
46 Khloé Kardashian's married name
47 Like St. Catherine
51 Rapper with the 2009 hit "Kiss Me Thru the Phone"
56 Classroom films, e.g.
57 Like opinion pieces
58 World of DC Comics

DOWN

1 Sprint competitor, once
2 Physical reactions?
3 "I'm such a fool!"
4 Deforestation, e.g.
5 Assorted
6 TV foodie Brown
7 Informal rejections
8 Rail construction
9 Say again
10 Nail site
11 Less direct, say
12 Steinbeck have-nots
13 It can kick back
14 Fermented milk drink
16 Souvenir shop purchase
20 Feminist with the 1984 book "Gender Gap"
21 Product under a sink
22 Dial-O-Matic maker
23 ___ van der Rohe
25 Animal whose tongue is more than a foot long
26 Brand that's a shortened description of its flavor
27 Topper of der Tannenbaum
28 Munchies, in ads
30 "Storage Wars" cry
31 Scrabble player's asset
32 Durango direction
33 Unlisted?
35 Dog breed distinction
38 Scapegoat for many a failure
39 Driver's warm-up
41 In a vulgar way
42 Día de San Valentín bouquet
43 Lefty out in left field
44 Cheese burg?
45 Fix, as some roofs
47 Stat for a pitcher
48 Term paper abbr.
49 Canon shooter
50 Stooge syllable
52 Insignificant amount
53 Blitzed
54 Japan's ___ Castle
55 ___ Explorer

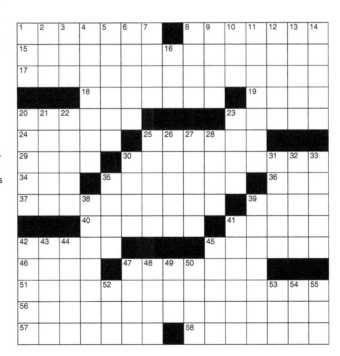

by David Steinberg

48

ACROSS

1 "Diamonds and Rust" singer, 1975
9 Add in large amounts
15 "Is that a gun in your pocket, or are you just happy to see me?," e.g.
16 Surround with light
17 Disappoints
18 More legible, say
19 Marvin Gaye's "___ Tomorrow"
20 Gambling
22 One often seen at the door
23 River of Hesse
25 Undermine
26 Wound around the body?
27 Reasons for some joyrides
29 Cause of an insurance increase, for short
30 National card game of Mexico
31 Call for a meeting?
34 Part of many a symphony
37 Visit
38 Many a Cape Cod locale
40 Multitudes
41 Multitude
42 Some settlers, before settling
46 H. G. Wells's "Empire of the ___"
47 Teatro Costanzi premiere of 1900
49 Kind of engr.
50 Pull (out)
51 New Testament money
53 ___ Andric, Literature Nobelist before John Steinbeck
54 Ornament at the top of a spire
56 Sign at the end of a freeway, maybe
58 Like God, in the olden days
59 Former Egyptian president Mohamed Morsi, for one
60 Team whose playing venue appears on the National Register of Historic Places
61 Dumps

DOWN

1 Dumped
2 Six Nations tribe
3 Provider of bang for the buck?
4 Greek consonants
5 Twins, e.g.
6 Make ___ of
7 Best Actor nominee for "American History X"
8 Fall asleep fast
9 Cylindrical pasta
10 Rare blood type, for short
11 Ching preceder
12 Asian capital
13 Wild olive
14 Boreal
21 Kojak's love of lollipops or Reagan's love of jellybeans, e.g.
24 Starts on a righteous path
26 Disobey directives, say
28 Gathers on a surface, chemically
30 Charms
32 Novel ending?
33 Time keeper?
34 "America's oldest lager beer"
35 First person outside NASA to receive a moon-rock award, 2006
36 Accelerated
39 1937 film based on a Gershwin musical
43 ___ of life
44 Work over
45 Nursery brand
47 Bringer of old news
48 Sitter's choice
51 Longtime soap actress Linda
52 "Take ___ a sign"
55 Group awaiting one's return, for short
57 Some rock

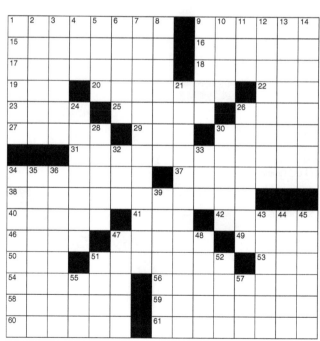

by Alex Vratsanos

ACROSS

1 Prepare to speak, say
16 Nurse
17 Not now
18 Puts somebody out
19 FICA fig.
20 ___ corde (piano direction)
21 Ganders, e.g.
22 "Bummer"
25 President's first name on "The West Wing"
26 Slicker go-with
29 With 35-Down, slightly stale
30 Choice for bow-making
33 Inexperienced
34 Their contents have yet to be dealt with
36 Tenor Vickers
37 Defense Department dept.
38 She played Detective Sasha Monroe on "Third Watch"
39 Greetings
40 Dummy in "Stage Door Canteen"
41 Cellphone feature, informally
42 Fr. religious title
43 Hotel waiter?
46 Florida preserve?
52 Keen insight, with "the"
53 Peak performance in 1953?
54 Focus of HGTV's "House Hunters"

DOWN

1 Philistine
2 "August: Osage County" playwright Tracy
3 Westphalian city
4 Looking down on?
5 DVD-___
6 Snack since 1912
7 Fish with iridescent blue stripes
8 Automaker Bugatti
9 German boys
10 The old you?
11 Snack since 1900
12 Named names, maybe
13 Crazy quilts
14 "Look ___ now!"
15 Alternative to cafés
22 Raid target
23 Top 10 hit for Eminem or 3 Doors Down
24 Eponymous German physicist
25 Aerosmith's titular gun carrier
26 Gandhi opposed it
27 ___, amas, amat
28 Crime writer Rankin
29 China shop purchase
30 Intro to biology?
31 Business bigwig Blavatnik
32 Composition of Accent seasoning
35 See 29-Across
39 Big name in oratorios
40 Scottish island that's home to Fingal's Cave
41 First stabber of Caesar
42 1930 tariff act co-sponsor
43 Joe, for one
44 "___ of Rock 'n' Roll" (1976 Ringo Starr hit)
45 Propensities
46 "Hug ___" (Shel Silverstein poem)
47 Exhibit upward mobility?
48 Some paddle wielders, briefly
49 Propose in a meeting
50 Bass line?
51 Romance novelist ___ Leigh

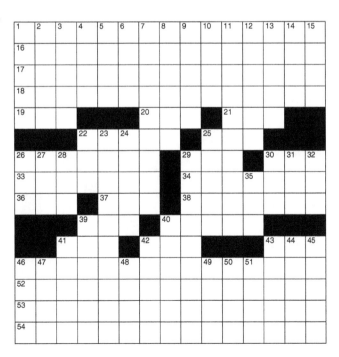

by Martin Ashwood-Smith

50

ACROSS

1 Keister
8 Soft drink company based in California
14 Comfortable way to rest
15 Cigar with clipped ends
16 Winter Olympics group
17 Edible in a cone
18 Onetime White House resident with a cleft palate
20 Onetime capital of the Mughal Empire
21 Only man ever to win an L.P.G.A. Tour tournament (1962)
22 Handy talent?
24 Govt. medical agency
25 Fountain spirits
27 Travelocity competitor
29 Saw home?
32 ___ d'agneau (lamb dish)
33 Harbors
34 El Greco, after age 36
36 Ate at
37 "Kramer vs. Kramer" novelist Corman and others
38 Crack, say
39 Energy company in the Fortune 100
40 Home pages?
41 Sierra Nevada evergreen
43 Like some verbs: Abbr.
44 Moon of Saturn
46 Strategic port raided by Sir Francis Drake in 1587
50 Anika ___ Rose, 2014 Tony nominee for "A Raisin in the Sun"
52 Java file, e.g.
54 Showed
56 Treats to prevent goiter, say
57 Delivers in court
58 Furthest stretched
59 Legs' diamonds?
60 Panel composition, often

DOWN

1 They rotate on Broadway
2 ___ Engineer (M.I.T. online reference service)
3 Gloria Gaynor's "I Will Survive," originally
4 Xenophobe's bane
5 Frozen foods giant
6 ___ Parker, founding president of Facebook
7 Author of the 87th Precinct series
8 Buff
9 One given to brooding
10 Bailiwick
11 Berlioz's "Les Nuits d'Été," e.g.
12 Printing on many concert souvenir T-shirts
13 Spots likely to smear
15 79, say
19 Onetime Toronado, e.g., informally
23 Game in which top trumps are called matadors
26 Certain tax shelters, for short
28 Stone coal
29 Setting for "One Day in the Life of Ivan Denisovich"
30 Helicopter-parent, say
31 University of Phoenix specialty
33 Dennis in "Monty Python and the Holy Grail," e.g.
35 Like roots, periodically?
36 Voter with a Green button, once
38 Array of options
41 Chancel arch icons
42 Slick, in a way
45 River bordering the Olympic host cities Grenoble and Albertville
47 Sleepy sort
48 Namely
49 Some garnishes
51 Annual race, colloquially
53 Soft-soap
55 Animation fan's collectible

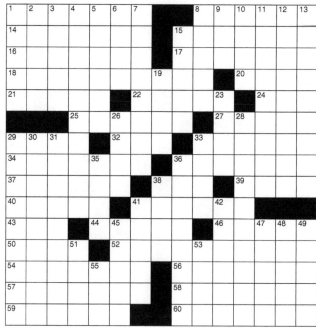

by Brad Wilber and Byron Walden

51

ACROSS

1 Hoping to get home?
7 Borrows without intending to repay
11 Therapy developers: Abbr.
14 In a slip
15 Government groups
17 Like many garments at the cleaner's
18 Hit the road
19 "I wouldn't lie"
21 Some linemen: Abbr.
22 Get in on the deal
23 Cross
25 Dreidel letter
26 It has a 30-min. writing skills section
30 Mtn. statistic
31 Surprising words from Shakespeare?
32 Ruined "rose-red city" of Jordan
33 Much of Mae West's wit
37 Line up
38 Mangrove menace, informally
39 It's often compounded: Abbr.
40 Lots
41 "___ to be!"
43 Approved
44 Language in which "talofa" means "hello"
46 What I can be
47 Sizzling
53 Celebrates wordlessly
54 Ferrari or Lamborghini
55 It may not be able to pick up something tiny
56 Bit of "Archie" attire
57 Elle's English-language counterpart
58 Bald-eagle link
59 One getting the picture

DOWN

1 Drop
2 ___ Barnacle, James Joyce's wife and muse
3 Drop in library use?
4 Will of "30 Rock"
5 Looks
6 Cause of some turbulence
7 Storied storyteller
8 "Casablanca" crook
9 Pea-brained researcher?
10 Real mess
11 Gucci contemporary
12 "Crucifixion of St. Peter" painter
13 Army E-6: Abbr.
16 Hoofed it?
20 Singer John with the 1984 #1 hit "Missing You"
23 Ready to dress down, say
24 Ecuadorean province named for its gold production
25 Bygone telecom
27 What half of a battery is next to
28 Concert itinerary listing
29 Easily taken in?
31 City on the Ouse
32 ___ Park (Pirates' stadium)
34 Its bottles feature red triangles
35 Big name in heating and air-conditioning
36 Hyperion's daughter
41 Suffuses
42 Cry when rubbing it in
43 Comparable (with)
45 Carne ___
46 Like some ancient Mexicans
47 Weapons inspector Blix
48 Hawaiian menu fish
49 No place for a free ride: Abbr.
50 Restaurant attachments?
51 It's at one end of I-79
52 Suez Crisis weapon

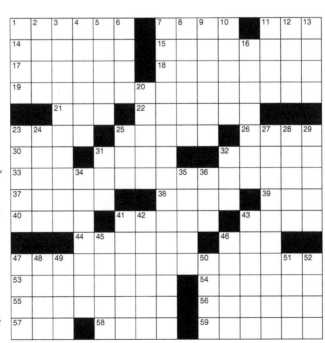

by Peter A. Collins

52

ACROSS

1 Tangy fruit pastry filling
11 Physical, say
15 There might be one after a bridge
16 The Rice Krispies mascots, e.g.
17 Georgia neighbor
18 Amazon icon
19 Raskolnikov's love in "Crime and Punishment"
20 City whose name is pronounced like the natives' word for "Where is . . . ?"
21 Something an aichmophobe fears, briefly
22 Old mount
24 Grandmotherly plaints
26 Abbr. at the end of some crossword clues
27 2003 Billy Bob Thornton crime film
32 Language of Middle-earth
34 Craigslist section
35 It's usually closed before leaving
36 Playground retort
37 Ax
39 Presidential debate mo.
41 Father of Paris
42 What may accompany a salute
44 With 51-Across, end of the London blitz?
46 Ruler with a palace near St. Mark's
47 San Diego's ___ Pines, site of the 2008 U.S. Open
48 Prerequisites for some overseas travel
50 On the q.t.
51 See 44-Across
53 New, informally
54 Valley girl's "no"
56 Cry over spilled milk?
58 Kung Pao chicken ingredient
63 Solstice time
64 Literally, "different lizard"
66 Some extracts
67 Advice of caution to a beginner
68 Midwest squad
69 Bizarre and alienating

DOWN

1 "What ___!" ("How fun!")
2 Two-time Oscar-winning screenwriter
3 Love at the French Open, essentially
4 Humble response
5 Changing place
6 Start of an "Ave Maria" line
7 Beer named for a port on the Yellow Sea
8 Guy from Tucson in a Beatles song
9 1960 historical film written and directed by John Wayne, with "The"
10 Well-off
11 Put on the surface, in a way
12 Superpower
13 Ventilation provider
14 Campers' relatives
23 Argentine ___
25 Spillover
27 Key of Schumann's Symphony No. 1
28 "Really?"
29 Not willing to give
30 "Popeye" cartoonist Elzie
31 Part of the Disney family, so to speak
33 "Falstaff" composer
38 Attention-getter, in some rooms
40 Company asset
43 Freebie on some airplane flights
45 Prefix with efficiency
49 Obsolescent media holder
52 It's around the mouth
55 Own (up)
57 Dedicatee of a famous Tallinn church
59 Runs smoothly
60 Setting for "Three Kings," 1999
61 Beaut
62 Vacation destination
65 "Come ___?" (greeting)

by Josh Knapp

ACROSS

1 Quickly gets good at
8 Summer hat
14 Restrained
16 "This isn't a good time"
17 First-century governor of Britain, whose name was Latin for "farmer"
18 Signer of the Kansas-Nebraska Act
19 Trade fair presentation
20 It means "council" in Russian
22 Apprehend
23 Roofing material
25 Cut short
26 Membre de la famille
27 Compact Chevys of old
30 G-rated oath
31 Poll calculation
34 "While we're on the topic . . ."
35 Marked by hostilities?
36 One of the Kennedys
37 Manhattan Project scientist
38 Emblem on Captain America's shield
39 All you can take with one hand
40 "Frida" actress Hayek
45 Williams nicknamed "The Kid"
46 Field strip
49 Automaker that introduced heated front seats
50 1950 short-story collection by Asimov
52 Cork bar
54 Dry up
55 Cause for complaint
56 Phalanx weapons
57 "Through the Dark Continent" author, 1878

DOWN

1 Witches' brew ingredients
2 Being in heaven
3 Cosmic payback
4 "I have measured out my life with coffee spoons" writer
5 Brief wait
6 Stop along the Santa Fe trail
7 Four-time host of the Nordic World Ski Championships
8 Upstanding one?
9 Pass over
10 Bart and Lisa's grandpa
11 Betrayed embarrassment
12 Not-so-fast food?
13 Amber-colored brew
15 Send-off for the dear departed?
21 To such an extent
24 Register
26 Empty
28 Creature outwitted by Hop-o'-My-Thumb
29 Tries to win
30 Columbian Exposition engineer
31 Addictive analgesic
32 Beauty magazine photo caption
33 Bit of paperwork
34 Call from home
35 Rouses to action
39 Finishing strokes
41 Pasty
42 Name tag location
43 "Never trust a woman who wears ___" (line from "The Picture of Dorian Gray")
44 "The Name of the Rose" setting
46 Two by two?
47 Veins' contents
48 Olympic skater Katarina
51 Burlesque accessory
53 Body treatment facility

by Patrick Berry

54

ACROSS

1 Neckwear slider
10 Domed dessert
15 "The highest result of education is ___": Helen Keller
16 Purpose
17 Continuing in its course
18 Hardly smash hits
19 Part of the Roman Empire in modern-day NE France
20 One forced into service
22 Bit of illumination
23 Tooth coating?
24 1994 Peace Prize sharer
25 Eschews money, say
26 Reduces the fare?
27 Big brand from Clermont, Ky.
28 Drill specialist, for short?
29 Minor documents?
30 "Poppycock!"
33 Producer of cheap shots?
34 "The Farm" painter, 1921
35 Dances with sharp turns
36 Biblical verb
37 What ruthless people show
38 Apollo, e.g.
39 Greek city where St. Paul preached
40 Los Angeles suburb once dubbed "Berryland"
41 ___ rock
42 "See!"
44 First name in the 1948 presidential race
45 About 90% of cotton fiber
46 "Magister Ludi" writer
47 Old-fashioned duds

DOWN

1 Greatly wanting
2 Good thing to keep in an emergency
3 A little of everything
4 Connects
5 Crunchy snack
6 Took for booking
7 "Young Frankenstein" girl
8 Drill specialist, for short?
9 Male issue?
10 Slums, e.g.
11 Not quite spherical
12 Winged prayer
13 Theodore of "The African Queen"
14 Computer programming command
21 Rather violent, perhaps
23 Old Pokémon platform
25 Woman in a leather jacket, maybe
27 Broadway inspector
29 Dot preceder
30 Consumed in copious amounts
31 Ignition technician?
32 Much-anticipated outings
33 Company with a game piece in its logo
34 1993 Peace Prize sharer
35 Orchard menaces
36 Get comfortable, in a way
37 Acapulco-to-Monterrey dirección
38 Château chamber
39 ___ crop
40 It's a blast
43 800s, e.g.: Abbr.

by David Steinberg

ACROSS

1 Displeases one's buds?
10 Dart maker . . . or dart
15 R.V. park hookup option
16 When New York's Central Park closes
17 Snack in a gym bag
18 Clog
19 Phrase cooed en español
20 Opposite of miniature
22 Uses a 49-Down
23 People thank God when it comes
25 What Kramer often called Seinfeld
26 Joseph of ice cream
27 Art ___, Steelers owner for 55 years
28 Cops, in slang
29 Moon views?
30 "Wiener Frauen" composer
31 They might like your comments
36 N.F.L. team that went 0-16 in 2008
37 Have an itch
38 Duncan of Obama's cabinet
39 Impound lot charge
41 Jump start?
44 Gomer Pyle, e.g.: Abbr.
45 Trees used to make shoe trees
46 Enfant bearer
47 Ad mascot in sunglasses
49 Spanish soccer club, for short
50 Spirit
51 Outerwear for moguls?
54 Battery for many a toy
55 Like a 1938 Andrew Jackson stamp

56 Writer featured in "The Electric Kool-Aid Acid Test"
57 409 and 410, but not 411

DOWN

1 Scary little sucker
2 12-book classic
3 Like many exercisers
4 The "2x" and "5" in 2x + 5, e.g.
5 Accordingly
6 Designing
7 Restaurant accessory
8 Knight who fell to the dark side
9 Knock sharply
10 Spot, to a tot
11 Large charge
12 Cousin of a carafe
13 It may cover a tear
14 Power line?

21 Unfavorable reply
23 Shot, informally
24 Tiller attachment?
27 Coats put on at barbecues
28 Part for a whack job?
29 Well, in Rome
30 Old change in the Vatican
31 Hotcake
32 Jet pack?
33 Cries uncle
34 What chickens have
35 Clothing, colloquially
39 Pro ___
40 Seat of Ector County, Tex.
41 Moved like a whiptail
42 Apprehended by a small group
43 Brewers' supplies
45 Pop singer ___ Rae Jepsen

46 Cry in a swimming pool game
48 He had a 1948 #1 hit with "Nature Boy"
49 Judge's perch
52 "___ no idea"
53 Kind of gravel

by Victor Fleming and Sam Ezersky

ACROSS

1 Army equivalent of a leading seaman: Abbr.
4 Lowered
11 Man on the street?
14 New England state sch.
15 Football helmet feature
16 Preposition with three homophones
17 Span since 1955
20 Middle of an Aeschylus trilogy, with "The"
21 Classic label in classical music
22 Try to pull off, say
23 Camera movement
24 Unwelcome neighbor
29 Get on board
30 Gouda and Muenster
33 Greeting at the head of a procession
34 Selfish response to a request
42 River that passes by the Hermitage
43 Wall hanging
44 Saint who is one of the Fourteen Holy Helpers
45 Squarely, informally
47 First name in late-night TV, once
48 Monumental
54 Pro athlete in a red-and-white uniform
55 Subway inits.
56 Bright spots
57 One being shepherded, say
58 It's double-hyphenated: Abbr.
59 Like many a sports car
60 Brutus' "but"

DOWN

1 Schnitzels, e.g.
2 Plain variety
3 Stick in a purse?
4 1950s–'70s defense acronym
5 Request often accompanied by "please"
6 Pasta eaten with a spoon
7 "That's enough," to a server
8 Banker/philanthropist Solomon
9 River into which the Vltava flows
10 Clear of vermin
11 Some corner shops
12 Move from A to B, say
13 Hero of 20-Across
18 Stanger a.k.a. Bravo's "Millionaire Matchmaker"
19 "You can't beat me!"
24 Sight-singing technique
25 54-Across, e.g., for short
26 Gender option on modern forms
27 Onetime center for the distribution of oranges
28 2008 World Series winners, to fans
31 Didn't get snapped up, say
32 Laura Nyro album "___ and the Thirteenth Confession"
34 They run up legs
35 Skips
36 Reproductive, in a way
37 Sportscaster Jim
38 Olympic gymnast Strug
39 Manhattan eatery referenced in Billy Joel's "Big Shot"
40 "Wow!"
41 Turned off and on
46 Shade
47 Ohio's ___ Point, home of the Top Thrill Dragster and Millennium Force roller coasters
49 Kind of day or job
50 Headlight?
51 Part of A.M.P.A.S.: Abbr.
52 Arum family member
53 TLC, e.g.

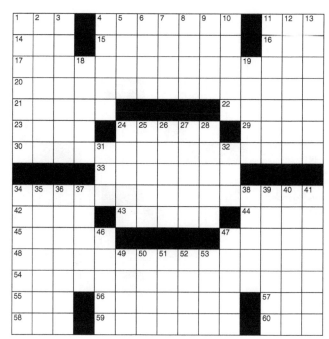

by Tim Croce and Alex Vratsanos

ACROSS

1 "Know what I'm sayin'?," in hip-hop slang
8 "Yep, alas"
15 Feature of many a reception
16 1998 N.F.L. M.V.P. Davis
17 Tablet alternatives
18 Laughed menacingly
19 Any of the Baleares
20 Political leader?
22 Bob of play-by-play
23 Squeeze
26 Kind of dye
27 Things that wind up on trucks
30 Sounded wowed
32 Days ___
33 Villainous organization in the 007 film "GoldenEye"
35 Sleep around
37 Like many Plains Indians
39 Football and basketball
43 Like innuendo
44 Electronics component
45 Ole Miss, athletically
47 What you might arrive two hrs. early for
48 Central American capital
49 Blue-flowered Mediterranean herb
52 Buff finish?
53 Nuzzling spot, maybe
57 Leader referred to as "His Imperial Majesty"
59 1994 memoir with a chapter on "New Robot Novels"
61 Oscar-nominated Greek-American actor
62 Crank

63 Certain solution holder
64 Figure in many a New Yorker cartoon

DOWN

1 Meditative sort
2 Big tree climbers
3 Something to catch from scolding parents
4 Box
5 Org. the Utah Stars belonged to
6 Public Enemy and others
7 Who wrote "Unless someone like you cares a whole awful lot, nothing is going to get better. It's not"
8 U.S. fraud watchdog
9 Breadth
10 ___ Arena (past Kings home)
11 Needles
12 Campus spot for Bluto, Otter and Boon
13 Scuzz
14 Motherland
21 Tender with Washington
24 Google browser
25 Ted Danson hit series
27 "Groovy!"
28 "All right already!"
29 Walk of Style locale
30 Flavorings in some root beers
31 Member of a loving trio?
34 Person on a mission?
36 Ordered
38 George Clinton was its first gov. (for 21 years)

40 K–12 grp.
41 "Whoops!"
42 Answers
44 Lower
46 "Quit your squabbling"
48 Switched to, as on a thermostat
50 Fictional boss of Stubb and Flask
51 River to the Colorado
54 Member of a loving trio?
55 Work for an artist, maybe
56 "Would I ___!"
58 Start of a kids' clothing line name
60 Letters on a track

by Ian Livengood

ACROSS

1 It has many giants and dwarfs
7 Profit-sharing figure: Abbr.
10 Part of the former Republic of Pisa
14 Run down a mountainside
15 Pour it on
17 One who winds up on a field
18 A kid might be punished for showing it
19 Scores
20 Marked up, say
21 Something pocketed in Italy?
24 Like Princess Leia vis-à-vis Luke Skywalker
27 Roller coaster feature with a food name
29 Celle-là, across the Pyrenees
30 Movie with the line "I'm a vulgar man. But I assure you, my music is not"
31 Be a very fast learner?
32 Title woman in a "Paint Your Wagon" song
35 Hybrid, maybe
36 Do a 35-Across chore
37 Romp
38 Brave, e.g.
40 "Who ___?"
41 1965 Yardbirds hit
45 Like many rodeo animals
47 Dweller near the Potemkin Stairs
48 Best seller
50 In
51 Track on "Beatles '65"
53 "Out!"
55 Scarab, e.g.
56 Tip for slips
57 Barreled
58 Like some broody teens
59 Folks working on courses?

DOWN

1 D preceder
2 Telescope part
3 Tuesday preceder
4 Be a juggler?
5 Ending of saccharides
6 Letters in old atlases
7 Seaweed derivative
8 Call for a timeout
9 Some body work
10 John in an arena
11 Chaises, in Cheshire
12 Flower child?
13 Had dogs, e.g.
16 Fail at falling asleep
20 Underdog playoffs participant
22 Character in many Baum works
23 Where Gray's "lowing herd wind slowly"
25 Biblical venison preparer
26 Artery connection
28 Noted acid studier
31 Noted 1-Across studier
32 Company with the King David Club
33 "Lost Horizon" figure
34 St. Patrick's Day order
36 "Saw" sights
38 Pity party plaint
39 Alternative to the pill, briefly
41 Snaps
42 Slip through, say
43 Like Cinderella's stepsisters vis-à-vis Cinderella
44 "___ Game"
46 Not iffy
49 Hungarian name meaning "sincere"
51 "___ me"
52 Battle-planning aid
53 Spring place
54 "Cap'n ___" (1904 novel)

by Barry C. Silk

ACROSS

1 It's part of a club
5 Place for vino
9 Like some floors and series
14 Ancient land east of the Tigris
15 Fur source
17 Repeated cry in a 1973 fight
19 High class
20 Mo. of Indian Independence Day
21 Annihilate, arcade-style
22 Many a New York Post headline
23 Geezers
25 Aptly named N.F.L. M.V.P. of the 1960s
28 Tudor who lost her head
29 The Glass Capital of the World
31 Thing, in Spain or Italy
35 Minority report?
36 Polish rolls
38 ___-eyed
39 Regardless of the repercussions
41 Fox in the Baseball Hall of Fame
43 Bring up to speed
44 They might become bats
47 Death, to Mozart
48 People often strain to make it
49 D.C.-based intercontinental grp.
50 Calls upon
54 Many Victoria Cross recipients
57 Heads with hearts
58 One hit on the head
59 Indian yogurt dish
60 "No ___ nada" ("It's all good": Sp.)
61 Journeyer through Grouchland, in a 1999 film

DOWN

1 Doc's orders
2 Palliation application
3 Demonstration of disinterest
4 Like God
5 Fall faller
6 Hens and heifers
7 "___ true"
8 Like God
9 Like yaks
10 Richard Pryor title role, with "the"
11 The "you" in "On the Street Where You Live"
12 Fold
13 Some cover-ups
16 Tanker's tankful
18 Currency of 46-Down
23 "Impressive!"
24 Elated
25 Touchstones: Abbr.
26 Bust a hump
27 Further
28 Liquor store, Down Under
30 Restrained
32 Beauvais's department
33 Institute in the 1997 sci-fi film "Contact"
34 N.R.A. member?: Abbr.
37 Agreement
40 Start of an alphabet book
42 Work first publicly performed at the Theater an der Wien in 1805
44 In open court
45 Junípero ___, founder of San Francisco
46 Where 18-Downs are currency
47 Home of minor-league baseball's Drillers
50 Ducky web sites?
51 Dollar bill feature
52 Quick cut
53 Europe's Tiger City
55 Cousin of a chickadee
56 The English Beat's genre

1	2	3	4		5	6	7	8		9	10	11	12	13
14					15				16					
17				18										
19							20				21			
			22				23			24				
25	26	27				28								
29				30						31	32	33	34	
35						36		37						
38				39		40								
			41	42					43					
44	45	46					47							
48				49			50			51	52	53		
54			55			56								
57								58						
59					60				61					

by Peter A. Collins

ACROSS

1 Faces facts
9 Cruise vehicle
14 Airline relaunched in 2009
15 A Ryder
16 Resort town near Piz Bernina
17 Like some migraines
18 "Home Alone" actor
19 Hot stuff
20 Schubert's "The ___ King"
21 Place for a shoe
23 Star material, maybe
24 Highlander, e.g.
28 Taking five
31 Public face
34 Scylla in Homer's "Odyssey," e.g.
35 Former hit TV show with the theme song "Get Crazy"
36 Eliza in "Uncle Tom's Cabin," e.g.
37 "Raising Hell" rappers
41 ___ de la Réunion
42 Phila.'s Franklin ___
45 Queenside castle indicator, in chess
46 Zigzag ribbon
49 Change for a C-note, maybe
53 Tops
54 Smashes to smithereens
55 Narrow soccer victory
56 Mark of affection
57 Undesirable element in the home
58 Deserve to be listened to, say

DOWN

1 Fixture in a chemistry lab
2 Las Ventas combatant
3 Opportune
4 Cry to a tickler
5 ___ bird
6 Whiffenpoofs, e.g.
7 Common aspiration?
8 Region of Italy that includes Rome
9 Material also known as cat-gold or glimmer
10 ___ probandi (legal term)
11 Set off easily
12 Caught
13 Bringing forth fruit, as corn
15 Provider of "!!!"
22 Voice actress in Disney's "The Princess and the Frog"
25 Horse ___
26 Feature of breakfast . . . or dinner?
27 Like the lifestyle of many a monk
29 African political movement
30 Fire sign?
32 Check for size, say
33 Some semiconductor experts: Abbr.
34 Set apart
35 Dutch queen until 1980
36 Reflect
38 Beaut
39 Some Renaissance music
40 Baby
43 Follow too closely
44 Siouan tongue
47 Subject of a Will Ferrell "S.N.L." impersonation
48 Court edge
50 Porto-___, Benin
51 Cousin of a goldeneye
52 Mr. ___

by Julian Lim

ACROSS

1 Very harsh
7 Cash flow statement?
15 Ultra 93 vendor
16 Winner of the inaugural Václav Havel Prize for Creative Dissent (2012)
17 Two-dimensional
18 The Hub
19 Meander
20 "I say" sayer
21 Ferrari rival, informally
22 Wildly cheering
24 Real joker
25 First talking pet in American comics
26 Steel-eyed one?
28 Horse whisperer, e.g.
29 Moves uncertainly
30 Boorish member of King Arthur's Round Table
32 Like dungeons, typically
33 Footprint, maybe
34 Tough to figure out
36 Paraphrase
40 Coin with a hole in it
41 First substitute on a basketball bench
42 Van Gogh's "L'Église d'Auvers-sur-___"
43 Chop-chop
45 Willy Wonka Candy Company candy
46 Flint-to-Kalamazoo dir.
47 "The X-Files" program, for short
48 Soft spot
49 Modern storage space
51 Flush
54 How Columbo often worked
55 Queued up
56 Be at the end of one's rope?
57 Principal part

DOWN

1 Ancient symbol of royalty
2 French bottom
3 Very succinctly
4 "No problem, I'm on it!"
5 "Been there"
6 One of a vocal pair
7 Hack
8 Sacred: Prefix
9 Anticipate
10 50 ___
11 Google unit
12 It means "sulfur island" in Japanese
13 Into crystals and energy fields, say
14 Redhead
22 Be part of the picture
23 Indian novelist Raja ___
24 Kind of business

25 Be a patsy
27 Hat-tipping sort
28 Catchphrase for the paranoid
30 Faux money
31 Holly
34 Deity with more than 16,000 wives
35 "Easy-peasy"
37 Rush home?
38 Soupçon
39 Nation's exterior?
40 Submit
41 Greeted someone
43 Time immemorial
44 Fast
47 "Dirtbag," e.g.
48 Remote
50 Revolutionary name
52 Kill
53 "The Partridge Family" actress

by Ashton Anderson and James Mulhern

ACROSS

1 Not too wimpy
10 Sensational effects
15 Begging, perhaps
16 David had him killed, in the Bible
17 Dish with crab meat and Béarnaise
18 Associate with
19 Allen in history
20 Many an event security guard
22 Say you'll make it, say
25 They wrap things up
26 Dangerous blanket
29 Craftsperson
32 Like a Big Brother society
34 Food order from a grill
38 K'ung Fu-___ (Confucius)
39 Charge at a state park
41 Zenith competitor
42 Hit the dirt hard?
44 Subject of the 2010 biography "Storyteller"
46 "Honest"
48 Regarded
49 Knowledge: Fr.
52 The very recent past: Abbr.
54 Sound reproducible with coconut shells
57 Left, on un mapa
61 Mall features
62 Portmanteau bird?
65 Shakespeare character who asks "To whose hands have you sent the lunatic king?"
66 Left part of a map?
67 Weather map feature
68 Smiley, e.g.

DOWN

1 Shake a leg
2 Operating without ___
3 Webster's first?
4 Swell
5 Electric shades
6 They're not forbidding
7 Perennial N.C.A.A. hoops powerhouse
8 Stick selection
9 "This is yours"
10 Completely bare
11 She came to Theseus' aid
12 ___-in-law
13 Bayou snapper, briefly
14 Mall features
21 Punch-Out!! platform, for short
23 Dance in triple time: Sp.
24 Snoopy sorts
26 They're often fried
27 Joanie's mom, to Fonzie
28 One in arrears
30 Alternative to tea leaves
31 Opprobrium
33 It helps get the wheels turning
35 Act like a jackass
36 Really long
37 Completely bare
40 Part of a C.S.A. signature
43 Perfect
45 Uncovers
47 It changes when you go to a new site
49 Bolt (down)
50 Let out, say
51 Labor Day arrival, e.g.
53 "Semper Fidelis" composer
55 Some parlors, for short
56 Trashy, in a way
58 It uses sevens through aces
59 First of many body parts in "Alouette"
60 Cabinet dept. since 1977
63 Chess's ___ Lopez opening
64 Frequent winner in a 66-Across: Abbr.

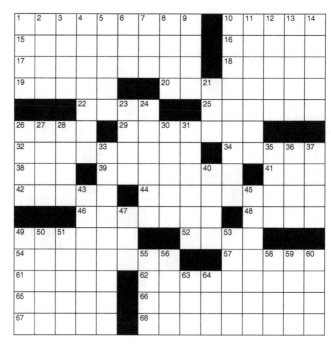

by Kristian House

63

ACROSS

1 "___ Style," first video with a billion YouTube views
8 Goes for enthusiastically
15 Home to "alabaster cities"
16 Like Saudi Arabia
17 "Hmmmmm . . ." [as hinted at by the three groups of black squares in the middle of the grid]
19 It may contain mercury
20 One of its flavors is Mud Pie
21 Starwort, e.g.
22 Sounds from some mall temps
23 Those south of the border?
25 ___ soup
26 Medical suffix
28 Bests
30 "___ am your father" (classic "Star Wars" line)
31 Things that ties never have
33 Last part
35 Mythical predator
36 Vietnam's ___ Dinh Diem
37 Excellent, in slang
41 Quintet comprising "Ode to the West Wind"
45 See 51-Across
46 "It was you," operatically
48 Dictator's beginning
49 ___ angle
51 With 45-Across, Thor's co-creator
52 Many a base player
53 Like 19-Across
55 No sophisticate
57 Ovid's others

58 Best Picture of 1954 [see 17-Across]
61 Hardly the assertive type
62 Gander
63 As part of a series
64 A wild card is unlikely to beat one

DOWN

1 Hybrid on the road?
2 Lovingly, on a music score
3 Greek goddess of vengeance
4 170 is its max score
5 Minute beef
6 Really long?
7 First
8 Closes a session
9 Rostock bar stock
10 "Bravo" preceder
11 Optical separator
12 Like some famous frescoes
13 Secretary of state before Dulles
14 Neighbor of the Adam's apple
18 Where Sotheby's is BID
24 "NCIS" actor Joe
27 Spanish muralist
28 They're clutched during some speeches
29 Sharp or flat
32 Mies van der ___
34 Anderson of "Nurses"
37 Dessert preference
38 Told, as a secret
39 Rough housing
40 Test the strength of, in a way
41 Where snowbirds flock
42 Corral
43 Cadet, e.g.
44 Under
47 Like a guitar string
50 Indian chief, once
54 Prefix with john
56 Suffix with switch
57 Refuges
59 Southeast Asian temple
60 Metrosexual sort

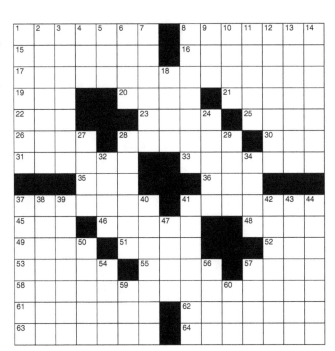

by Bruce Haight

64

ACROSS

1 Colonel's charge, once
4 Conventioneers: Abbr.
8 Washington, once, so they say
13 Creature that moves by jet propulsion
15 Loses one's shadow, say
16 Like John Belushi, ethnically
17 Spelunking supply
18 High level
19 Couscous ingredient
20 Ones working over the holidays?
21 Try to stop
22 Part of Austin Powers's attire
23 Big beat?
26 "Mad Men" award
27 One getting stuck in a horror movie
29 Powder holder
30 French locale of prehistoric cave paintings
31 Bellwether sound
32 Image on many an old map
34 ConocoPhillips competitor
35 Like top-shelf liquor
36 Place to walk to
37 Tired
38 "The Divine Comedy" has 100 of them
39 Ski lodge fixtures
42 Digression
43 Going in circles
44 Lear's youngest
45 British footballer Wayne ___
46 Inconvenience
47 Some modern fads
48 Reckon
49 Curtains

DOWN

1 Contents of some lockers
2 Drop off
3 Bolívar, Cohiba or Juan López
4 Patronize, in a way
5 Mount St. ___ (Alaska/Canada border peak)
6 Common dance theme
7 Fig. on some shredded documents
8 Case for a bootblack
9 Weak, with "down"
10 Drug dealer on "The Wire"
11 Many a flier under a door
12 Alternative to an elbow
14 Tomahawk for Andrew Jackson, surprisingly
15 Quickly produces in great quantity
19 One might have a cameo at the end
21 Bishop's place
23 Biblical quartet
24 Arlington House is his memorial
25 Monocle, in British slang
27 How Mount Etna erupts
28 The Battle of Thermopylae, for the Spartans
30 Some gatherings in halls
33 Raphael's "___ Madonna"
34 Swinging joints
36 Group of lovers, collectively
38 "___ mañana" (procrastinator's jokey motto)
39 "What's the ___?"
40 Shakespearean lament
41 Fashion designer Browne
42 A–F or G–K, maybe
44 Conqueror of Valencia, with "the"

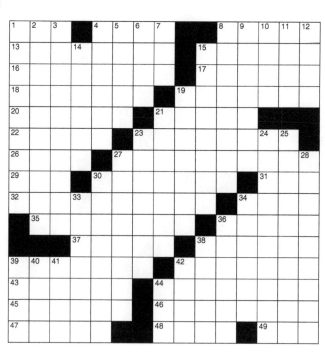

by Josh Knapp

ACROSS

1 "The Lion King" bird
5 Environmental pollutants, for short
9 Easter cake
14 Remote
15 Writer ___ Stanley Gardner
16 "Sounds like ___"
17 Staples of Americana
19 Iraqi P.M. ___ al-Maliki
20 One end of the [circled letters], which opened on 8/15/1914
22 Quanta
24 First female athlete on the front of a Wheaties box
26 Brew that gets its color from oxidation
27 Capillaceous
29 What a check might be delivered in
30 Tribal wear, for short
31 Part of the conjugation of "être"
32 Fiery eruptions
35 Features of many drive-thrus
39 Chicago market, with "the"
40 One with a once-in-a-lifetime experience?
45 Elation
47 ___ Wuornos, "Monster" role for which Charlize Theron won an Oscar
48 "Whew!" feeling
49 Was behind
50 The other end of the [circled letters]
53 Sonatas have four of them
54 What never lets go?
57 Hip place?
58 Second issue?
59 Prefix with zone
60 Gives it up, so to speak

61 N.B.A. coaching great George ___
62 Nobel pursuits?: Abbr.

DOWN

1 When doubled, onetime name in Hollywood
2 Pinnacle of "The Sound of Music"
3 Letter number
4 Deutsch marks?
5 Seed in Mexican cuisine
6 Homie's homes
7 Air bubble
8 Zaire's Mobutu ___ Seko
9 Ad form
10 Evangelist
11 Bird that, curiously, has a yellow breast
12 Bars in a bar?
13 Darth Vader's boyhood nickname
18 ___ Rutherford, the Father of Nuclear Physics
21 Result (from)
22 A pop-up has one
23 So-so
25 The Legend of Zelda platform, briefly
27 Trite
28 Electrical inits.
30 Stable role on TV?
33 "Ta-ta"
34 Boxing souvenir
35 Flight board abbr.
36 Medical product with no conceivable use?
37 Central American danger
38 Enliven
41 Family-friendly category

42 TV's Capt. Picard
43 Fountain feature
44 Suffix with opal
46 They'll rock your world
47 Remote power source
49 Rodeo performer
51 "Out of Africa" writer Dinesen
52 Island sometimes called El Cocodrilo
53 Peculiarity
55 Location of the William Tell legend
56 Lover of Orion, in Greek myth

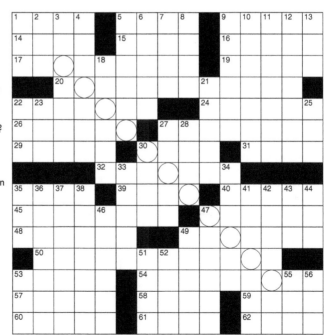

by Jeff Chen

66

ACROSS

1 Genre for Django Reinhardt
10 Spaceship Earth setting
15 "Has the whole world gone mad?!"
16 Recipient of a major downgrade in 2006
17 Clicking point
18 Musical Hall of fame collaborator?
19 Stretch before giving birth
20 Islamic repub.
21 Not 100% sold
22 "The ___ true for . . ."
24 Winner of an annual "posedown"
26 One of saintdom's Fourteen Holy Helpers
28 Windbags beat them
29 Ones with low class standards?
32 Speaker connectors?
35 Thing pulled by a "hoss"
36 Her poison killed Creon
37 "The Next President" comedian
38 Boatload
39 Rude response to "Excuse me?"
41 Like some horror films, in modern lingo
42 Maternally related
43 What's round due to too many rounds?
48 2009 Grammy winner for "Crack a Bottle"
50 Giant in jets
51 "Pretty Little Liars" actor Harding
53 Give a powerful electric guitar performance
54 Convalesces
55 Hague Conventions topic

57 Shakespearean title role for Anthony Hopkins
58 Render unwell
59 Farm call
60 Spots for company cuisine

DOWN

1 Campers' annoyances
2 Cry that helps people pull together
3 Prey for an Arctic fox
4 Palindrome property
5 Start of an attention-getting cry
6 Sudden start
7 Starting lineup
8 Crashes, with "out"
9 "B.C." sound effect
10 Louis Braille and Les Paul
11 Cell interiors
12 Card
13 1995–2000 "S.N.L." cast member
14 Where captains go
21 Lament loudly
23 Not tolerate injustice, say
25 Gives elevator eyes
27 Phoenicians, e.g.
29 Sask. doesn't observe it
30 Cross you wouldn't mind bearing?
31 First name in tyranny
32 People's 2007 Sexiest Man Alive
33 Least dismal
34 Shooter's choice, briefly
37 Tacky television transition
39 He said "Music is the space between the notes"
40 Wiener link?
41 1959 #1 hit for the Fleetwoods
43 Southeast Asian coins
44 What goes after cows, ducks and pigs?
45 Close relative of Clio
46 Eric Cartman's mom on "South Park"
47 Packers' measurements
49 "Someone ___ Dream" (Faith Hill country hit)
52 It has a "Los Angeles" spinoff
55 Film director Wenders
56 Character string

by Peter Broda

ACROSS

1 Something that goes from a pit to your stomach?
12 Snarky sound
15 It has billions of barrels
16 Queen of Thebes, in myth
17 One may tell a conductor to slow down
18 Sound of a slug
19 Sashimi selection
20 Buckled
21 Dos little words?
23 Esther of "Good Times"
25 Large part of some herds
28 Brand of bait pellets
29 Fix
30 Walt Disney Concert Hall designer
32 Cop
34 Monarchial support
35 G squared?
37 Spotmatic, e.g., briefly
38 Unhelpful reply to "How did you do that?"
43 Screen entertainers with many gigs?
47 "All the President's Men" figure
49 Like many hipsters
51 Actress Blanchett
52 Pie hole
53 Parts of kingdoms
54 Juan's sweetheart
56 ___ rock (some George Harrison music)
58 & 59 Race that's not very competitive
60 Pill holder
64 Occasion to do a late shift?: Abbr.
65 Member of a "great" quintet
66 ___ Gonçalo, Rio de Janeiro
67 Mideast president who wrote "The Battle for Peace," 1981

DOWN

1 Regulus A and Bellatrix
2 Gets rounds around town?
3 Show fear of
4 Govt. project whose logo depicted a shield in space
5 Danny of the Celtics
6 Curiosity producer
7 First course selection
8 Do battle
9 Counterpart of "abu"
10 "Burn Notice" grp.
11 Freeze
12 Literally, "fire bowl"
13 Doesn't just attract
14 Cache for cash, say
22 1963 Pulitzer winner Leon
24 It's KOH, chemically
26 "The Killing" star Mireille ___
27 Like some lobbies
30 Trip up?
31 T. S. of literature
33 Member of a Latin trio
36 Line to Jamaica in N.Y.C.
38 Bar necessities
39 "Dream" group in Barcelona in 1992
40 Mounted below the surface of
41 Quick Time or RealPlayer format option
42 Like boors vis-à-vis gentlemen
44 Masseur gratifier
45 Raise crops on the Plains, maybe
46 So-called "Helen of the West Indies"
48 Director of the 2012 comedy "This Is 40"
50 Try to pull off, say
53 Epic start
55 Cutting it
57 Replicator, e.g.
61 ___-Boy
62 Old White House nickname
63 Guerra's opposite

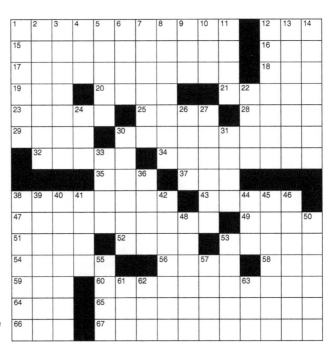

by Sam Ezersky

68

ACROSS

1 Rage
6 Hardly ice outside
10 Places for sprigs
14 Quiet parter?
15 Pie cutter's tool
16 Umber at the opera
17 First part of a hit for this crossword
19 Relative of "Hey, ma"
20 Arc's target, maybe
21 Plat pouch
22 Easter floor mat
24 Pog or Pogs, formerly
26 Lives
29 Bad member to pick?
30 Fly of film
32 Hit, part 2
34 Olympia with a watery realm
36 Perform peace
37 Fried with four legs
38 Covered with slug mud
40 Sorters' quarters
43 Dramatically scored sorceress
44 Ager
46 Hit, part 3
50 Cagey parts, e.g.
51 Early
52 Part of a euro
54 Tige, say
55 Adds a little toe to
57 Like a great bod
59 Bled for a social affair, perhaps
61 Dramatic cry from people who get subbed
62 Last part of the hit
66 Caker, for example
67 Car whose logo is liked?
68 Ever lost to
69 Starts of some chorus lies
70 Eve
71 Chia growth area?

DOWN

1 Crow
2 Vegas would love this type of world
3 Casio game
4 Kat's "I"
5 Slag for sleuths
6 Product made by Moe
7 Kid of poetic work
8 Arm from a Mideast lad
9 Did a baker's job
10 Covert, maybe
11 Margarie might be described thus
12 Grad's opposite
13 Gere of "Gulliver's Travels"
18 User's circuit
23 I pieces
25 You might board yours at the keel if you take a cruise

27 Wig of the old Greek army
28 Program that asks "Are we aloe?," for short
30 Metal worker's claim?
31 Abruptly becomes violet
33 Doe, e.g.
35 Bombs without bags
39 Sci-fi character remembered for her large bus
40 Strad part that becomes frayed
41 Wet like a seesaw
42 Spas that last 52 wks.
43 Bugled strokes
45 Deadly gag
46 Mesa prerequisite
47 Guy who may offer a girl a rig
48 Mystical chat

49 H.L. player
53 Refusal from a boy lass
56 "Ow!"
58 O
60 Murray who's highly raked
63 Be-___
64 Ed of some school addresses
65 Old rival of America

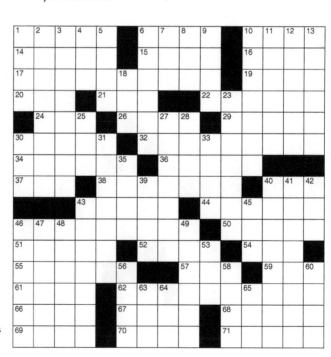

by Timothy Polin

69

ACROSS

1 Poll Internet users on, perhaps
12 Inn stock
15 Code often used for take-home tests
16 W. Coast airport one might think has poor security?
17 Summed up
18 Middle-earth baddie
19 Short order?
20 Kiwi's companion
21 Longtime N.F.L. coach whose name is French for "the handsome"
23 Ordinary person
25 Soprano Grist
27 Neighbor of St. Kitts
28 Symbol of sentimentality
30 Anti-Mafia measure, briefly
32 Eliot title surname
33 Budgetary concern
35 "Miss Julie" composer, 1965
37 Ray often seen over a range
41 As surplus
42 He played John Glenn in 1983 and John McCain in 2012
44 Bo Jackson was one in '89
45 Mideast's Gulf of __
46 Department store chain founder
48 Like un bébé
52 Costa __
54 Whaler's direction?
56 Angela Lansbury, e.g.
57 Group sharing a culture
59 Year Bush was re-elected
61 Kroger alternative
62 Mark, as a survey square
63 Singer known as "La Divina"
66 Natural rock climber
67 Words following an understatement
68 Leaves on a trolley, say
69 "Don't worry . . ."

DOWN

1 In-flight calls?
2 Doc Savage portrayer
3 Cousin of a donkey
4 Secured
5 One expected to get beaten
6 Cool red giant
7 The world, to a go-getter?
8 Mark the start of
9 Travel option: Abbr.
10 Word with wall or tower
11 Football Hall-of-Famer Tunnell
12 Juice source for a trendy drink
13 Bo Jackson was one in '89
14 Response to an insult
22 Played like Bird or Trane
24 Notable lifelong bachelor in U.S. history
26 Player of Fin Tutuola on TV
29 Host of 1950s TV's "Bank on the Stars"
31 Longtime Laker Lamar
34 Salon job
36 Answer, quickly
37 Means of furtive escape
38 12-Down, often
39 Neighbor of Georgia
40 "South Pacific" girl
43 Political theorist Carl
47 Steinway competitor
49 Suitable job?
50 "Count me in"
51 Like big hair, often
53 ESPN analyst Garciaparra
55 Sieves, in a way
58 Not unhinged
60 Relocation transportation
64 Travel options: Abbr.
65 Fighting Tigers' sch.

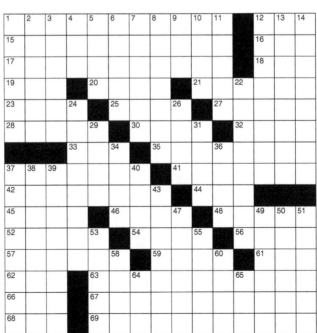

by Daniel Raymon

ACROSS

1 ___ Street, London's onetime equivalent to New York's Wall Street
8 Lurid nightspot
15 Synthetic purplish colorant
16 Took too many courses?
17 Vicks product
18 Rap type
19 Assn. with a "100 Years . . . 100 Movies" list
20 Bygone Acura
22 Non-Roman Caesar
23 Have a dependency
25 "Would you look at that!"
26 Musical title character who "made us feel alive again"
27 What the Sup. Court interprets
29 "___ in '56" (old campaign button)
30 Plantation machine
31 Hid
33 Sybill Trelawney, in the Harry Potter books
35 Gorp, e.g.
36 Like some projects, for short
37 Mesh with
41 Piece of trash?
45 Slightly ahead
46 "___ man can tether time or tide": Burns
48 Tim Tebow, in college football
49 "Sweet" girl of song
50 Ones with issues?
52 Person holding many positions
53 Ox- tail?
54 Trattoria specification
56 Key holder?
57 Mercury's winged sandals
59 Outlook alternative
61 Parasite
62 Cash in a country bar
63 Parallel bars?
64 Onetime "Lifts and separates" sloganeer

DOWN

1 "The Raising of ___" (Rembrandt painting)
2 Annual heavy metal tour
3 Big name in browsers
4 Popular chip flavor
5 Parisian possessive
6 Kicking oneself for
7 Trapezius neighbor
8 Welders' wear
9 Egg maker
10 Rowlands of "A Woman Under the Influence"
11 Assn.
12 Beverage with a triangular logo
13 Occasionally
14 Kindles, e.g.
21 Pride : lion :: gang : ___
24 Bleeth of "Baywatch"
26 Avon competitor
28 "Do I have to?," for one
30 Extraterrestrial, e.g.
32 Abbr. on a business card
34 URL ender
37 Japanese electronics giant
38 Download from Apple
39 "Funky Cold Medina" rapper
40 Not entirely of one's own volition, say
41 "Cloud Shepherd" sculptor
42 Ferocious Flea fighter, in cartoons
43 Producer of a hair-raising experience?
44 Certain movie house
47 Aldous Huxley's "___ and Essence"
50 Worked with
51 Common comedian's prop
54 Best Picture before "12 Years a Slave"
55 Wife of Albert Einstein
58 Party concerned with civil rights, briefly
60 "If I ___ . . ."

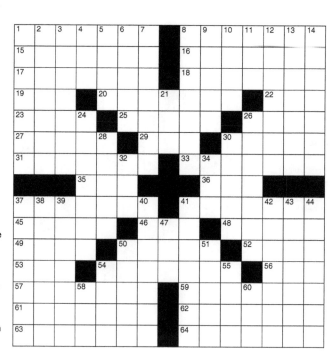

by David Steinberg

71

ACROSS

1 Elderly person on a fixed income
16 Propagandists' detention site
17 Deterioration of standards by competitive forces
18 1957 Patrick White novel adapted into a 1986 opera
19 Comprehends
20 Didn't clash (with)
21 What a chicken feels
24 G.P. grp.
27 Diversified investment strategy
32 Corp. whose name is also its stock symbol
33 L. Frank Baum princess
34 Title heroine of a Wagner opera
35 Ford from the past
37 It's easy to swallow
38 "Beats me"
39 Go outside the calling area, say
41 Dawg
42 Charging for every little thing
45 With 11-Down, become a part of
46 With 53-Down, many Marcel Duchamp works
47 Ray of old pictures
48 It's a mouthful
51 Silents actress Negri
52 Political machine practice
59 Eugenia Washington (co-founder of the Daughters of the American Revolution), to George Washington
60 Tumblers

DOWN

1 Bruin legend
2 Heartlessly abandons
3 Break down
4 Hymn opener
5 Courage
6 Friendly start?
7 Word that is its own synonym when spelled backward
8 Biblical ending
9 Baseball Hall-of-Famer Phil
10 PepsiCo brand
11 See 45-Across
12 Fall mos.
13 D.C. player
14 Like some broody teens
15 Dash letters
20 On hold . . . or what the seven rows of black squares in this puzzle's grid spell in Morse code
21 Pasta ___ (Italian dish, informally)
22 Smooth-leaved ___
23 Much like
24 Some backwoods folks
25 Alvin Ailey's field
26 "Just about done"
28 Metric weight
29 One coming out of its shell?
30 "Me too"
31 Best
36 Contents of a well
39 It's stranded, for short
40 Head-scratching
43 Televised fights?
44 Native New Zealanders
48 Pack (in)
49 Lanford Wilson's "The ___ Baltimore"
50 Messenger de Dieu
51 ___ colada
52 "War and Peace" has a lot of them: Abbr.
53 See 46-Across
54 Silkscreen target
55 Oomph
56 Lang. class
57 Blood test letters
58 Some appliances, for short

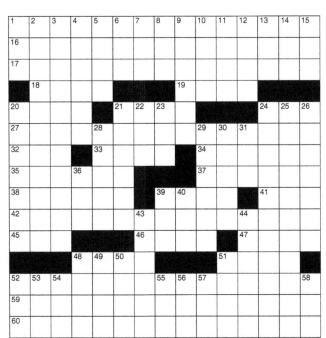

by Joe Krozel

ACROSS

1 Big chain closed on Sundays
10 Person lacking foresight?
15 Version of a song that's shorter or cleaner than the original
16 Point of origin for some flights
17 Nobody's opposite
18 Overly talkative
19 Cause of many unwelcome lines
20 "Uh-huh"
21 Ratso's given name
22 First name at the U.N., once
24 Predigital beeper?
27 Display
29 Seem forthcoming
30 Malt finisher?
31 Hit Showtime show
32 Nasdaq member?: Abbr.
34 An early Disney cartoon had one
35 BBC World Service std.
36 Contact briefly electronically
39 Like throwbacks
41 You might strain to produce them
43 Chief Chono Ca Pe, e.g.
46 Harmonica piece
47 Part of a funeral procession
48 Use a two-digit confirmation code?
51 Neighbor resort of Snowbird
52 Undergo induction
53 Silver Buffalo Award org.
55 "___ shall live your epitaph to make": Shak.
56 Type of white wine

57 One may soak a competitor
60 "Panic 911" airer
61 Tables or shelves
62 Position
63 Zippy

DOWN

1 Was hoarse
2 It can be a headache
3 Preoccupation
4 "Profiles in Leadership" publisher, briefly
5 "___ 2012" (viral video)
6 Completer of a career Grand Slam in 2009
7 Snake River Plain locale
8 Much-used epithet in hip-hop
9 P.R. setting

10 Prime piece
11 Jones
12 Duke of Illyria, in Shakespeare
13 Final sign
14 Kid-lit character with a long face, in more ways than one
21 Libido
23 National leader?
25 Stylish
26 "___ not thou fear God . . .": Luke 23:40
28 Ingredient in many salad dressings
33 Near
35 Opposite of contracted
37 Linguistically adventurous
38 "Most seeming-virtuous queen," in Shakespeare

40 Try
41 Go on
42 Like some teeth and glass
43 Leitmotif settings
44 Stereotypical wear for the paranoid
45 Connected
49 "Ish"
50 Meets
54 Give ___ (have any interest)
57 Burn prevention stat
58 As
59 Grp. with rules about carrying on?

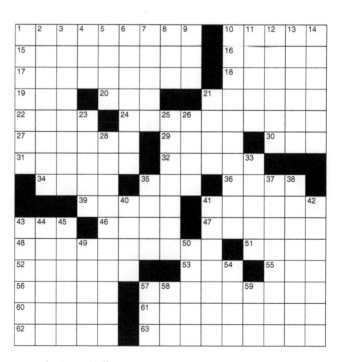

by James Mulhern

ACROSS

1 Queen's music
12 Film developer?: Abbr.
15 "Hasta la vista!"
16 Musician with the 2012 album "Lux"
17 Allows someone to walk, say
18 Big gun on a ship: Abbr.
19 Oxford, e.g., to its students
20 Michael of "Juno"
21 Oxide used in picture tubes
23 "A person who talks when you wish him to listen," per Ambrose Bierce
24 Lead
25 Shots
28 Coddle, e.g.
29 Shack
30 Artistic friend of Zola
31 Sharpshooter's skill
32 Poet Wilfred __
33 Out of gear?
34 Buchanan in a bookstore
35 Word of logic
36 Moving day multitude
37 Governor or senator follower
38 Caught in a web
40 Certain book, sizewise
41 Makes out
42 Secure neatly, as an umbrella
43 Pioneer in the Nevada gaming industry
44 One of its categories is Agency of the Year
45 With 46-Down, two-in-one movie players
48 It's often an oxide
49 Something avoided in a factory outlet
52 Washington and McKinley: Abbr.
53 Commute, in a way
54 Replies of confusion
55 Stick here and there

DOWN

1 Archaeologists often find what they're looking for in this
2 Counterfeiter fighter, informally
3 Isao of golf
4 At full term
5 "No worries"
6 Comes out with
7 Skiing twins' surname
8 Sister of Phoebe, in myth
9 "Or softly lightens __ her face": Byron
10 Like many kids' self-made greeting cards
11 Didn't let oneself go, say
12 Lead-in to some written advice
13 Blurred
14 Option for a marinara base
22 Not too big a jerk
23 Old bomber
24 A lot of what makes you you
25 Checked in with loved ones, say
26 Exclamation that might be punctuated "¿¿!?"
27 Put too much weight on
28 Like some potato chips
30 Ceilings
33 From the Union
34 Hebrew for "to the skies"
36 Rival of Captain Morgan
37 ABBA's music
39 __ Tamid (ever-burning synagogue lamp)
40 Thick spreads
42 Ace on a base
44 Give up
45 One of its fragrances is Poison
46 See 45-Across
47 Rink fooler
50 Small warbler
51 Inits. of Thoreau's mentor

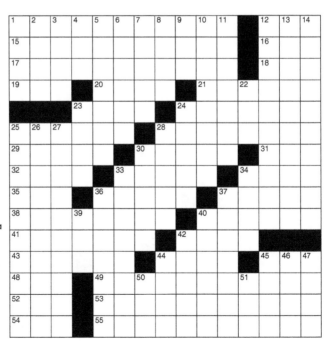

by Michael Wiesenberg

ACROSS

1 Pro
6 Paper job
15 Words repeated after "I shall no more," in "The Tempest"
16 Say
17 When bars close in Boston
18 TV screen format
19 Subject of a standing order?
21 ___ COIN
22 Super-corny
26 Pair
27 Font menu choice
28 It's between =1 and +1
29 Bag
30 Source of conflict, in antiquity
31 Film, e.g.
33 12/
34 Biker chick, perhaps
35 Dude
38 Invention that prompted NBC to adopt the peacock logo
39 ___ seeds, ingredients in some health drinks
40 "Gotcha," in old lingo
43 Star followers
44 Something that's fallen off a shelf?
45 What an article may refer to
46 Herb used in Thai food
48 Fair
50 Italian after-dinner drink
51 Party to a tryst
55 Toy company that introduced Rubik's Cube
56 Like bulldogs
57 Finely prepare

58 Something on either side of a bridge
59 One advised to take two tablets

DOWN

1 Beset
2 Call from the cellar
3 Like most philosophy dissertations
4 Ones involved in an elaborate courtship
5 Breaks
6 Radar's rank on "M*A*S*H": Abbr.
7 Bank deposit?
8 Universal area
9 Through
10 Kitchen brand
11 Like many new mothers
12 Still being tested

13 One running home, maybe
14 Modern-day "Let's stay in touch"
20 Agave product
23 Montreal eco-tourist attraction
24 Anemone, to name one
25 "Just relax, will you?!"
29 Chase scene producer, for short
32 Classic storyteller who wrote under the pseudonym Knickerbocker
34 Punch
35 Depreciates
36 Valuable commodity in New York City
37 What some homemade signs announce

38 Anchors of some malls
39 Box in a cab
40 Spark
41 Comedian Paul
42 Kind
46 Words that are rarely spoken
47 Teller of many tales
49 Unscrewed
52 [Thumbs up]
53 End of many a long race: Abbr.
54 P.E.I. setting

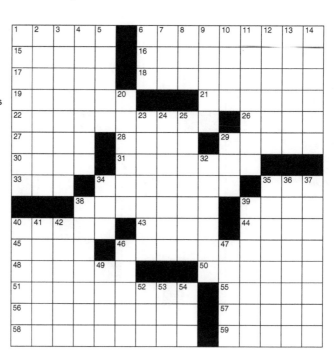

by Josh Knapp

ACROSS

1 Self-praise couched in self-deprecation, in modern lingo
11 Story lines
15 Wanting
16 What marketers might follow
17 2013 Golden Globe winner for "Girls"
18 Colony in ancient Magna Graecia
19 "Downton Abbey" title
20 Four-star figs.
21 Risotto relative
22 Refrain syllable
23 Going green?
24 South American cowboy
26 Animal that may swim on its back
28 It's often checked on a cell
30 ___-soul (style of Erykah Badu and Lauryn Hill)
31 Talent scout's find, informally
33 Public
35 Beginning of a process of elimination
37 One who gets numbers by calling numbers
40 Bathes
44 Coach Parseghian
45 44-Across's "Fighting" team
47 Between, to Balzac
48 One living in urban poverty, pejoratively
50 Baby docs
52 ___ pop
53 Contemporary and compatriot of Debussy
54 You may drop a big one
56 Toon toned down for the 1930s Hays Code
57 Resort options
58 A nerd may not have one
60 Some tributes
61 Alcopop relative
62 Christie novel title that, without spaces, is a man's name
63 New lease on life

DOWN

1 There's no place to go but down from here
2 Make public
3 Obamacare obligation
4 Fourth of July, for Calvin Coolidge, informally
5 Was up
6 Level
7 Unit of energy?
8 First name in Chicago politics
9 Not level
10 Peach
11 Eschewed takeout, say
12 Stuffed chili pepper
13 How you may feel after taking allergy medication
14 Shore dinner
21 Spots where artists mix?
23 Nickname for Oliver Cromwell
25 Turkish dough
27 Unstable compound
29 Ties up in a slip
32 ___ desk (newsroom assignment)
34 Either director of "True Grit"
36 Negligee
37 Fire
38 Sentinel's place
39 Taylor of "Twilight"
41 Chef de cuisine's shout
42 Publishing house employee
43 Dr. Ruth, for one
46 Bros
49 "Divine" showbiz persona
51 Bad place for a whale
55 Spots annoying teens
56 Stain
58 Match.com abbr.
59 ___ Lonely Boys (2004 Grammy winners)

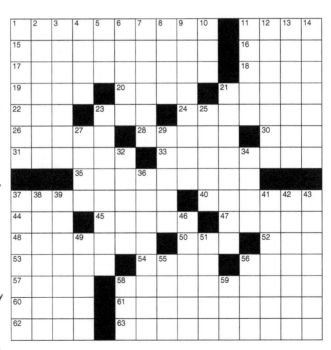

by Finn Vigeland

76

ACROSS

1 Goes quickly after takeoff?
8 Series of antecedents
14 Professor who tries to kill Harry Potter
16 ___ pectoris
17 One not favored
18 Randomly distributed
19 PBJ filling?
20 16:9, say
22 Muscles for some fraternity guys?
24 Shake
25 Mo. of National Grandparents' Day
26 Raft
27 Height
29 Viewfinder?
30 Some nerve!
32 Nobelist Frederick ___, pioneer in radiochemistry
33 Fashion series since 2004
37 Asner's "Elf" role
38 Browning, for one
39 It might be found in a café
40 Spanish interrogative
41 All-nighter, maybe
45 Writer Rand
46 Cold-shoulder
48 Mackenzie of "The Facts of Life"
49 Legerdemain
53 Cooperstown inst.
54 Words before and after "Am too!"
55 Longest continuous corporate partner of the Olympic Games
57 Get misty
58 Fall guy?
59 Galley slaves, e.g.
60 Least abundant

DOWN

1 Teams
2 Smuggling aid
3 Judges 14:14 has the only one in the Bible
4 "Maid of Athens, ___ we part": Byron
5 Hamlet takes a stab at it
6 Some gym shoes
7 Spill
8 Holds up
9 Word with deux or nous
10 Home of the Unesco World Heritage Site Fatehpur Sikri
11 Light refreshment
12 Hard to handle
13 Splendid array
15 "Life's Good" sloganeer
21 Sportsperson who may take a bow?
23 Situation that makes a double play impossible
27 Tucked away
28 Snap
29 Dungeons & Dragons attributes
31 Wear for the weary
32 TV inits. since 10/11/75
33 Feature of many a McDonald's
34 Macs and such
35 Part of a crater
36 Saucer, perhaps
37 Red juice hybrid
40 Contemptible sort
42 In
43 They take bows
44 Terrible one?
46 Comb
47 Certain address starter
48 Yoga pose
50 About
51 Some Red Cross supplies
52 Single-serving coffee holder
56 Abbr. found at the 56-Down of this puzzle's four longest answers

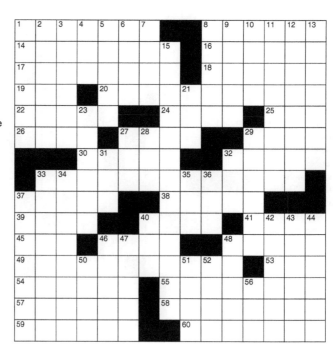

by Erik Agard

ACROSS

1 "Ninotchka" setting
6 Fad dance of the 1930s
10 Swedish Air Force supplier
14 Hollywood job
15 Water bearer
16 Lady Antebellum, e.g.
17 Someone might call your number this evening
19 Asian tourist magnet
20 Delayed sensation?
21 1920s–'30s debate opponent of Einstein
22 15-Across shape
23 "The road of excess leads to the palace of ___": William Blake
25 Succumb to drowsiness
26 Exceed 21 in twenty-one
28 Orchard Field, today
30 Spending time unprofitably
34 Little homewreckers?
35 Some carved Victorian toys
36 Strong and durable, in a way
37 Maid
38 Deli offering
39 Gin cocktail
43 They're on during the wee hours, briefly
46 Arab League member
48 Lengthened unnecessarily
51 Roofing material
52 1963 song investigated by the F.B.I. for supposedly obscene lyrics
53 Cartridge fillers
54 Forever, basically
55 In the intervening time
56 Cole Porter's "___ Magnifique"

57 Three-player card game
58 Wound up

DOWN

1 Brewer of Schlitz, nowadays
2 Catlike, in a way
3 Soprano Fleming
4 "Splendor in the Grass" screenwriter
5 Telegraphy word
6 Secretly carrying (off)
7 Weathercast numbers
8 Fruit grower's bane
9 Reach
10 Uninformed guess
11 Ancient mariners
12 Banned items at Wimbledon
13 Left the gate, say
18 Post office workers?

24 Hard-to-escape situation
26 Philosopher who wrote "Superstition is the religion of feeble minds"
27 Working while others play?
29 Improves
30 Answers wrongly?
31 Ultimate degree
32 Fault finder?
33 Systematize
34 Where firedamp can form
35 Like Tik-Tok in the Land of Oz
40 Runs without moving
41 Small tributary
42 Ritzy gym feature
43 Egyptian monetary unit
44 Power, slangily

45 Jousting need
47 First flight locale
49 "Somethin' ___" (Eddie Cochran song)
50 Dispatch

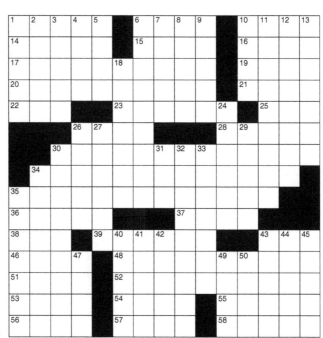

by Patrick Berry

78

ACROSS

1 Start of a weird infraction?
9 Sushi offering
14 First Indian tribe to sign a treaty with the U.S. government
15 Hand in hand
16 Eskimo wear
17 Hike, e.g.
18 Mideast pops?
19 Smoke without fire?
21 Naval petty off.
22 What was once cool?
23 Gray figures?
27 One-man Broadway hit of 1989
29 Only one U.S. prez has had one
32 Straight talker's slangy phrase
37 Country standard
38 Words from a good buddy
39 On the side
40 X or Y preceder
41 Site of class struggles?: Abbr.
42 Floor
43 One N.B.A. All-Star Game team
46 One telling you where to get off, for short?
49 High ranking?
55 Introductory ballet instruction
56 Whence the word "alcohol"
57 Listen here!
59 Words of support from an organization
60 Reacts to, as a nagging request
61 Game keeper?
62 Tiramisu ingredient

DOWN

1 Guesstimate opening
2 Deep-sea explorer William
3 Explain
4 Beginning of a seasonal refrain
5 Hurtful outbursts?
6 Playboy
7 Shortstop Aybar who was a 2011 Gold Glove winner
8 Start of an elimination
9 Time that little Susie is woken in the 1957 hit "Wake Up Little Susie"
10 Lo-cal
11 Military group
12 Canterbury's home
13 Beat by a whisker
15 Who said "I have a wonderful psychiatrist that I see maybe once a year, because I don't need it. It all comes out onstage"
20 Easily passes
24 Name in 2000 headlines
25 Mates
26 Old age
28 Early online forum
29 Inane
30 Spangle, say
31 "___ trifle!"
32 Having much at stake
33 ___ asada
34 Parade V.I.P.
35 Cockeyed
36 Song that ends "O dolcezze perdute! O speranze d'amor, d'amor, d'amor!"
44 Challenge for defenders
45 Bygone royalty
47 Measures of one's writing?
48 Mind
49 Shooters
50 Israeli conductor Daniel
51 Rain forest rodent
52 Aid in an uphill climb
53 Country name pronounced by natives in two syllables
54 Atlantic City resort, informally, with "the"
55 Common cleaning scent
58 Hole number

by Martin Ashwood-Smith and George Barany

ACROSS

1 Ones who get lighter sentences?
10 1983 action comedy with the tagline "When these guys hit the streets, guess what hits the fan"
15 "Hold on one cotton-pickin' minute!"
16 Band-Aid inventor Dickson
17 Situation that's gone absurdly out of control
18 Car or cellphone feature
19 Relative of Cie.
20 Exchange words
22 Land of the poet Máirtín Ó Direáin
24 Doctors' orders
25 Order (around)
26 City on the Seine
28 Ill-tempered
30 Victor at Gaines's Mill and Cold Harbor
31 One whose word is gospel?
33 Steadiness in leadership
35 ___ scale
37 Corn bread
38 Pfizer cold and flu medicine
42 Result of equal opposing forces
46 Number of African countries with español as an official language
47 Mild cigar
49 Pioneer of Dadaism
50 Auto parts giant
52 Pope Francis and others
54 "There!"
55 Leading lady?
58 Country with a red, white and blue flag: Abbr.
59 Dianne of "Parenthood," 1989

60 Musical "Mr."
62 Like much slapstick
63 Either way
64 Choice words?
65 Combined Latin/Jamaican/hip-hop genre

DOWN

1 Casting directors?
2 Horticultural problem caused by overwatering
3 Kind of rock
4 Direction from Luxembourg to Nürnberg
5 "Me neither," formally
6 Response to a lousy deal
7 Pitiful group
8 Sub-Saharan tormentors

9 Amasses
10 No longer working
11 Carr who wrote "The Alienist"
12 Company that makes Silly Putty
13 The Hebrew Hammer of Major League Baseball
14 Puzzled
21 Minute Maid Park team
23 Ronald who directed "The Poseidon Adventure"
27 College org. for sailors-to-be
29 Musical matchmaker
32 Muslim name that means "successor to Muhammad"
34 Sympathy
36 Thumb key

38 "Chinatown" co-star
39 Queued
40 Children
41 Talk up
43 Menace, in a way
44 Results from
45 Onetime Minnesota governor who ran for the G.O.P. presidential nomination nine times
48 Continuing obsessively
51 Bret Harte/Mark Twain collaboration
53 Urban Dictionary fodder
56 Record label for Cream and the Bee Gees
57 "And Winter Came . . ." singer, 2008
61 M.A. hopeful's hurdle

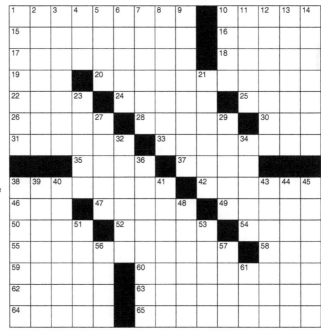

by Tracy Bennett

80

ACROSS

1 Two-man band?
9 Blush-inducing
15 Anti-spill, say
16 Green machine
17 Exponential unknown
18 "Anticipate the difficult by managing the easy" philosopher
19 Cause of a stinging breakup?
20 Less significant
21 Sonnet extender?
22 Enjoyed muchly
23 Mount ___, Charley Weaver's hometown
24 See 41-Across
27 Partner of many
30 Lambs, to Lucius
31 One being strung along?
35 Decline dramatically
37 180s
38 Title subject of a search in a 2003 film
39 "Twilight," e.g.
40 Gets a clue, with "up"
41 With 24-Across, barbecue finger stainer
44 "___ really help"
45 Storm designation
46 To whom Charles Darwin dedicated "Different Forms of Flowers"
49 Bartending tool
53 In-flight
54 Mixer for losers?
55 Pioneer in literary realism
56 "Servant of the Bones" author
57 "Really?"
58 Ditch

DOWN

1 Like some straws
2 Have prestige
3 Org. that, when spelled backward, is an old-timey exclamation
4 What Gollum calls the Ring in "The Lord of the Rings"
5 Nadir's opposite
6 Dove's dream
7 Aids after blanking out
8 Slip
9 Service providers?
10 Statement of confidence
11 Musical component
12 Last part of "Waiting for Godot"
13 Was a slug
14 ___ Lane, London theater locale
20 Southeast Asian fruits with large, thick spines
22 Burgundy or claret
24 "Twilight," e.g.
25 Oodles
26 "Adventure most ___ itself": Emily Dickinson
27 Empty-headedness
28 Word with deep or dead
29 Newest fashion
31 Mother superior?
32 It's named for a Scand. god of battle
33 "Pencils down!"
34 Nonhuman Earth orbiter of 1961
36 Trip planner's option: Abbr.
40 More like a sheet?
41 Fanatically militant sort
42 "Veep" actor ___ Whitlock Jr.
43 Very much
45 Widening agent in medicine
47 Goggle
48 Gold-certifying grp.
49 0.5, for 30°
50 ___ rage (result of juicing)
51 Sister brand of CorningWare
52 Shipping hazard
54 The U.N.'s ___ Hammarskjöld

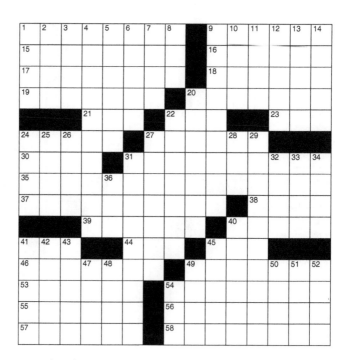

by Julian Lim

ACROSS
1 Major artery
8 No longer under consideration
12 "Absolutely!"
13 Raid target
14 Something a bride brings to a marriage
15 Originate
16 Like some nuts
17 Black-and-white
19 Sunroof, maybe
20 Count at the breakfast table
21 Golden Gophers' sch.
22 Woman's shift
23 Guilty sensation
24 Italian red
25 Bath site: Abbr.
26 Number 10-Down
27 Routes: Abbr.
30 Indian condiment
31 Sugar source
32 Was a hit, say
33 Ballerina descriptor
34 Blackened
35 Showed unhappiness, in a way
36 Mars, notably
37 1949 show tune with the lyric "Here am I, your special island!"
38 Olympian's first name that sounds like another Olympian's name
39 Site of the largest sports arena in Europe
41 Cupid's teammate
42 Ranch dressing?
43 Small change
44 Quickly reproduced

DOWN
1 Suggesting, as an idea
2 Extending the life of
3 City where the Lehigh and Delaware Rivers meet
4 Scene of W.W. II airstrikes
5 Do some yard work
6 Org. concerned with bridges and canals
7 "Unfair!"
8 Persian ruler dubbed "the Great"
9 Strand, in a way
10 See 26-Across
11 One changing locks?
12 Stage assistant
13 Dearth
14 Play group
18 Presidential candidate who wrote "No Apology"
20 Pulled up to a bar
22 Yakker
24 Spanish/Mexican pastry
26 Transportation for Helios
27 Judge of movies
28 Slights
29 Large bowls
30 River that flows past four universities
31 Touch-type?
32 2014 Kentucky Derby winner California ___
33 Low-tech hacker?
34 Dinner chicken
35 Certain shortcut
36 Only major U.S. city with a radio station whose call letters spell the city's name
37 Title in children's literature
40 Hail and farewell

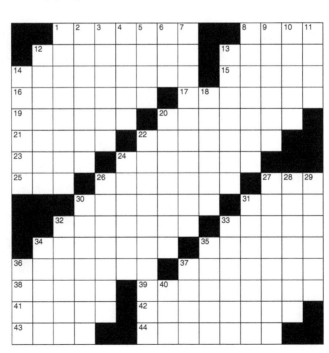

by David Steinberg

ACROSS

1 Quite cheaply
12 Green piece
15 Guinness record-setter for "highest-rated TV series" (scoring 99 out of 100 on Metacritic.com)
16 Org. with a radon hotline
17 Ones in praise of angels?
18 Burmese greeting
19 Times in classifieds
20 Looking up to
22 Tom Petty's "___ So Bad"
23 Game of pure chance
25 Group of very small stars?
26 Third party label: Abbr.
27 Green piece?
29 Aid for collecting some samples
31 It's shown in much storm reportage
35 Biblical land in what is now Yemen
36 Get rid of jerks?
38 Mess (around)
39 Ripens
40 Tourist city on the Yamuna
41 Common scale topper
42 Spanish 101 verb
43 Country that includes the islands of Gozo and Comino
45 Bit of censure
46 Laotian money
49 Manhattan architect?
52 Spread of book and film
53 N.L. West team, on scoreboards
54 Far from scarce
57 Place for a monitor, for short
58 2014 N.B.A. M.V.P.

59 Omega, in physics
60 Millions of people swipe them

DOWN

1 Austen's "Northanger ___"
2 Architectural crossbeam
3 100,000,000 maxwells
4 Makes bale?
5 Clears
6 Year before the emperor Trajan was born
7 Key key?
8 They may be in a mess: Abbr.
9 Help complete a job
10 City in old westerns
11 Villager station wagon, e.g.

12 Like some chocolate
13 Restaurant availability
14 Bud, slangily
21 Catch badly?
23 Having gone south
24 Cartoon supplier
26 It's relatively lacking in iodine
27 "Benson" actor Phillips
28 Baker with a trumpet
30 Deep end?
31 Eastern leader
32 Force to walk with the arms pinned behind
33 Turtle locale, maybe
34 "Look ___!"
35 Animated hero of 2001
37 Big chicken
41 One after another?
44 Some desk materials
45 16th-century council site

46 Best Director of 1947 and 1954
47 Memorable hurricane of 2011
48 Gauchos, e.g.
49 "Soap" actor Jimmy
50 Many an exploding star
51 Eastern leader
52 Ring combatant
55 Big payroll service co.
56 "Of course!"

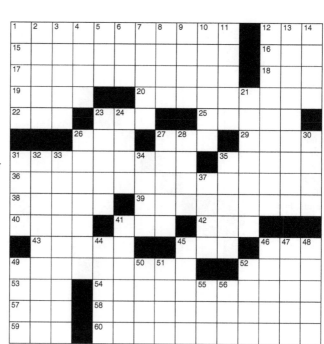

by Evans Clinchy

ACROSS

1 Something running on a cell
10 "The Waltons" co-star Ralph
15 Starting to succeed
16 Opera title boy
17 Been exposed to an awful lot
18 Like Royal Albert Hall
19 Roofing option
20 "Palindromania!" writer Jon
21 Male duck
22 Be up
24 Ones hanging around delis?
26 Flashers at a rock concert
30 Let up
31 Superslim
34 Some QB protectors
35 Out of service?: Abbr.
36 Gouge, e.g.
37 Dog tag?
38 Thespian Thurman
39 One who's often 31-Across
43 Orbiting Galaxy, e.g.
45 Hulu offerings
46 Like a cat-o'-nine-tails' nine tails
48 Spitfire org.
49 Paul who pioneered in quantum mechanics
50 Means to deep spiritual insight
53 Malaria-fighting compound during W.W. II
56 Development sites?
57 "V for Vendetta" writer
60 "Le Bassin aux Nymphéas" painter
61 Tabs, e.g.
62 Lead character in seasons 1–3 of "Homeland"
63 One-run homers

DOWN

1 Start of many records
2 Prime draft pick
3 Two-time belligerent against the British Empire
4 Country ___
5 "Magnum, P.I." wear
6 Things dealt with in passing?
7 Like many dogs' tails
8 Faint
9 TV's Goober and others
10 Was ducky?
11 Lacking scruples
12 2007 satirical best seller
13 2007 Jamie Foxx film set in Saudi Arabia
14 Many future monarchs
22 What atoms may have
23 Oakland Oaks' org.
25 Consist of
26 Overawed
27 Church-owned newsweekly, for short
28 Only Hispanic performer with an Emmy, Grammy, Oscar and Tony
29 ___ Club
32 Player motivator
33 Olympian troublemaker
37 Person's sphere of operation
39 Easy street's location?
40 Had
41 Town at the tip of Italy's "heel"
42 Carrying people, for short?
44 Didn't just peek
47 Couples
51 Potpourri
52 Fine ___ (Irish political party)
53 Dummy
54 "Consarn it all!"
55 Danny Ocean's ex-wife in "Ocean's Eleven"
58 Some mail for a mag
59 "Will ya look at that!"

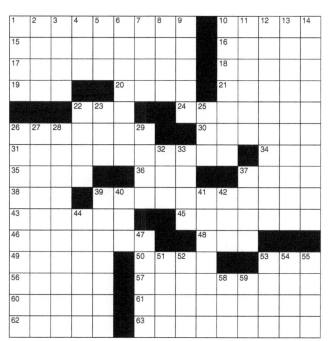

by Michael Ashley

ACROSS

1 Some military settings?
9 Pants part
15 Part of a bar code?
16 "Annie ___," old Scottish love song
17 Atlantis section
18 Sharp
19 Car radio button
20 Droids have them
22 When repeated, aerobics class cry
23 The Joker, e.g.
26 Certain punch
29 One in a one-on-one session
30 With 14-Down, literary yes-man
33 Connecting word
34 "Wait ___!" ("Hold on there!")
35 Strong ale, in British lingo
36 One who didn't make it to the office?
38 Classic British cars that pioneered in rear engines
39 They may be picked up by dogs
40 Integral course of study, briefly?
41 "The thing is . . ."
42 Bakery purchase
43 Competition where the last one standing wins
44 Current setting
45 Scorpio hunter of film
48 Noted avoider of the color red
50 Be full
51 Court star Nadal, informally
54 Really move
56 Oner
59 Parts of the Navy's full dress blues

60 Actor with Adam Sandler in "Funny People"
61 Leave one's company?
62 Like some business letters

DOWN

1 "Sheesh!"
2 Big things on Capitol Hill
3 Former Zairian leader Mobutu ___ Seko
4 "A hint of lovely oblivion," per D. H. Lawrence
5 Modern kind of campaign
6 Letters with a view
7 Brand once plugged by John Madden
8 First Christian martyr
9 Grip
10 "Batman" villain ___ al Ghul
11 Exceed
12 Subject of "The Wørd" on the first episode of "The Colbert Report"
13 Recognize
14 See 30-Across
21 Literary figure whose name is a letter short of something he wrote
24 Native Arizonans
25 Aid for clumsy thumbs
26 "Stop" at 44-Across
27 "Consider it done"
28 Abandoned storage units?
31 Say "amen," say
32 Gomer's biblical husband
35 Cobbler, at times

37 Walking very quietly, say
38 Dish whose name comes from the Latin for "ink pot"
40 Stuck
43 Kvass component
46 Statistical method for comparing the means of two groups
47 Start of a cartoon cry
48 Waste of a vote?
49 Wile
52 Order
53 Egg chair designer Jacobsen
55 Xerox option: Abbr.
57 Wrestler Flair
58 Pap

by Evan Birnholz

ACROSS

1 Times for speaking one's mind?
10 Coarse
15 Spot for shooting stars
16 Finish putting on pants, say
17 Became a bachelor, maybe
18 Onetime Coleco competitor
19 Rom-___ (some films)
20 Up to the present time
21 Beyond blue
22 Trivial Pursuit board location
23 Agreements
25 Richard March ___ (inventor of the rotary printing press)
26 Remotely monitored event, informally
28 Plum or pear
29 "Sharknado" channel
30 Save
32 Sleep on it
34 "Ash Wednesday" poet
36 Groups with play dates?
40 "Brokeback Mountain" role
42 "Hurry up!," en español
43 Henchman first seen in "The Spy Who Loved Me"
46 Stationery store stock
48 Pusillanimous
49 ___ Aduba of "Orange Is the New Black"
50 Stop obsessing
52 Not just a pop group, for short?
53 Tilting poles
55 Triton's domain, in myth
56 Dart
57 Two-time N.B.A. All-Star Brand

58 Free
60 Flowering plant named for a Greek god
61 Saloons
62 Onetime sponsor of "I Love Lucy"
63 "Boy, am I having fun!"

DOWN

1 Diagram showing company positions, briefly
2 Detours
3 Title carpenter of an 1859 novel
4 Watch things, for short
5 Condensed vapour
6 Patient looks?
7 Most fitting

8 People with signs at airports, e.g.
9 Part of E.S.T.: Abbr.
10 Bygone emperors
11 "Lovely" one of song
12 It may elicit a shrug
13 Not doubting
14 ___ sense
21 Nissan offering
23 Took courses at home
24 "Faster than shaving" brand
27 Yugoslavian-born winner of nine Grand Slam tournaments
29 One with a short hajj
31 $, € and £
33 Johnny Depp role of 2013
35 Formatting palette choice
37 Site of an annual encierro

38 They think they're special
39 Least excited
41 Outfit worn with goggles
43 Things downed at Churchill Downs
44 Rhododendron relative
45 Chinese appetizer
47 Rear ends
50 Actress/singer Lotte
51 Pot
54 Bop
56 Thwart
58 ___ Friday's
59 Start of an alley-oop

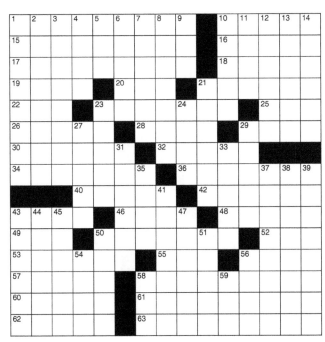

by Patrick Blindauer

86

ACROSS

1 Sting, e.g.
5 100th anniversary of Disney's "Fantasia"
9 Singer Aguilera's nickname
14 Not well, say
15 Second
16 Conventions
17 Coming or going
19 Shows of appreciation for services provided?
20 Characters from Sophocles
21 Prideful?
22 "Born again" woman
23 Figureheads?
24 Most laggardly
26 Pabst product
29 Some Arabian food
30 ___ Lumpur
31 Needles
36 "Huh?!"
38 How Marilyn Monroe sang "Happy Birthday" to President Kennedy
39 Blank
40 City near Arches National Park
41 Queen's "We Will Rock You" and others
42 Requiem Mass part
46 Musical partner of DJ Spinderella and Salt
47 Bit of writing that's slashed?
48 Household brand that's an anagram of 47-Across
50 Homophone of 55-Down
53 Minute hands, in a way
54 Sci-fi disturbances
56 Early Trinity College affiliation: Abbr.
57 It's hair-raising
58 When Hamlet says "The rest is silence"
59 Leaves in
60 Actor Bean of "Troy"
61 Grate

DOWN

1 Colorful breakfast option
2 Mysore Palace resident
3 Focus of some philanthropy
4 So says
5 They come and go
6 Sushi bar servings
7 Double-crossed?
8 Fraternity house cry
9 Map phrase
10 Rourke's co-star in "The Wrestler"
11 Greek goddess of peace
12 Leche drinkers
13 What you will?
18 Certain character set
23 They're easily caught
25 Ear-related
26 Lift things?
27 Sassiness, slangily
28 Spring fall
29 Bathroom brand
31 1977 PBS sensation
32 Pair of hearts?
33 Trumpeter Jones
34 What a soldier may be at?
35 Heads of some towns in Quebec?: Abbr.
37 ___ Pueblo (Unesco World Heritage site)
41 Half of a cigarette?
42 Cuts down
43 A little off
44 Fast ___
45 Ceiling support
46 Black-and-white creature
49 Skip it
50 Black-and-white creature
51 Some N.F.L. workers
52 Do something polite
55 Thrust provider

by Patrick Blindauer

ACROSS

1 Boston and Chicago, but not Seattle
10 Diddly-squat
14 Inuit's transport
15 Oscar nominee for "Fiddler on the Roof"
16 Recommended
17 Photoshop effect
18 Bright lights
19 What naturals have
21 With 24-Across, witchcraft, e.g.
22 Up
23 Sea-___
24 See 21-Across
25 Ring of islands?
26 Barely clear, in a way
29 Expert
32 Like Fortunato, in Poe's "The Cask of Amontillado"
33 "The Cask of Amontillado," e.g.
34 Ease
35 Predators in the "Predator" films, for short
36 Some I.R.A.'s
39 "Be on the lookout" signal, in brief
40 ___ country (rustic locale)
43 Gallows ___
44 Anthrax cousin
47 Prey for a dingo
48 Helpful
49 Get ready to click, maybe
51 Ora pro ___
52 Having human form
53 ___ chic
54 Didn't kill each other

DOWN

1 Where primatologist Dian Fossey worked
2 "We're in trouble now!"
3 Gambol
4 TV colonel
5 20th-century first lady
6 Grp. with suits and cases
7 Easy decision
8 Start of an Eastern title
9 Fusses
10 Book after Hosea
11 Desire
12 Introduction to English?
13 Social gathering
15 Grp. with a lot of baggage
20 British kitchen accessory
22 Like the words "hoagie" and "kitty-corner"
25 Actor with the line "Rick! Rick, help me!"
27 Small dams
28 "___, like lightning, seeks the highest places": Livy
29 Base men?
30 Some E.R. cases
31 Topping for skewered meat
32 Idiot box
33 Desire
34 The son on "Sanford and Son"
36 Adam's apple coverer
37 X
38 Blackened
41 Parrot
42 Prefix with -graphic
43 Betty Boop and Bugs Bunny
45 "The way things are . . ."
46 Tous ___ jours (daily: Fr.)
47 Actress Russell of "Felicity"
50 Adolphe with an instrument named after him

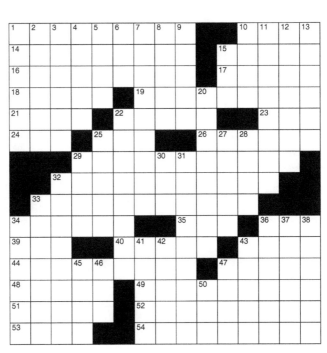

by Mary Lou Guizzo and Jeff Chen

88

ACROSS

1 Send
6 Future works?
11 Apricot or eggplant
16 Reveal
17 Husband of Elisheba
18 Laughable
19 81 ÷ 27
21 Lists for
22 Bee relative
23 Kind of sleep
24 Get out of the line
26 Supertrendy
27 It's conducted in a theater
28 Old Memorial Coliseum player, for short
30 Utter
32 Staff with notes
34 61 + 86
39 He is one
41 National Junior Tennis League co-founder
42 Supervising
43 The Apostle of Cuban Independence
46 Checkout line?
48 Upgrade, as a shower
50 Explicatory words
51 Powerful guy
53 Digs near the ocean, perhaps
54 Miss dismissal
56 ___ a time
57 Ends of scissors?
58 Like illegal charades clues
59 1977 law school memoir
61 Flip
63 56 × 42
66 European Parliament locale
70 Blanket material
71 Crude
73 Wicked
74 Block number?: Abbr.
77 1989 AP Female Athlete of the Year
79 Sans le ___ (broke: Fr.)
80 "Go ask your mother" elicitor
81 Cul-de-sac, in some addresses
83 33 − 21
86 Match
87 Like some coincidences
88 Wind stopper?
89 Sentence units
90 Cans
91 Lay low?

DOWN

1 Jabbers, at times
2 Unhesitatingly go for
3 Threads
4 Word with bag or board
5 Developing option: Abbr.
6 Comparatively trouble-free
7 South American reptile
8 Eruption cause
9 Turn down a raise?
10 Comprehensive
11 "Academica" author
12 Subject of the tribute album "Every Man Has a Woman"
13 Eye liner?
14 Well aware of
15 Hinge (upon)
20 Cut from a log, maybe
25 Lorelei, notably
28 Novel about Dolores Haze
29 1979 comedy set at Camp North Star
31 #1 fans
33 Take after all?
35 Bolt with gold
36 Utopias lack them
37 ___ Porter, "Ally McBeal" role
38 Belts
40 "Newhart" production co.
43 No big deal
44 Be crazy about
45 Change the plot of
47 Carrying
49 Pop's ___ Brothers
52 Fleece
55 Tool along
60 John Tesh fan, maybe
62 Be crazy about
64 Team once owned by Gene Autry
65 & 67 Signer of the Oslo Accords
68 Like boxers
69 Paper cutter?
72 Shakes off
74 Not at all creaky
75 Ballet move
76 ___ bean
78 Not taken
80 Either "Inside Llewyn Davis" director
82 Tilt-A-Whirl part
84 "Che ___ è?" ("What time is it?": It.)
85 Abbr. on a Topps card

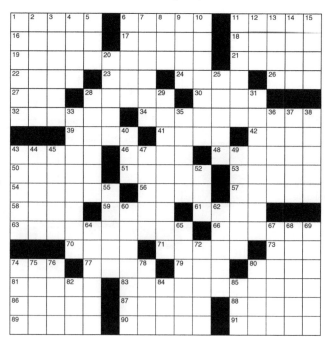

by Trip Payne

ACROSS

1 Kierkegaardian concept
6 Discharge from the R.A.F.
11 Org. that regulates tobacco products
14 Archibald ___, birth name of Cary Grant
15 Commercial blockers?
17 Title film character whose last name is Patel
18 Observances of the law
19 Car door feature
21 Rancho ___ (famed fossil site)
22 Very flexible
25 Like some humor
26 Place to stay
27 Into very small pieces
28 Essence
29 Horn of Africa native
30 Was bossy?
31 It might be beneath your notice
34 Really tired
35 Put right on paper
36 "That was unexpected!"
37 So far
38 1970s fad items
41 English channel
42 Two-person matchup on ice
44 University dubbed "The Country Club of the South"
46 Talking-to
47 California city whose name describes its location
50 TV producer Michaels
51 "Will do!"
52 Word with city or circle
53 Brief reproach
54 Regions
55 Mariachi's earnings

DOWN

1 Basic thing
2 Electrical cell
3 Decisive board game victory
4 Warrior's collection
5 Again and again?
6 Ticket info
7 Stretcher carrier, for short
8 Wharton deg.
9 Buffalo Bill's Wild West Show performer
10 Gluten-rich food
11 Typical sedan
12 Checked
13 Put to trial
16 Mouth, slangily
20 Viscous stuff
23 Girl's name that begins the lyrics of Neil Diamond's "Solitary Man"
24 Lines of reasoning that go nowhere
28 Mackinaw or Norfolk
29 Malamute's burden
30 Green keeper
31 Amount in six figures, say
32 In dire straits
33 Davis of "Of Human Bondage"
34 Penguin part
37 Muscle type
38 Rustic agitators
39 World's third-largest island
40 Changes directions, say
42 The San Diego Zoo's Gao Gao or Zhen Zhen
43 Hearth material
45 Are allowed to
48 "Alibi ___" (Ring Lardner story)
49 D.O.J. division

by Patrick Berry

ACROSS

1 Up-coming world phenomenon?
10 Material for a float
15 Anthrax, potentially
16 Big name in old strings
17 Notable switcher from Democrat to Republican to Independent
18 Not ripped
19 Offensive observance?
20 Binder?
21 Really into something
22 See 4-Down
24 It's turned before bolting
26 Like emissions from some 40-Down
27 Put out
29 Life preserver?
31 Puts in
33 Some notes
34 Adversaire's opposite
35 Aid in creating a part
37 Phils' rivals
39 Settings for donors, briefly
42 Pick, say
44 Allama Iqbal International Airport locale
48 Searchlight in comics
51 Searchlight element
52 Number line
53 1914 Belgian battle line
55 Searchlight element
56 Eisner's successor at Disney
57 Cause of temporary blindness
59 "Die Fledermaus" soprano
60 A tiny bit strange?
62 Banking facilities?
64 Still to be attained
65 First-and-second track options
66 "Sleepless in Seattle" quartet
67 Bureaucratic environmental regulations

DOWN

1 Cyclic recession
2 Banking facilitator
3 Get rid of
4 With 22-Across, obsolescent club
5 Eco-chic clothing option
6 Capital across the river from its sister city Salé
7 Drug used in aversion therapy
8 Assaults
9 Like Spender and Spenser: Abbr.
10 Relief may follow it
11 Libertine
12 Song whose title follows "Para bailar"
13 Harry and Wills acquired one in 2005
14 Puddle-jumper
23 Minute minute part: Abbr.
25 Author Hubbard
26 Pump add-on
28 Hot
30 Literally, "skyward"
32 Blanket produced in Mexico City
36 Too thin
38 Wooley of "Rawhide"
39 Like some references
40 Futuristic fryers
41 Goes with the flow?
43 One pulling a calf, say
45 A tiny bit
46 Detailed plan
47 How bands move
49 Bob may follow it
50 "Sainted maiden" of literature
54 Jamestown colonist
58 Cousin of a gnatcatcher
61 Some chessmen: Abbr.
62 N.B.A. scoring stat
63 Alternative to 10

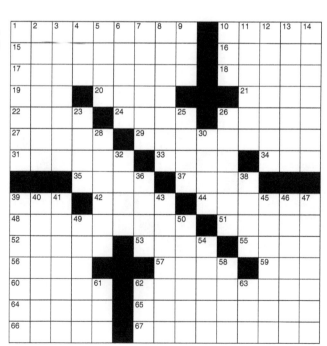

by Barry C. Silk

ACROSS

1 ___ Store (debut of 2008)
4 Space on a bookshelf?
9 Bush found in Florida
12 "___ funny!"
13 Stray away
15 Short coming?
16 Boring thing
17 Part of a bridge truss
18 Apology opener
19 10th-century pope
21 War room topic
23 "The Alphabet" artist
24 ___ itself
26 Sponges, say
27 Fly in the face of someone?
29 Mau ___ (forever, in Hawaii)
30 It may have a high grain content
31 B, for one
34 B♭, for one
35 Bb6, for one
36 Score at the half?
38 "You've got mail!" and such
41 Cry of innocence
42 Caesar's force
44 Notable 1979 exile
46 Invisible thing that's inflatable
47 They often succeed
51 States on a game board, e.g.: Abbr.
52 Soap of a medical nature
55 Fancy invitation feature
56 They might catch some rays
57 Some 24/7 facilities
58 Spanish for "basket"

DOWN

1 "Ben-Hur: ___ of the Christ"
2 Basis of the Nintendo Wii's processor
3 It has four mounted players
4 Gandhi who heads the Indian National Congress
5 Longtime luxury sedan
6 Sitter hitter, maybe
7 Pat Patriot and Billy Buffalo
8 Hypothetical example opener
9 Curtis of the screen
10 Player with Legos, for example
11 Authority figures
13 Big outdoor gear retailer
14 What might break people's trust?: Abbr.
20 Discoverer of the Amazon's mouth
22 Giggles
25 "Copacabana" showgirl and others
28 ___ b'Av (annual Jewish fast day)
30 Place for a glowing element
32 20-20, e.g.
33 Hydroxyl-bearing compound
36 Turned-over part of a leaf
37 Alternative to Avia
39 See 49-Down
40 Wise one
41 Opposite of blanco
43 "___ Shoes" (2005 Cameron Diaz film)
45 Frequent Wyeth model
47 One aboard Marine One: Abbr.
48 "Wicked!"
49 Id ___ (39-Down)
50 Provide technical details for
53 Spanish demonstrative
54 Burning feeling

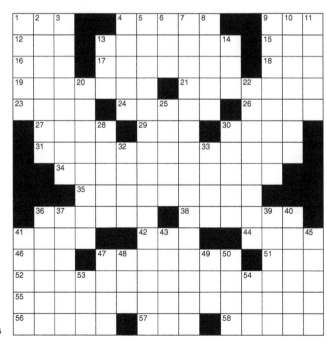

by Joe Krozel

ACROSS

1 "Eureka!"
10 Home tech product discontinued in 1987
15 Pants extender?
16 Request for a hero
17 Source of inspiration for Sir Isaac Newton, famously
18 Locked up
19 Drudges
20 "Illness" affecting the wealthy
22 What a gate change might affect: Abbr.
23 Join in the attack
24 Washed out
25 Nereus, Proteus, Glaucus and Phorcys, to the ancient Greeks
27 A little night music
28 "Can this be?!"
30 "Y" athlete
31 Speeding
32 Hit
34 "The Painter of Sunflowers" setting
35 "That's terrible!"
36 Classic Jaguars
37 Who said "Genuine poetry can communicate before it is understood"
39 Life force, in meditation
40 Chops meat
41 Terrain maker
44 Animal with a sweet tooth
46 First video game character to be honored with a figure in the Hollywood Wax Museum
48 Make a bank withdrawal?
49 Author who was the title subject of the Best Picture of 1937
51 Grant presenter?
52 Endgame
53 Freezing temps
54 Social butterfly, e.g.

DOWN

1 Emulate a King or Senator
2 High, in a way
3 Muted
4 "A half-filled auditorium," to Frost
5 Some early astronauts
6 Gang symbol, for short
7 Plain-spoken
8 Something fallen off a shelf?
9 Market leader
10 Not seriously
11 Hollow out
12 Excursions for some rock collectors?
13 Certain party deliveries
14 Did a week-long juice diet, say
21 ___ Pollos Hermanos ("Breaking Bad" restaurant)
23 Some dog rewards
25 Good ones are never cracked
26 HHH
27 Silent
28 Tireless sort
29 Ace
30 High-seas cry
31 Al Capone, famously
32 One doing the highlights?
33 Cut off the back
35 Loser in a 1970s–'80s "war"
37 Sight in an ice cream shop
38 Literary contemporary of Addison
40 Bristol's partner in pharmaceuticals
41 Place for a 17-Across
42 Meet someone?
43 Put in minimal effort
45 Locale painted in the Sistine Chapel
46 Note
47 Eastern Europe's Sea of ___
50 Printer setting: Abbr.

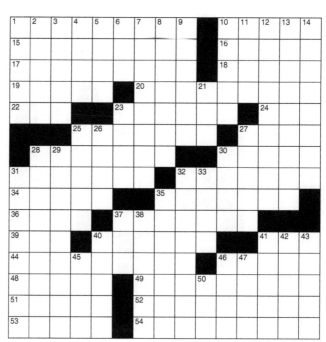

by Peter Wentz

ACROSS

1 Having a big itch
9 Giant jet
15 Sideways look?
16 "Swann's Way" novelist
17 Marinara, e.g.
18 When to put all your eggs in one basket?
19 Late legend in countdowns
20 Bell part
22 Fertiliser ingredient
23 Neighbor of 10-Down
24 Underlying
26 "Country Girl" memoirist O'Brien
27 Capital player, briefly
28 Fire
30 Soy, north of Mexico
31 Elves, in poetry
32 Heat loss, maybe?
34 Home of minor-league baseball's Brewers
37 Like lizards and lizardfish
38 Tennis since 1968
40 "Give this ___"
41 It can be dry or sparkling
42 Title woman of a 1977 Neil Diamond hit
44 Org. of sisters
47 Bit of design info
49 Not still
50 Where a ducktail tapers
51 Paroxysm
53 Looney Tunes devil, for short
54 Ceilings, informally
55 Refuse to leave alone
57 Farmers' market frequenter, maybe
59 Novelist Shreve and others
60 Hoosier
61 Key figure?
62 Spark

DOWN

1 Close-fitting, sleeveless jacket
2 1998 Masters champ Mark
3 Acknowledges without a sound
4 Footnote abbr.
5 Neighbor of India and China in Risk
6 Post-O.R. stop, maybe
7 What a boor has
8 Rock with colored bands
9 Boor
10 Neighbor of 23-Across
11 Good name for an optimist?
12 Call from the rear?
13 Avatar accompanier
14 Like music on Pandora Radio

21 Hassle
24 Giants' environs
25 Source of the delicacy tomalley
28 Like many mirrors
29 Nautilus shell feature
31 Home for a sedge wren
33 Like the out crowd?
34 "Come again?"
35 Moment when the fog lifts
36 "Go for it!"
39 Second: Abbr.
40 Major copper exporter
43 Slanted
44 State bordering Poland
45 Unlikely fare for philistines
46 Mind a lot
48 Kinkajou's kin

50 Like some forces
52 Those, in Toledo
54 Hermes' mother
56 Boomer for nearly 35 yrs.
58 Setting for many Card games

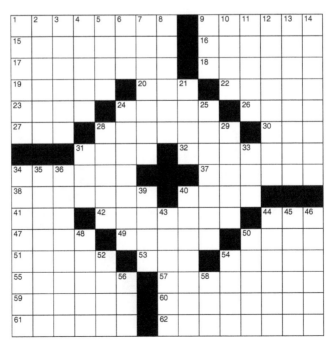

by Kevin Christian

94

ACROSS
1. Dated agreement?
10. Cognizes
15. Comment to an unapologetic burper, say
16. Cosmetics dye
17. Hawk
18. Q preceder
19. Fashion designer Saab
20. Mexican couple
21. Something locked in a cell?
22. Neuralgia : nerve :: costalgia : ___
23. Lightly towels off
25. Dickens pseudonym
26. Woman's name that sounds like a repeated letter
28. First name in design
29. Turn off, maybe
30. School basics, facetiously
32. Succeeded
34. Donnybrook
37. Moon named after the Greek personification of terror
38. SALT signer
40. Adèle, for one: Abbr.
41. Page, e.g.
42. Juice name starter
44. Letters at the top of a page
47. Brick, for example
48. Fictional locale of a John Wayne western
50. Eagle's place: Abbr.
52. Attacked verbally
54. Something most Americans won't take, for short
55. Destiny's Child, e.g.
56. Olympian Moses
57. iPhone competitor
59. Uniform
60. Where El Nuevo Herald is read

61. Classic sea adventure of 1846
62. Straight man of old comedy

DOWN
1. "The ___ the words, the better the prayer": Martin Luther
2. ___ acid (bleach ingredient)
3. Old record keeper
4. "An Enquiry Concerning Human Understanding" philosopher
5. Film speed letters
6. Castle town in a 1937 film
7. Start of something big?
8. "Hoop-Dee-Doo" lyricist
9. USD alternative
10. Writer in "The Electric Kool-Aid Acid Test"
11. A follower?
12. Slow-cooked Italian dish
13. Handy things in the game world?
14. Exhibited sternutation
21. Feels (for)
23. Lake catch
24. Stowe antislavery novel
27. It's temporarily hot
29. David who wrote the screenplay for "The Verdict"
31. Bad, and then some
33. Art purchase
34. Warm
35. Grocery product with a multiply misspelled name
36. Hematology prefix
38. Stool, typically
39. Jarrett of the Obama White House
43. "Ain't happening!"
45. "Boom" preceder
46. Lipitor maker
48. Taylor of "The Nanny"
49. String bean's opposite
51. Product once pitched by Ronald Reagan
53. Lake catch
55. Disneyland sight
57. Part of a certain cease-fire agreement, for short
58. Roman divinity

by David Steinberg

ACROSS

1 Gaping opening
4 Tees off
10 Salon service
13 Hoo-has
15 "Easy Rider" ride
16 Beginning to mature?
17 Christian symbol used during the Crusades
19 Coastal feature
20 Expert
21 Bit of electric guitar play
23 Epoxy, e.g.
24 Trading insider Boesky
26 Ages ago
27 Results of refrigerator raids
29 Fathered
30 Prime or crime follower
33 Small amount of liquor
34 Many an informative tweet
35 Wordsworth's "___: Intimations of Immortality"
36 New England architectural style
38 Best effort
39 Early Stephen King thriller
41 Charles, for one
42 Ball opener?
43 Gulf of Aqaba resort city
44 ". . . And God Created Woman" actress
46 Its highest possible score is 240, for short
47 Jam
48 Space blanket material
52 St. Francis of Assisi, for one
54 Chain owned by Wyndham Worldwide
55 Hit animated film of 2011

56 Time of annual madness . . . or a hint to four squares in this puzzle
59 Colorful carp
60 One way to study
61 Falsetto-voiced Muppet
62 It has many famous alums
63 Some NASA designs
64 Big Sur institute

DOWN

1 Epic
2 Singer who was awarded an M.B.E. in 2013
3 An argument
4 Ordinary guy: Var.
5 XXX part
6 Misidentify, e.g.
7 Warm greetings?
8 Unstable physics particle
9 Alphabetizing, e.g.: Abbr.
10 Cracks, as piping
11 "The Very Hungry Caterpillar" author
12 It whistles while it works
14 Flat on one's back
18 Italian port on the Tyrrhenian Sea
22 Theater magnate Marcus
24 "Come hungry. Leave happy" sloganeer
25 Expert
28 Assists, e.g.
29 Sack
30 Mother of the Freedom Movement, to friends
31 What a ticket is good for

32 Electrical transformer
34 Reason to be barred from a bar
36 Simple 29-Down
37 Part of a tennis net
40 One way to be running or working
42 Stonewall, say
44 Tummy soother
45 Baseball All-Star Infante
47 Tolkien protagonist
49 Big dipper
50 Water
51 So-called "laboratory's first gift to the loom"
53 Way up?
54 Country addresses, for short
57 Baby's sound
58 "2 Broke Girls" actress Dennings

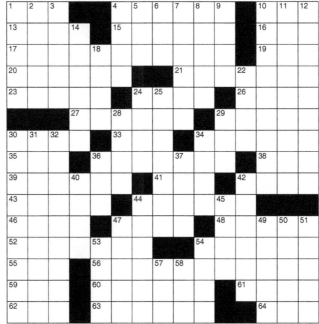

by Tracy Gray

ACROSS

1 Likes a lot
8 It's not to be believed
15 Ones clearing for takeoff?
16 O.K.
17 Like one of Brunei's two main languages
18 Less experienced
19 It might give you a headache
20 Hunting party?
21 Boobs
22 Continental Congress delegate from Connecticut
23 Quads, e.g.
24 Onetime host of CBS's "The Morning Show"
28 "__ doing . . ."
29 Alternative to quotes: Abbr.
30 Cry at a revival
32 Something not found in this puzzle's answer
37 She played Wallis Simpson in "The King's Speech"
38 But, in Bonn
39 Be a Debbie Downer
41 "King __" of old comics
42 Height of fashion
43 Boxer who won 1980's Brawl in Montreal
44 Grammy-nominated Franklin and others
45 Giant with a big trunk
48 Flunkies
50 "Let me repeat: Forget it!"
51 Historic residential hotel in Manhattan
52 Part of a 14-Down's harness
53 Putting away
54 Registers
55 Spray on a dress

DOWN

1 Comes clean
2 Handle
3 Small unit of atmospheric pressure
4 Insomniac's lament
5 Kings of León
6 Noteworthy times
7 Payroll dept. info
8 Fairy tale figures
9 Fairy tale figure
10 Less likely to give
11 They play hard on Saturday and Sunday
12 Principal lieutenant of Hector in the "Iliad"
13 Portable heater
14 You can bet on it
24 Mount, with "up"
25 Formless life form
26 Bloom in Robert Frost's "A Late Walk"
27 Nickname in the Best Picture of 1969
31 Block from the White House
33 They're 50–50
34 Enthusiasm shown during a 2008 race
35 Wining and dining
36 Olympic sport that includes passades and pirouettes
39 Food whose name means "little purée"
40 Transition to fatherhood
43 Tiny amounts
44 "Masks Confronting Death" painter, 1888
46 "No __ think is in my tree" ("Strawberry Fields Forever" lyric)
47 Michael who played Worf on "Star Trek: The Next Generation"
48 Like Italian "bread," e.g.: Abbr.
49 Inside opening?

by Elizabeth C. Gorski

ACROSS

1 "Perish the thought!"
12 Many a delivery participant
15 It has a "Complete My Album" service
16 It'll slow down traffic
17 He played Maxwell Smart in 2008
18 Energy
19 Idée origin
20 The end of Samson?
21 "Absolutely"
23 Ingredients in bowstring waxes
25 Marks, as a box
26 One-sixth of diciotto
27 What may drop in disbelief
30 Certain union member
31 Show signs of life
33 Kind of acid used in fireproofing
35 "Encore!"
36 Made a comeback, say
39 Greenwich-to-New Haven dir.
40 They might come with trains
41 Old show horse
42 Athletic conf. for UMass
44 Title bird in a Rimsky-Korsakov opéra
45 One may be smoked out
46 "If I Were a Carpenter" singer
48 Province : Canada :: ___ : Russia
51 Part of a large kingdom
53 Umami source, briefly
54 16-season N.H.L.'er Fleury
56 Start to sense?
57 Totally break up

60 One smoked, informally
61 Renowned long jumper
62 Causes of street rumbles?
63 National coming-out day?

DOWN

1 Drift
2 Furry oyster cracker
3 By dint of
4 Get a share of, say
5 Chuckle bit
6 Of songbirds
7 They have 125 questions and last 130 mins.
8 French soliloquy starter?
9 Arche de ___ (boat in la Bible)
10 General-aviation alternative to Le Bourget
11 Early text messager
12 Like any number by itself
13 Soured
14 Succubus, e.g.
22 Secure, with "up"
24 Like "come" and "go": Abbr.
27 2002 Denzel Washington thriller
28 Frequent foe of Wonder Woman
29 What "many a man hath more hair than," in Shakespeare
31 Browning selection?
32 Aids for dating
33 Riboflavin, familiarly
34 Transport over dry land?

36 Social event in "No, No, Nanette"
37 Rx writer
38 Showed signs of life
43 Ancient game much studied in game theory
45 Options for target practice
47 Early touter of air bags
48 Home to baseball's Orix Buffaloes
49 Sanskrit for "the auspicious one"
50 Canon element
52 Unexploded
53 "___ Modiste" (Victor Herbert operetta)
55 Eyeball, in a way
58 Gulper ___
59 Bestow, to Burns

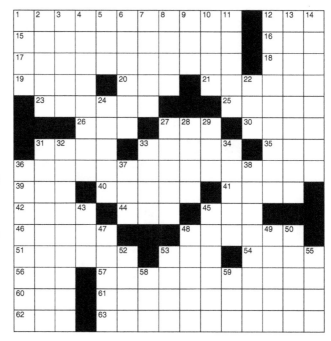

by Tim Croce

ACROSS

1 Site of a 1789 rebellion
10 Nickname for a lanky guy
14 Classic brewing ingredient
15 It can wrap things up
16 Nursery bagful
17 Gap competitor
18 Chided, with "off"
19 "No Exit" has one
20 Cloth with tears in it?
21 Enterprise adversary
22 Dimwitted title character of a 2001 comedy
24 Burrow, say
25 Deodorant brand
26 Middle marker?
28 Boon
29 Four-time Pro Bowler Michael
30 It might give you a buzz
33 Score in Italy
34 Meh
35 Gives one's approval
40 Law enforcers, slangily
41 Puma, for one
42 Dig
45 Bygone Asian dynast
47 "The Bicycle Thief" setting
48 Giant article of clothing?
49 Like soon-to-be-frescoed plaster
50 Contend
51 Number one number two
52 Songlike
54 Ends of some board meetings?
55 Some end-of-the-year dramas, informally
56 Bygone bomber whose name is a call in bingo
57 First Fox show to finish in Nielsen's top 20 for a season

DOWN

1 The "Harry Potter" books, e.g.
2 "Darling"
3 Give no escape
4 Investment category
5 "Jesters do ___ prove prophets": "King Lear"
6 Serene
7 Some righties, for short?
8 Like most semaphore flags
9 Abbr. among stock listings
10 Elegant pool maneuvers
11 Job-hunter's aid
12 Glancing
13 Twitter trending topic, maybe
15 Other ___
20 Assistance
23 Author Deighton
25 What everyone has at birth
27 One of a sporting pair
28 Union attendants
30 Death on the Nile creator?
31 Considered
32 What Eliza didn't do for 'enry 'iggins?
33 One calling the shots?
35 Certain street dancer, in slang
36 Director Justin of the "Fast and the Furious" franchise
37 Mixture brushed onto pastry dough before baking
38 "The poetry of reality," per Richard Dawkins
39 Gandhi marched to the sea to protest one
42 Full of high spirits
43 2001 French film that was nominated for five Academy Awards
44 Green ___
46 The new girl on TV's "New Girl"
47 Wedding party, sometimes
48 Hinge holder
52 Something that may be rolled out for company
53 Newfoundland cry

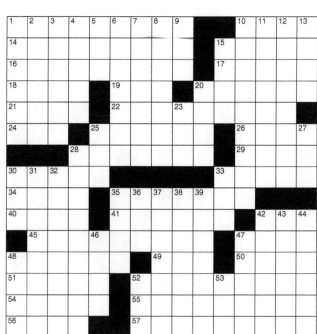

by Josh Knapp

ACROSS

1 Person at the top of the order
7 Excited
14 Fan's output
16 Brand behind the mouthwash Plax
17 Tex-Mex item
18 Robert Goulet, e.g.
19 Annual event held in the Theresienwiese
21 Certain tube filler
22 Slangy goodbye
27 Relative of a harrier
28 All hits all the time?
29 Reply on the radio
30 Person with important clerical duties
31 Tuber grown south of the border
32 Tomfoolery
35 Ones trying to prevent stealing
36 Stud muffin
37 Certain branches
38 The tropics and others
39 Uses maximally
40 Ceiling
43 Influential figure in upward mobility?
45 ___ Ball (event at Hogwarts during the Triwizard Tournament)
46 Their best-selling (23× platinum) album had no title
48 Series of drug-related offenses?
52 Politico who wrote "The Truth (With Jokes)"
53 Skin cream ingredient
54 Square snack
55 Licensing requirement, maybe
56 Wee

DOWN

1 Start to play?
2 Talk show V.I.P.
3 Common ground?
4 John in a studio
5 9–5, e.g.
6 Talk show V.I.P.'s
7 Put up with
8 Mohamed ___, Egyptian president removed from power in July 2013
9 Thickening agents?
10 Psych 101 subject
11 Judo ranking
12 Trojan competitor
13 So says
15 21-Across, e.g.
20 N.H.L. players' representative Donald
23 Reduces to bits
24 Land east of Babylonia
25 Fictional corporation that made a jet-propelled unicycle
26 It has points of interest
28 This is the end
30 Tree huggers?
31 Half a nursery rhyme couple
32 Run through the gantlet, say
33 Pop ___
34 Iowa politico Ernst
35 Credo
37 ___ bath
39 Car modified for flying in "The Absent-Minded Professor"
40 "Home Alone" star, 1990
41 Time Lords on "Doctor Who," e.g.
42 Big name in retail
44 Planes, quaintly
45 Broadway character who sings "The Rumor"
47 Not that bright
48 Number of weeks in il Giro d'Italia
49 "Stop right there!"
50 When le Tour de France is held
51 Romeo's was "a most sharp sauce"

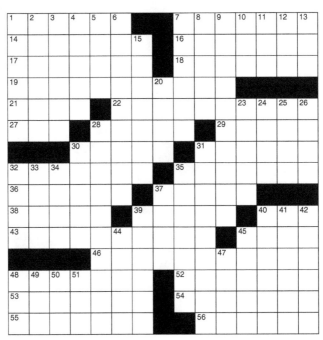

by Evan Birnholz

ACROSS

1 Cheeky couple?
9 Opposite
15 Many a pickup game
16 Zero chance
17 Become ripped
18 Needing to sit for a minute, maybe
19 Lakers commentator Lantz and others
20 Met someone?
22 Minute, briefly
23 Caesar's predecessor?
24 Deliverer of thousands of monologues
25 City known for its traffic violations
26 See 36-Across
29 Larrup
30 Fat Tire and Full Sail
31 Ballerina Rubinstein who commissioned Ravel's "Boléro"
32 Business end?: Abbr.
34 Target target?
36 With 26-Across, somewhat
37 Exotic juice ingredient
38 Big marble
41 Thataway
42 With 54-Across, spa town on the Lahn River
45 Bachelor's least favorite radio station?
46 Glace, essentially
48 Action figure released in 1997
50 Basse-Californie, e.g.
51 Fashion designer Knowles, mother of Beyoncé
53 Climbing figs.
54 See 42-Across
55 Hurrier's words
57 Progressives, e.g.
58 __ person
60 Kangaroo Point is a suburb of it
62 Illumination indication
63 Online aid for job-hunters
64 H.S. challenge with 1-to-5 scoring
65 Beach book, typically

DOWN

1 Where Prokofiev's "Cinderella" premiered
2 1-Down wear
3 1958 #1 hit whose only lyric is its title word
4 Ruffle
5 Mackerel variety on Hawaiian menus
6 Langston Hughes's "__ Unashamed"
7 Small projecting ridge
8 Menorah's branches, e.g.
9 Celery topped with peanut butter and raisins
10 Codger
11 Mass-over-volume symbol
12 "Mm-mmm!"
13 Surprise giveaway?
14 What keeps order at a concert?
21 Somewhat
25 Derived (from)
27 A.T.M. feature
28 Kebabs sold curbside, say
33 Throw a monkey wrench into
35 Anderson of sitcomdom
36 Big name in bubbly
38 Comics boy with the given name Scooner
39 Modern request for contact
40 Somewhat
42 Chopin dedicated one to Schumann
43 Title girl in literature's "Prairie Trilogy"
44 Derive (from)
47 Powerless
49 Yap
52 Some lobbies
55 Classes
56 Beethoven's first?
59 11-Down's shape
61 Hit high in the air

by James Mulhern and Ashton Anderson

ACROSS

1 There's the rub!
4 Novel subtitled "The Parish Boy's Progress"
15 Lot
16 Underground waves?
17 Animal on the Michigan state flag
18 Is beyond compare
19 Plea opener
21 Heading from Okla. City to Tulsa
22 Gown maker's supply
23 Tests that accommodate claustrophobes
25 "Ella giammai m'___" (Verdi aria)
26 Pretend to be
27 Casts a wide net?
30 Rarin' to go
31 Lot, maybe
33 Tiresias in "Oedipus Rex," e.g.
35 Heading: Abbr.
36 Major media event of '95
39 "Star Wars" boy, informally
40 Vacuum maintainer
42 "Scimitar-horned" creature
43 Find a spot for, say
45 Flowering shrub whose name comes from the Greek for "coil"
47 Chorus of approval
48 Big name in chips
49 Play house?
51 Coin with a picture of un rey
54 About 28% of the U.N.: Abbr.
55 Indigestion cause
56 Fictional school bully with henchmen named Crabbe and Goyle
59 Volume 1 starter, maybe

60 Practice swizzles and twizzles, say
61 Dr. Watson portrayer on CBS's "Elementary"
62 Track star of 1977
63 Craft that must overcome wave drag, in brief

DOWN

1 Quaint office supply
2 Ones involved in horseplay?
3 Stiletto attachment, perhaps
4 Ending with psy-
5 Some bottled water purchases
6 Almost any character in Jon Stewart's "Rosewater"
7 Turbine blades
8 Gate approx.
9 Where you might see someone walk the dog
10 ___ center
11 Indulges oneself, in a way
12 Fan fixation
13 0, for 180°
14 Tips of wingtips
20 Common notes
24 Subway option
27 Cereal that reverted to spherical shapes in 2007
28 Frontman's assignment
29 Certain drop in motivation
31 Gillette brand
32 "Extra! Extra!," e.g.
34 No longer sudsy, say
37 Pack animal?
38 Never-seen neighbor on "The Mary Tyler Moore Show"
41 Black-and-white engraving
44 Table filler
46 Shoot back
47 Mechanically
49 Part of SALT
50 Some haggis ingredients
51 Many email attachments
52 County name in three states
53 Novel format
57 Enzyme suffix
58 Tree whose name sounds like a letter of the alphabet

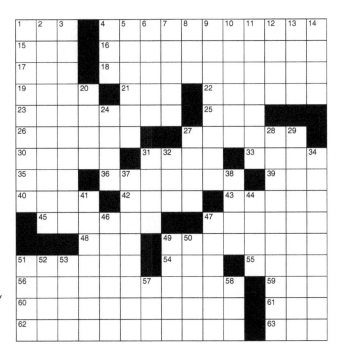

by Brad Wilber and Doug Peterson

102

ACROSS

1 Where much grass grows
9 Moolah
15 Jazz/funk fusion genre
16 Creature with a crest
17 Enterprise headquarters
18 Tap
19 Place for a sucker
20 Faiths
21 Rosetta Stone symbol
22 Betty's sister on "Ugly Betty"
24 One ferried by Charon
25 Plato portrayer in "Rebel Without a Cause"
26 Org. seeking to catch 11-Down
27 Cork's place, maybe
31 Tameness
35 In abundance
37 "Le Bourgeois gentilhomme" playwright
38 Positive response to "How ya doin'?"
40 Sherlock Holmes cover-up?
41 Rugby four-pointer
42 Flying female fighters in W.W. II
44 Orange side dish
46 Hip, with "in"
47 Lolcats, e.g.
51 Kind of bullet
53 Before making one's debut?
55 Photoshop command
56 Cross words?
57 Tip-offs, maybe
58 Nexus 7 rival
59 "No doubt!"
60 Important figure in business

DOWN

1 Tagliatelle, e.g.
2 A lot
3 One delivering a knockout, informally
4 Into the open
5 Ones repeating "I do" in 1976?
6 Access, as a pocket
7 Literary/film critic Janet
8 Girded
9 Practice with the Book of Shadows
10 Stabilizing kitchen supply
11 See 26-Across
12 Faddish food regimen
13 Italian count?
14 Murderer
23 Dr. ___ (archenemy of the Fantastic Four)
25 ___ bean
27 Caterer's preparation
28 Figaro, e.g.
29 Ones with recess appointments?
30 What keeps a part apart?
32 Power outage?
33 Shangri-la's lack
34 Symbol of purity, in Lille
36 Caterwaul
39 Heir apparent to a French king
43 Wear for Clint Eastwood in "The Good, the Bad and the Ugly"
45 Blood-curdling
46 Garden ___
47 Her "little baby loves clambake," in a 1967 Elvis song
48 Cyber Monday activity
49 Home for Deer Isle and Moosehead Lake
50 Dock ___, Pirate who claimed to have thrown a no-hitter on LSD
52 Novel's end?
54 "___ Declassified" (old Nickelodeon show)

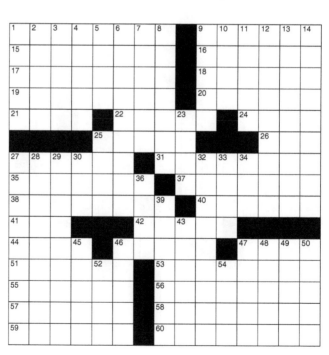

by Kevin G. Der and Ian Livengood

ACROSS

1 Take measures
4 Deeply offended
9 Did a little housekeeping
14 One who gets upset twice?
16 Thick smoke
17 Ladylove
18 Love ballad from the 1973 album "Goats Head Soup"
19 Way to bear arms
20 Frank Capra title character
22 Oscar nominee Rowlands
23 They're often underfoot
25 Bobs, e.g.
26 Some slurry stuff
27 Vessels of the Napoleonic Wars
29 Silent "ick"
30 Based on instinct and guesswork
33 Letter's capital?
34 Thrift
39 Page with many views
40 Most treacherous for driving, maybe
41 Trendy
43 Fitting
44 Hides
45 Maximum on a hurricane wind scale
46 Detail-oriented
48 Caduceus carrier
50 Soft white mineral
51 Operation Neptune Spear group
54 Like aspen leaves
55 Stand-up guy Dave
56 First inert gas made into a compound
57 In the pit of one's stomach?
58 Instrument in Glenn Miller's "Pennsylvania 6-5000"

DOWN

1 Often-grated cheese
2 Game played by British schoolkids
3 Recent staff addition
4 Home wrecker?
5 John Deere rival
6 Ryder Cup side
7 URL ending
8 Record holders of old
9 A whole bunch
10 "It makes a man mistake words for thoughts," per Samuel Johnson
11 Given encouragement
12 Disbursed
13 Head set?
15 Miss Woodhouse of Highbury
21 Forwards
23 Psychology or sociology
24 Web-based service succeeded by Outlook in 2013
27 Acronymic weapon name
28 Winter underwear, informally
29 Ingredient in Marie Rose sauce
31 Uninteresting
32 Hide
34 Something to express views on
35 O.K.
36 Longtime
37 Fabled characters?
38 Steinbeck's "Of Mice and Men," e.g.
42 Alfred the Great's kingdom
44 Yuletide team member
45 Not occupied
47 Punic War agitator
48 Talk up
49 "Outside the Lines" broadcaster
52 Sound of a light going on?
53 Tanyard sight

by Patrick Berry

104

ACROSS

1 Clichéd sequel catchphrase
8 Economist who wrote "An Essay on the Principle of Population," 1798
15 Like Rome, supposedly
16 How one might play a love ballad
17 19-season Yankee Rivera
18 Batting targets
19 Batting targets
20 Go on foot
21 Assuage
22 Any miss
24 Manchester man
27 With 46-Down, common canvas coater
29 Red three-year-old of TV
31 "Verily"
32 Event with the categories Best Kiss and Best Fight
36 Raced
37 Savage
38 Ninny
39 & 42 2001 video game set in Liberty City
43 Senate majority group, maybe?
44 Ascension Isl. setting
45 Quite like
47 Slush for eds. to wade through
49 They can get excited
53 "Damn Yankees" Tony winner
55 "The Girl Who Kicked the Hornets' Nest" novelist
57 Dressing type
59 Popular pop-up preventer
60 Ninnylike
61 Above all others

62 Without even cracking a smile, say
63 Big name in air circulation?

DOWN

1 Some rope sources
2 Net sales
3 Comfortaire competitor
4 Place for a Neapolitan pizza
5 Home to "The Happiest Place on Earth"
6 Quaint stage dancing accessory
7 Supermodel Karlie
8 11-pointed national symbol
9 Mon ___
10 It may be drawn in a forest
11 A dog may pick one up
12 Turned on
13 Its seal has an olive branch
14 Sign of trouble
23 Brooke Astor, e.g.
25 Bud
26 Standard offshoot
28 Like many ideals
30 Its one-euro coin depicts a cross
32 Elaborate underground complex in "The Lord of the Rings"
33 Limited expense?
34 Fire
35 Sister of Cartoon Network
36 Office whoop
40 "The best value under the sun" sloganeer
41 Serene calmness
46 See 27-Across
48 Comes to a sudden close?
50 First name of a 10-year manhunt target
51 ___ support
52 Tackle box accessory
54 Junk mover
56 Alaskan island or its principal town
57 Pre-texts?
58 Playskool product tester

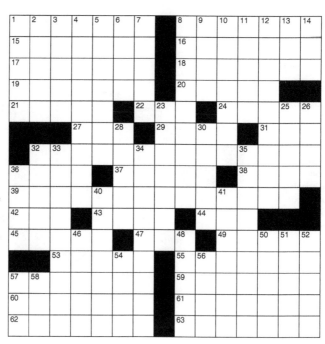

by David Phillips

105

ACROSS
1 Utah's ___ Range
8 Snatches
15 Where to check for prints?
16 Kind of pie
17 What a blog provides
18 Cornish knight of the Round Table
19 Bud of Nancy
20 "Ghost" character Brown
22 The working girl in "Working Girl"
23 Euro dispenser
25 Freshwater predator
26 Semester, e.g.
27 "That ___ stupid!"
28 Richard Gere title role
29 Addresses shrilly
31 1980s TV outfit
34 "Am ___ blame?"
35 Date shown on the tablet of the Statue of Liberty
39 Blood-typing system
40 Converses
41 Situated near the middle line of the body
43 Formed a junction
44 Gypsy people
48 $2 to $2,000, in Monopoly
49 Actor Hamm of "Mad Men"
50 "The accuser of our brethren," per Revelation
51 Digital imaging brand
52 ___ oil
54 Port vessel
55 University of Cincinnati athlete
57 Former Colts arena
59 Bend backward
60 J, F or K
61 Turner backers
62 Scale often used in a laboratory

DOWN
1 Condiment that can make your eyes water
2 Coffee and fresh-baked cookies have them
3 Adds color to
4 "Antony and Cleopatra" prop
5 Banned
6 Lug
7 "I Ching" figures
8 Orange dwarf
9 German possessive pronoun
10 "___ ever!"
11 Jet wing warning
12 When to wear a cocktail dress, traditionally
13 Sports bar feature
14 Aid and abet: Abbr.
21 Oscar winner once named Sexiest Man Alive by People
24 20th-century French leader
26 Record label for the Miracles and Stevie Wonder
28 Former Massachusetts governor ___ Patrick
29 Entry in a celebrated international sports competition since 1851
30 French pronoun
32 Drum kit part
33 Odd
35 Preserves, perhaps
36 Epithet for a computer whiz
37 Eat crow
38 Bonus, in ads
42 Mired
45 Holy Roman emperor known as "the Red"
46 Fighters for Kenyan independence
47 Little dears
49 Early invaders of Britain
50 Slow racer
51 Shelter dug into a hillside
52 Pitching stat
53 Middle school marks?
56 Monitor, for short
58 Shakes

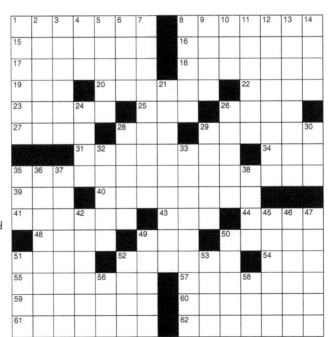

by Paula Gamache

106

ACROSS

1 "Moses" novelist
5 Home to Morro Castle
9 Rigging pros
14 Hoops nickname
15 Its prices are determined by competition
17 Rafts
18 "Red pottage" in Genesis
19 Gun
20 Sharks' place
21 Neighbor of Telescopium
22 "___ Obama" (epithet used by Rush Limbaugh)
24 Criticize in a small way, informally
25 Circulation problem
26 "Just ___ Love Her" (1950 hit)
28 Granny, to Gretel
30 Central figure of a country
38 1978 punk classic
39 Transcript, e.g.
40 What many married couples bring in
41 Finnair alternative
42 Blowout, e.g.
43 With 5-Down, bygone beverage
46 Sort who isn't safe around a safe
50 "Women Ironing" artist
53 English Channel feeder
54 Land above, to Sonorans
56 Honor for Harry Potter's creator: Abbr.
57 Acid Queen player in "Tommy"
59 1998 Spielberg title role
60 "Two Tickets to Paradise" singer

61 Domino getting played
62 They take up some measures
63 Squat
64 Gonitis target

DOWN

1 1960s TV dog
2 Walk-ins?
3 It may cover all the bases
4 C.E.O.'s places
5 See 43-Across
6 Knock for a loop
7 Dog star
8 Composer Arensky
9 Roll in the grass?
10 Sites for system repairs, briefly
11 Toasting option
12 Intro to chemistry?
13 Parade honoree, familiarly

16 What a bad ruler does
20 Parting word
23 Mizzen neighbor
25 Dressage half-turn
27 Put away, maybe
29 1970s
30 Sots' shots
31 ___ bit
32 Look out for, say
33 Singer Lovich
34 Sparkling white
35 "Chloe" director, 2009
36 "Chicago" Golden Globe winner
37 Teaching degs.
43 2012 major-league leader in hits
44 Quicklime, e.g.
45 Furnishes
47 ___ Field (Minute Maid Park, once)

48 Fixin' to
49 "Wall Street" theme
51 Drop off
52 What a yo-yo lacks
54 Tour de France times
55 Sam Cooke's "___ Little Love"
58 British isle
59 Subj. of the 2006 film "Bobby"

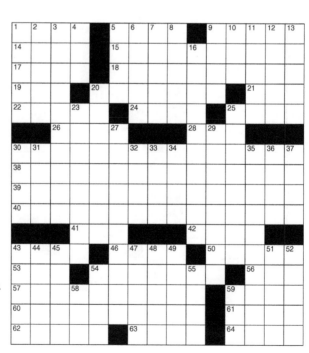

by Martin Ashwood-Smith

ACROSS

1 "Not much at all for me, please"
10 Bare
15 Director Michelangelo
16 Big name in movie theaters
17 What gets the shaft?
18 Struck, as by God
19 *Basketball area
20 Unlike Iago
22 *100%
23 Not run, maybe
25 Co. that introduced Dungeons & Dragons
26 Cane material
28 Abhorrent
30 Symbol of modesty
32 *Water cooler
33 British critic Kenneth who created "Oh! Calcutta!"
34 Women, old-fashionedly
36 Bit of flimflam
38 Third-place candidate in the 1920 presidential election who ran his campaign from jail
39 Skiing mecca
43 *Submerged
47 Outwits
48 Alternative indicator
49 Ageless, in an earlier age
50 Portmanteau food brand
52 Microscopic messenger
54 Sets (on)
55 *Had charges
56 Pizarro contemporary
59 Cousin of a cistern
60 Messed (with)
62 Many British mathematicians
64 Came (from)
65 So that one might
66 Wood fasteners
67 Revolutionary invention for restaurants?

DOWN

1 Something good to hit
2 Asleep, say
3 What an agoraphobe does
4 Big load
5 Symbol of life
6 Daisies and the like, botanically
7 Stable colors
8 Even or close to even, in a tennis set
9 Circlegraph shapes
10 '14s in '14, e.g.
11 Lead on
12 Relatives of guinea pigs
13 Grind
14 Product that might be used with a blessing
21 Like "Have a nice day," for example
24 Takes off
27 Nearly
29 Left over
31 ___ of the earth
34 Gets set
35 Feudal thralls
37 Table leaves?
39 Target, in a way
40 Like Europe in 1945
41 Cry in hide-and-seek
42 Image
44 Those who should follow the advice in the sounded-out answers to the five starred clues
45 Wikipedia precursor
46 Uses for support
49 Grill, e.g.
51 Words of explanation
53 Cramming aid
57 ___ Zátopek, four-time Olympic track gold medalist
58 Delta 88, e.g., informally
61 Paris's Avenue ___ Champs-Élysées
63 Money of Romania

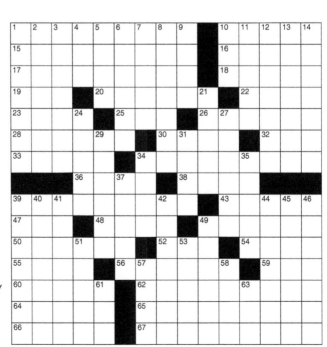

by Matt Ginsberg

108

ACROSS

1 Back order?
7 Main means of defense?
15 First city bombed in W.W. II's Baedeker Blitz
16 Opted to duck
17 1954 Audie Murphy western
18 Prom amenity
19 It comes with lots of extras
21 "Every hero becomes a ___ at last": Emerson
22 W's is 74
23 Not hunched over
24 Biased writing?: Abbr.
25 Pounded side
26 Scrooge's portrayer in "The Muppet Christmas Carol"
27 Soul
28 Pens
30 Jaguar, for one
31 Classic brand in men's apparel
32 Occur
33 Occur
36 Christ the ___ (Rio de Janeiro landmark)
40 Grace
41 Small, round and shiny
42 Letters on some overseas packages
43 Person taking drugs
44 Dark green?
45 Automotive plural selected in a 2011 promotion
46 Court position
47 They're off on casual Fridays
49 ___ chicken
51 Indignant denial
52 Frozen treat with Alexander the Grape as one of its flavors

53 2010 U.S. Open winner McDowell
54 Setting of the Levant
55 Tito's successor as head of the Non-Aligned Movement

DOWN

1 Superman accessory
2 Apply to
3 Of pions and kaons
4 When clocks are set back for the end of daylight saving time
5 Pi Day celebrant, perhaps
6 Late October to March, in West Africa
7 Malaria enlarges them
8 It might be in a jam
9 Not satisfied
10 Midori on ice
11 "White Christmas" singer, informally
12 Beyond silly
13 Obama descriptor
14 Show reverence to, in a way
20 Called out
26 Deceive
27 "Revelations" choreographer
29 Expert in facial recognition?
30 Recall reason
32 They may be stoked
33 Jazz legend who turned the Benny Goodman Trio into the Benny Goodman Quartet
34 Worship
35 Cornmeal mush
36 It often comes with a "Thank You"
37 Devil dogs
38 Height
39 Whoop it up
41 Unpaid mine workers
44 One of two components of the drug Sinemet
45 Some athletic shoes
48 Manhattan's ___ D. Roosevelt Park
50 A heavy metal band may have it

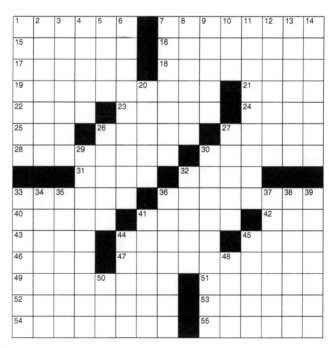

by Byron Walden

ACROSS

1 Winning smile, e.g.
6 International cricket event
15 Too-familiar
16 Road built during the Samnite Wars
17 Press conference segment
18 Game ender, possibly
19 Working for
20 Republican who won Bentsen's vacated Senate seat
21 Band with a person's name
23 1970 Kinks album title starter
24 Afternoon reception
25 Orange growers
26 Joe who was retired in 1997
27 Folk medicine plant
29 Music genre prefix
30 Clears the mind, with "up"
31 Chow
33 Chase off
34 "Things Fall Apart" novelist
37 Escort, as to the door
38 What the name "Rhoda" means
42 Trying minors
43 What repellent might prevent
45 New Deal program, for short
46 Heady feeling
47 She and Clark Gable were known as "the team that generates steam"
49 Surrounded with foliage
51 Impressive, as accommodations
52 Player of Sal in "The Godfather"
53 Call to mind
54 "Don't decide right away"
55 Parties with mai tais, maybe
56 Titan's home
57 Shrill cries

DOWN

1 British P.M. when W.W. I began
2 One who's unseated?
3 Land line?
4 Tribal bigwig
5 Claw
6 Five-time N.C.A.A. basketball champs from the A.C.C.
7 Uniform ornament
8 Thwarts for petty reasons
9 Add color to
10 1968 novel set in Korea
11 Opposed to the union, say
12 Couple
13 Performer on the road?
14 Note books used in church?
22 Stevedore's burden
26 Gentle murmur
28 "Music should strike fire from the heart of man, and bring tears from the eyes of woman" speaker
30 Undercover item?
32 Exercise target
33 Begin planning the nuptials
34 Way to walk while conversing
35 Fall apart
36 Fallen star
37 How Congress might adjourn
39 Major error in soccer
40 "Louder!"
41 Seal classification
43 Magna Carta's drafters
44 Without doubt
47 Largely hollow bricks
48 Flo Ziegfeld offering
50 Erase

by Patrick Berry

110

ACROSS

1 1993 hit with the lyric "Keep playin' that song all night"
8 Credit
15 Gross, to a toddler
16 Blue dress wearers
17 A guillotine is used to remove them
18 Good with
19 Cause for cardiological concern
20 Something to hop on
22 Not cut, say
23 Took to the ground?
25 Shed material?
27 Friday, e.g.
31 Successor to Gibson on "ABC World News"
34 It's in general circulation
35 Oriente
36 Subject for Gregor Mendel
37 Shows some emotion
40 End up short
41 Ends up short, maybe
43 Grp. with the motto "Deo vindice"
44 Seeking
46 1957 Dell-Vikings hit
49 Paris Hilton, e.g.
50 [Why me?!]
54 Area of need
56 It's feedable
58 Speaker of the house, perhaps
59 Famed kicker born with a clubfoot
61 Fashion designer behind the fragrance Rock Me!
63 Hydrocortisone producer
64 Gets on the line?
65 ABC's first color program, with "The"
66 Big spinning effort

DOWN

1 Tow bar
2 Place for une faculté
3 "See what I'm talkin' about?"
4 What often comes with a twist?
5 Sch. with a Hartford campus
6 Sweets
7 Nez Percé war chief
8 Org. that endorsed Obamacare
9 He hit 106 more home runs than Barry Bonds
10 Like "Zorba the Greek" novelist Nikos Kazantzakis
11 Concern for a lifeguard
12 Concerning
13 Think piece?
14 Abbr. before a year
21 Take in more
24 Take in less
26 What you see here
28 Some-holds-barred sport
29 Audi model retired in 2005
30 "So sweet was ___ so fatal": Othello
31 It may be submitted to an architect
32 México lead-in
33 Meanie's lack
38 ___ speak
39 Cousin of a jaguarundi
42 Gets hot
45 Infusion aid
47 Jordache alternative
48 Literary son of Jenny Fields
51 "Orfeo" composer Luigi
52 Wear during re-entry
53 It's known for its varieties
54 Setting of "Love Me Do": Abbr.
55 Need to tan
57 Standout
60 Real Salt Lake's org.
62 Tortoise's beak

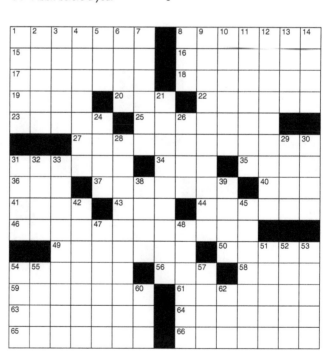

by Tim Croce

ACROSS

1 First rock band whose members received Kennedy Center Honors
7 Jiffy
11 Shade of black
14 Fix, in carpentry
15 Undoubtedly
17 Dropped a line?
18 Olympians' food
19 Figures for investors
20 Animal that catches fish with its forepaws
21 Ward on a set
22 Shade of gray
24 Work __
25 Annual with deep-pink flowers
28 Miles off
30 Tailor
33 Part of the Dept. of Labor
34 All-Star Martinez
35 "Guys and Dolls" composer/lyricist
37 Like dirty clothes, often
39 Secondary: Abbr.
40 The muscle of a muscle car, maybe
42 Soup scoop
43 Fill
44 ABBA's genre
46 "Alice" actress Linda
48 Kyrgyzstan's second-largest city
49 Game discs
53 Uncopiable, say
55 Quick session for a band
57 Springsteen hit with the lyric "Only you can cool my desire"
58 Noted graffiti artist
59 Viking, e.g.
60 Philosophize, say
61 Strike leader?
62 Breather
63 Trained groups

DOWN

1 Sights at the dentist's office
2 Three-time Olympic skating gold medalist
3 Georgia of "The Mary Tyler Moore Show"
4 1955 Pulitzer-winning poet
5 Rushed
6 Maxim
7 Pot and porn magazines, typically
8 Norton Sound city
9 Diplomat who wrote "The Tide of Nationalism"
10 Reform Party founder
11 Legitimate
12 Construction project that began in Rome
13 Rush
16 "Yeah . . . anyway"
23 Ultra sound?
26 Boolean operators
27 Charging things?
29 Ensnare, with "in"
30 "It wasn't meant to be"
31 Literally, "the cottonwoods"
32 Those with will power?
36 Exactly 10 seconds, for the 100-yard dash
38 Spanish greeting
41 Tending to wear away
45 Illogically afraid
47 Draw (from)
50 Actor Werner of "The Spy Who Came in From the Cold"
51 Heroic tale
52 Lid afflictions
53 Cleaner fragrance
54 They're sometimes named after presidents
56 Squat

by Brendan Emmett Quigley

ACROSS

1 Fictional amnesiac portrayer
10 Out
15 Mix and match?
16 Total
17 Identifies with
18 Old computing acronym
19 Head Start program service, briefly
20 Some drillers, for short
21 Prefix with gram
22 Stay (with)
23 Turned on a friend, maybe?
24 Painting surface
28 Proscribed
30 Destination in the "Odyssey"
32 "No need to go on"
37 Without embellishment
39 Vitamin in meat, milk and eggs
40 Resolve a bromance spat, say
42 Crime scene sight
43 Muscle Beach sights
45 Backs
46 Garden decorations
50 Evade
52 2007 horror sequel
53 It may be hard to reach
54 Fool
58 1970s subcompact
59 Member of a medical minority
61 British running great Steve
62 Start of a Dickensian request
63 Clipped
64 Emulate Ferris Bueller

DOWN

1 Dealer's amt.
2 Parrot
3 Communications leader?
4 Big Indonesian export
5 "Silent Spring" topic
6 Gland: Prefix
7 Costumed figure
8 Suleiman the Magnificent, for one
9 Modernists
10 Difficult sort
11 Addition
12 Common subject of medieval art
13 Blank ___
14 Title role for Charlton Heston
22 Election-related nonprofit since 1990
23 Cymbal sound
24 "Mystic Pizza" actress Annabeth
25 Dramatic accusation
26 Cut with more than one layer
27 Bit of Bollywood attire
29 Mac
31 Base for some incense
33 Dry
34 Tynan player in "The Seduction of Joe Tynan"
35 "Severn Meadows" poet Gurney
36 Retreats
38 "Delish!"
41 Presentation by Bill Clinton in 2007 or Bill Gates in 2010
44 Cores
46 Sensitive subject?
47 Green
48 Sports league V.I.P.
49 Paws
51 Tawdry
53 They're a handful
54 What might put you through your paces?
55 Minor opening?
56 Wave function symbols
57 Suffixes with mountain and cannon
60 Grp. involved in the Abbottabad raid

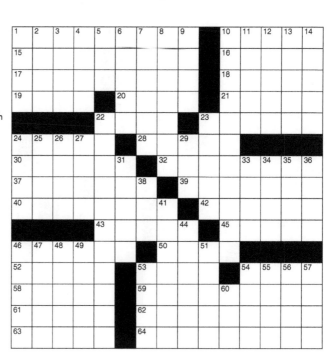

by John Lieb and David Quarfoot

ACROSS

1 Food item resembling an organ
11 Not long-departed
15 Question after a public shellacking
16 Plutoid just beyond the Kuiper Belt
17 Many a detective film cover-up
18 Squire
19 Lack of authorisation?
20 "Casablanca" carrier
22 It really stands out
25 Be loud at a funeral, say
26 Many 56-Across users
29 It may have check marks
30 General exercise?
31 Stretches out
35 "We're in trouble now!"
36 Abbr. on a sports ticker
37 Topics at some religious retreats
41 Cousin of a screwdriver
44 Largest city in the South Pacific
45 Go back on
46 Six bells in the morning watch
49 Prefix with geek
50 Hand picks?
52 Monogram of the author of "A Charge to Keep: My Journey to the White House"
55 Kind of block
56 It replaced the Indian rupee in 1932
60 Winnipeg's ___ Franko Museum
61 Ithaca is at its southern end
62 Be inclined
63 His Secret Service code name was Providence

DOWN

1 Classic name in New York delis
2 Subject precursor
3 Like some eggs
4 Intro to Euclidean geometry?
5 Letter abbr.
6 Casual assent
7 As
8 Weena's race, in fiction
9 Generally speaking
10 Big name in video streaming
11 Five and ten, e.g.
12 Ticketmaster info, maybe
13 Coloring
14 Compact first name?
21 Formation on 28-Down
22 About 186,282 miles
23 Marathoner Pippig
24 NASA's Aquarius, e.g.
26 Done some strokes
27 Routine reaction?
28 See 21-Down
32 Home of the Black Mts.
33 Crow relatives
34 Stock mover
38 Shrimp
39 Midas's undoing
40 Katana wielder
41 Curt
42 Beauregard follower
43 GPS abbr.
46 Cheerleader's move
47 Relative d'un étudiant
48 Many an animal rights activist
51 Baseball Hall-of-Famer who played for the Giants
52 Bother, with "at"
53 After-life gathering?
54 Backwoods relative
57 Starting device: Abbr.
58 Code word
59 Publisher of World of Work mag.

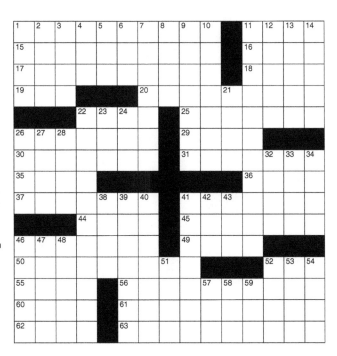

by Barry C. Silk

114

ACROSS

1 Bar fixture
4 Person who might suit you well?
15 Start of many a "Jeopardy!" response
16 Transported
17 Org. with an Office of Water
18 "Poor Little Fool" hitmaker, 1958
19 Danny who composed the theme music for "The Simpsons"
21 Eponymous Dr. Asperger
22 Onetime Michael Jackson bodyguard
23 Benders
24 Sight on a "Hee Haw" set
25 Hindu god often depicted with a bow and arrow
26 A choli may be worn under this
27 "Star Trek: T.N.G." role
28 Name on the cover of "Yosemite and the High Sierra"
29 Verb suffix?
30 Ancient scribe's work surface
32 Treadmill runners, maybe
34 "Sex is an emotion in motion" speaker
37 Not reliable
39 Empire State tech school
40 "Pride ___ before destruction": Proverbs
42 Be uncooperative
43 Showroom window no.
44 Discipline
45 European hub
46 Show stoppers?
47 Leipzig-to-Zurich dir.
48 Columnist Collins
49 Was triumphant in the end

50 Inventor's undoing?
53 Mineralogical appendage?
54 Avatar setting
55 Base man
56 Image on Utah's state quarter
57 Baker's dozen for the Beatles, for short

DOWN

1 Tree also known as a sugar apple
2 "You've got to be kidding!"
3 Perfectly
4 Wedding rings?
5 Have ___ (be advantageously networked)
6 Secret attachment, for short
7 South Bend neighbor
8 Court group
9 Dominick who wrote "A Season in Purgatory"
10 Some Snapple products
11 Conan O'Brien's employer from '88 to '91
12 1899 painting used to promote gramophones
13 Massive, as a massif
14 National service
20 Internal investigation, for short?
24 Hybrid menswear
25 Grasped
27 Texas Ranger Hall of Fame and Museum site
28 Many are blonde
30 Among
31 Enjoy the moment

33 Copier giant absorbed by the Kyocera Corporation
35 Appear suddenly
36 Track consultants
38 Banana Republic defender, maybe
40 Ersatz blazer
41 Speaker of Shakespeare's "If music be the food of love, play on"
43 Calculus calculation: Abbr.
45 Like some gruel
46 Pioneer in cool jazz
48 Mapped item
49 "Marjorie Morningstar" novelist
51 Got out of the way
52 Head of state?

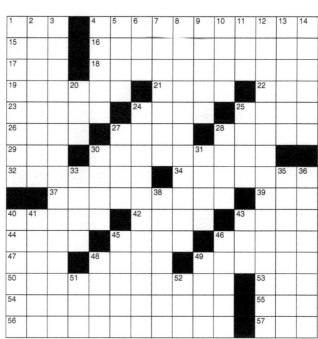

by Brad Wilber and Doug Peterson

ACROSS

1 Where Union Pacific is headquartered
6 Chinese ___ (popular bonsai trees)
10 Medieval drudge
14 Sister of Castor and Pollux
15 Fighter getting a leg up?
17 Site of Tiberius' Villa Jovis
18 Page on the stage
19 Comfortable
21 Taking place (in)
22 One-point throws
24 Appliance sound
25 Checkers, for instance
26 Play critic?
28 Hype
32 Onetime Arapaho foe
33 Grooming tool
36 Vietnamese holiday
37 O-shaped
38 Priest in I Samuel
39 Dread Zeppelin or the Fab Faux
41 Sports div. that awards the George Halas Trophy
42 Gold Cup venue
43 Quote qualification
44 Coin of many countries
45 Pretension
48 Get more inventory
50 Country whose flag is known as the Saltire
54 Bubble handler?
55 Foundation devoted to good works?
57 Uniform
58 Bag lady?
59 Less often seen
60 Deep black
61 Twist
62 America's Cup trophies, e.g.

DOWN

1 Broadway musical with two exclamation points in its name
2 They might have bones to pick
3 Like characters in a script
4 Some wetlands wildlife
5 Miyazaki film genre
6 Hosp. record
7 Creates an account?
8 Fast-food debut of 1981
9 Go along effortlessly
10 Vending machine drink
11 What to do when you have nothing left to say?
12 Peace Nobelist Cassin
13 Dance-pop trio Right Said ___
16 Symbol of happiness
20 Off the mark
23 English Channel feeder
27 Bad line readings
29 Launched the first round
30 Narcissistic one
31 Hand-held "Star Trek" devices
33 Sea creature whose name means "sailor"
34 Huxtable family mom
35 Surgical cutter
40 Gondoliers, e.g.
44 Like a poli sci major, maybe
46 Woodworking tools
47 Underhanded schemer
49 American Airlines hub
50 Drink served in a masu
51 Zodiac symbol
52 Palindromic man
53 "My man!"
56 Plaintive pet sound

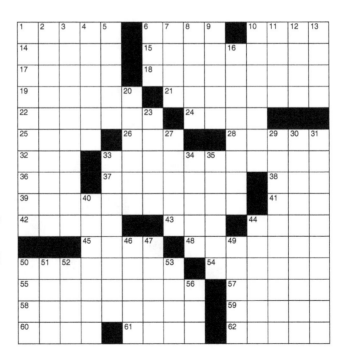

by Patrick Berry

116

ACROSS

1 Title trio of a 1980 Pulitzer winner
16 One-on-one with a big shot
17 Gist
18 French preposition
19 "Just what I need"
20 Stamp purchases
23 "Cool dad" on "Modern Family"
24 Hill minority: Abbr.
28 Top honors for atletas olímpicos
29 They're often taken on horses
30 Happening
31 ". . . we'll ___ a cup o' kindness . . .": Burns
32 First name in Harlem Renaissance literature
33 Quail
34 Winged it
37 Napkin material
38 Son of 30-Down
39 "___ wise guy, eh?"
40 Very little (of)
41 A quarter of acht
42 Second-largest city in Nicaragua
43 Tree-hugger?
44 Youthful and fresh
45 Longtime late-night announcer
46 Breakout company of 1976
48 Spearfishing need
49 Moment's notice?
56 Vetoes
57 Some government checks

DOWN

1 It might tell you where to get off
2 Sch. founded by a Pentecostal preacher
3 Turn down
4 Dances around
5 Dangerous things to weave on
6 Ballparks at J.F.K.?
7 Her, to Henriette
8 Grabbed some sack time
9 Self-confidence to a fault
10 Vehicular bomb?
11 Romance novelist's award
12 Looking ecstatic
13 One of the Romneys
14 New Deal inits.
15 Snicker bit
20 Home of Sanssouci Palace
21 Wind River Reservation native
22 Hiawatha's grandmother in "The Song of Hiawatha"
23 Philatelist's concern, briefly
25 Clean type
26 Lab growth need
27 Designer Gabbana of Dolce & Gabbana
29 Stamp purchase
30 Father of 38-Across
32 Limoncello ingredient
33 K. J. ___, 2011 Players Championship champion
35 Univ. in Manhattan
36 Smaller cousin of a four-in-hand?
41 100 bits?
42 San Diego suburb
44 Russian retreat
45 One trying to avoid a banking crisis?
47 Loss from a guillotine
48 They're issued to cruisers, briefly
49 Little chances?
50 Fruitcake
51 It's H-shaped
52 First year of the Liang dynasty
53 "Kung Fu" actor Philip
54 Part of U.S.S.R.: Abbr.
55 Charlotte-to-Raleigh dir.

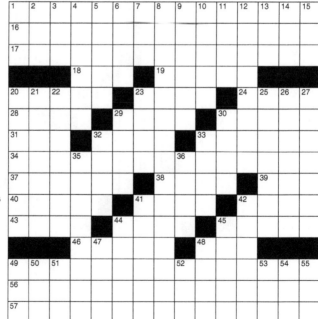

by Chris A. McGlothlin

ACROSS

1 Fighting
6 Amscray
10 They get taken easily
14 ___ Road (W.W. II supply route)
15 Hospital bed feature
16 Nail
17 Circular side?
19 Unisex name meaning "born again"
20 Many a security point
21 Straight
23 Form of "sum"
24 Sound name
25 Tom who won a Tony for "The Seven Year Itch"
26 Ones keeping on their toes?
29 The City of a Hundred Spires
31 Triage determination
32 Home of "NerdTV"
35 Line of rulers
37 Big game plans?
39 Argument-ending letters
40 Short distance
42 Occasions for bulldogging
43 Hot-and-cold menu item
45 Mathematician Cantor who founded set theory
48 Going without saying?
49 Aid in getting back on track
52 Means of reducing worker fatigue
54 Kraft Nabisco Championship org.
55 Color also known as endive blue
56 Classic Hitchcock set
58 Quiet place to fish
59 Suffixes of 61-Across
60 Rich of old films
61 Contents of some ledges

62 "___ Wedding" ("The Mary Tyler Moore Show" episode)
63 Occasioned

DOWN

1 Flat, e.g.
2 Fixes flats?
3 Hospital patient's wear
4 See 5-Down
5 With 4-Down, lost control
6 Feature of some western wear
7 Pathfinder?
8 Reagan was seen a lot in them
9 Word after who, what or where, but rarely when
10 Things driven on construction sites
11 Anti-inflammatory product
12 Authorities might sit on one
13 Wonderful
18 Kind of wheel
22 One putting the pedal to the metal
24 Summer symbol?
27 One of the Eastern elite
28 Aviation safety statistic
29 Straightaway
30 Manhattan choice
32 Broken into on TV?
33 Kind of lab
34 Nemesis of some dodgers: Abbr.
36 Fellow chairperson?
38 Use a 24-Down
41 Like pigtails
43 Talks tediously

44 Hacker's achievement
45 American company whose mascot has a Cockney accent
46 Diamond flaw
47 Diagonal rib of a vault
50 One getting cuts
51 Early: Prefix
53 Exit lines?
54 Ethnologist's interest
57 254,000 angstroms

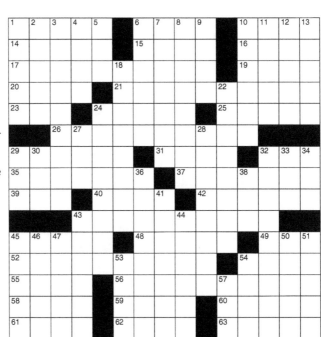

by Dana Motley

ACROSS

1 Baker's predecessor
5 "The Daily Rundown" carrier
10 Steinbeck siren
14 Vindaloo accompaniment
15 Admission about a story
16 Skillful, slangily
17 Brother's keeper?
20 In thing
21 In place
22 What one should take in: Abbr.
23 Engagement rings?
25 Muhammad, e.g.
27 Ready for another round
28 Packer in a bookstore
31 Young turkey
32 Strong order?
35 Compliment to the chef
36 Drawers hitting the pavement?
42 County whose seat is La Junta
43 Means of changing one's mind
44 One way to catch the game
45 Quaint letter-opening abbr.
47 Took the wrong way
48 13th Spanish letter
49 Ear plug?
53 Big inits. in power
54 Remark after holding someone up
57 War head?
58 Thrill
59 Strauss's "Tausend und __ Nacht"
60 Backwoods agreement
61 Many a Madrileño
62 Walked all over

DOWN

1 Where to observe some workers
2 Napa Valley setting
3 Clipboard's relative
4 One way to fly: Abbr.
5 "Carota" and "Blue II," for two
6 Start of many an operation
7 Trivial objections
8 Blast from the passed?
9 Software box item
10 Peck, e.g.: Abbr.
11 Den mother's charge
12 Tony with an Emmy
13 Like many sonatas' second movements
18 Mad person's question
19 Leave to scrap, maybe
24 Indigent individuals
26 Numbered relations
28 "__ wind that bloweth . . ."
29 Bass parts
30 Legendary spring figure
33 Pier grp.
34 Bras __ Lake (Canadian inland sea)
36 Rumor opener
37 Agenda opener
38 They're thirsty much of the time
39 What gobs take in
40 The Merry Mex of golf
41 Feeling no pain
46 Jewel cases?
47 Bill with barbs
50 Fruit giant
51 Home of the daily Hamshahri
52 Raiders Hall-of-Famer Jim
55 Coin feature
56 Unlike 38-Down

by Ed Sessa

ACROSS

1 Human-powered transport
8 Lingerie enhancements
15 Japanese "thanks"
16 Consumed
17 Like some Mideast ideology
18 Grammy-winning singer from Barbados
19 "___ me later"
20 Barrister's deg.
21 Belief opposed by Communists
22 Hammer and sickle
24 Small arms
25 "Be right there"
29 Labor outfits
30 Bubbly brand, for short
34 Oral reports?
35 Des Moines-to-Cedar Rapids dir.
36 It's known to locals as Cymraeg
37 "Money" novelist, 1984
38 Orange entree, informally
40 Not take a back seat to anyone?
41 Diner freebies
45 Fisherman's Wharf attraction
46 Young colleen, across the North Channel
48 Browns' home, for short
49 Bring to a boil?
52 By the boatload
53 Wastes
55 Cubs' home
56 Improbable victory, in slang
57 Potentially embarrassing video
58 Mezzo-soprano Troyanos

DOWN

1 Quebec preceder, to pilots
2 Meaningful stretches
3 Soft touch?
4 Supermarket inits.
5 Some bank offerings
6 Totally flummoxed
7 Spring figure?
8 Pitcher Blyleven with 3,701 strikeouts
9 Oatmeal topping
10 Close
11 Unit of wisdom?
12 "Little Girls" musical
13 Actress Kirsten
14 Hits with some trash
22 Sporty auto options
23 Torch carriers
25 Capital of South Sudan
26 Old one
27 Her voice was first heard in 2011
28 It's already out of the bag
30 Parts of a school athletic calendar
31 Designer Cassini
32 "Mi casa ___ casa"
33 Segue starter
36 Everything, with "the"
38 Trip
39 Fried tortilla dish
40 Landlocked African land
41 Collectors of DNA samples
42 Hides from Indians, maybe?
43 Chill
44 All-points bulletin, e.g.
47 Final word in a holiday tune
49 Locale for many political debates
50 Perdition
51 Site of the Bocca Nuova crater
54 Poli ___

by Ian Livengood

ACROSS

1 Start of a phobia?
5 All the best?
10 Five-time U.S. Open winner
14 Immensely
15 Leisurely
16 Sign of virtue
17 Malted alternatives
20 Be ruthless
21 Run-___
22 Pair of word processors?
23 Instinctive reaction
24 Verbal gem
25 Bygone country name or its currency
28 Safe to push off
34 It springs from Monte Falterona
35 Brush off
36 Place for tiger woods?
37 Get going
39 Not at all sharp, maybe
40 A shot
41 Plant production: Abbr.
42 "Go figure!"
48 One of the muskrats in the 1976 hit "Muskrat Love"
51 Play savior
53 Dual diner dish
54 Stickler's citation
55 "Or else ___ despiser of good manners": Shak.
56 Newton, e.g.
57 Event with body cords
58 Not at all sharp
59 Lands

DOWN

1 Brand of blades
2 Brand of literature
3 Where seekers may find hiders
4 Almost never
5 Go-for-broke
6 Proceeded precipitately

7 IV component
8 Chain of off-price department stores
9 Guzzle
10 Home of the world's largest artificial lake
11 Ground crew gear?
12 Like prairie dogs, notably
13 "Pippin" Tony winner
18 As if scripted
19 "Get the lead out!"
23 Get inside and out
25 Director/screenwriter Penn
26 "Exodus" character
27 Magazine with an annual "500|5000" conference
28 Likely result of excess 17- and 53-Across
29 Prefix with 36-Across
30 Seemed to be

31 Bit of chiding
32 Not dally
33 "That's fantastic news!"
35 One bound to hold notes?
38 Venom
39 Spot ___
41 Actress Matlin
42 Words of support
43 Do the final details on
44 Not coming up short
45 Frost, to François
46 Human Development Report publisher, in brief
47 About 50% of calls
48 Turnover alternative
49 Tax burden?
50 Measures up to
52 Like many a goody-goody

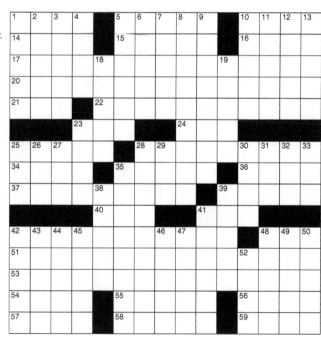

by Frederick J. Healy

ACROSS

1 First female candidate to win the Ames Straw Poll
16 War paths
17 It airs in the morning, ironically
18 Case builders: Abbr.
19 Copy from a CD
20 Understood
21 Show featuring special agents
22 Red Cloud, e.g.
24 Player of the bad teacher in "Bad Teacher"
26 Rear
27 Possible rank indicator
29 Overseas relig. title
30 Big name in car monitors
32 Beat it
34 "Keep dreaming!"
36 Word after a splat
37 Like some lovers' hearts
41 Strikes
45 She may be fawning
46 Colorful cover-ups
48 Brandy letters
49 Grilling test
51 Misses abroad: Abbr.
52 Newborn abroad
53 ___ Hedin, discoverer of the Trans-Himalaya
55 Folman who directed the 2013 film "The Congress"
56 Comcast Center hoopster
57 Alternative to a breakfast burrito
61 Big source for modern slang
62 Some critical comments from co-workers

DOWN

1 Yellowstone setting: Abbr.
2 Odysseus, e.g.
3 Dopes
4 Knocks off
5 Control tower info
6 Re-serve judgment?
7 Female adviser
8 Ill-humored
9 Norwegian Star port of call
10 Old oscilloscope part, briefly
11 Turns over in one's plot?
12 Was reflective
13 Its adherents are in disbelief
14 Formula one?
15 Neighbor of Victoria: Abbr.
21 Top kick, for one: Abbr.
22 Puck and others
23 Some exact likenesses
25 Part of Queen Elizabeth's makeup?
27 Certain league divisions
28 Forerunners of discs
31 Kind of cross
33 They may be returned with regrets: Abbr.
35 458 Spider and F12 Berlinetta
37 Production
38 Definitely
39 Give some space, say
40 Grind
42 Stormed
43 Modern mouse hole?
44 Ring bearer, maybe
47 Emulates Homer
50 Actor Burton
52 Competitor of Lauren and Klein
54 Numerical prefix
56 First name in footwear
57 "Two, three, four" lead-in
58 Org. with a clenched fist logo
59 Org. created right after the cold war
60 MS-DOS component: Abbr.

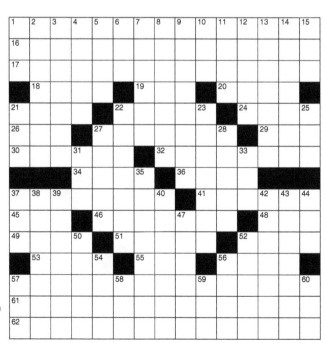

by David Steinberg

ACROSS

1 TV host who won a Best Comedy Album Grammy
12 Vegan lunch option, informally
15 Cry used to pump up a crowd
16 Following
17 Fortune
18 Beast in a Marco Polo tale
19 Old station name
20 Abbr. in a birth announcement
21 Request in pool or beer pong
23 Hudson River school?
25 "Eww!"
27 Soundtrack to many a bomb-defusing scene
28 Prizes given to good docs?
31 "Kazaam" star, informally
32 Crying need?
36 A wedge might come out of it
37 Beast hunted by Hemingway in "Green Hills of Africa"
38 Work set mostly in Cyprus
40 Herbal quaff
42 Wilde wrote "De Profundis" in one
43 Lion runner
45 Unlike a showboat
46 Rash application
47 Reception opening
49 Hull sealer
51 1-Across's home, once: Abbr.
52 Resistance figure
57 Like pickle juice
59 Dated
61 Many a donor, in brief
62 Go around, but not quite go in
63 W.W. II defense

66 Sun ___
67 Fall fallout, some believe
68 Short agreement
69 Scorsese film before "Alice Doesn't Live Here Anymore"

DOWN

1 "The Two ___" ("Chinatown" sequel)
2 Like 1-Across, by descent
3 Quick set
4 "Oh no!"
5 His, modern-style?
6 Roll up and bind
7 Source of the word "alcohol"
8 Glass protector
9 Velázquez's "___ Meninas"
10 Repute

11 Orange and blue wearer, for short
12 It opens during the fall
13 Some trade barriers
14 Nada
22 On the line
24 Dangerous thing to sell
26 Humphries of the N.B.A.
29 Southern site of an 1865 battle
30 Weak spots
32 Wrap session?
33 Slant one's words, in a way
34 Picture with a lot of gunplay
35 Game controller button
39 Cholesterol-lowering food
41 First-choice

44 Hand over (to)
48 Self-titled debut album of 1991
50 Sign at a game
53 "Au Revoir, Les Enfants" writer/director
54 Sporty Lotus model
55 Put one's foot down, in a way
56 Accord indicators
58 Protection
60 "I ___ tell"
64 1998 Angelina Jolie biopic
65 49-Across source

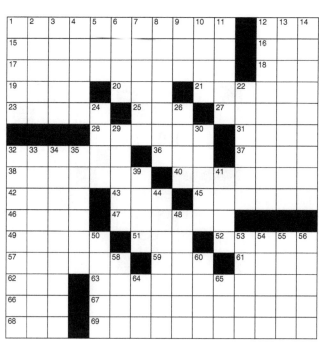

by Josh Knapp

ACROSS

1 Old Hollywood low-budget studios, collectively
11 "Oh, God!" actress
15 Wine bottle contents in Hitchcock's "Notorious"
16 Only event in which Venezuela medaled at the 2012 Olympics
17 Dessert often with cream cheese icing
18 Ironwoman org.?
19 Singer born Eithne Ní Bhraonáin
20 Map inits. created in the wake of the Suez Crisis
21 Now-rare connection method
23 Blather
25 Big name in markers
26 Nitroglycerin, for one
29 Director's alternative to a dolly
32 It was dissolved in 1991
34 Time in TV ads
35 Fused
36 Fortify
38 Domingo, e.g.
39 Onetime TV music vendor
41 Kind of community
43 Avocado relative
45 Ross Sea sights
46 Interrupts
47 Strike out
48 Excoriates
49 "Revolution 9" collaborator
51 It may slip in the back
55 L.B.J. biographer Robert __
56 One-third of a triangle, maybe
59 Hindi relative
60 The goddess Kali appeared on its first cover
61 Bygone
62 New Jersey childhood home of Whitney Houston and Queen Latifah

DOWN

1 Brownish purple
2 Port where Camus set "The Plague"
3 Fluctuate
4 Brings to a boil
5 Rock in __ (major music festival)
6 "Coppélia" attire
7 Hit from the 1978 disco album "Cruisin'"
8 More than chuckle
9 Planet first mentioned on "Happy Days"
10 It's used to define a border
11 Colorful dessert
12 Press production
13 Doing a government agency's job
14 Garner
22 Not the party type?: Abbr.
24 Part of 20-Across
25 Substance that citrus peels are rich in
26 Endor natives
27 Site of the last battle of the Cuban Revolution
28 Barriers used in urban renewal projects
29 Ire
30 Get a hint of
31 Party tray array
33 Vexing
37 Country name
40 Releases
42 Baseball's __ Line (.200 batting average)
44 Prime meridian std.
47 Skip
48 Smallish lingerie spec
49 Electrical units
50 Ordered
52 "You can count on me"
53 Provided backup, in a way
54 Deep or high lead-in
57 Org. with inspectors
58 "A defeat for humanity," per Pope John Paul II

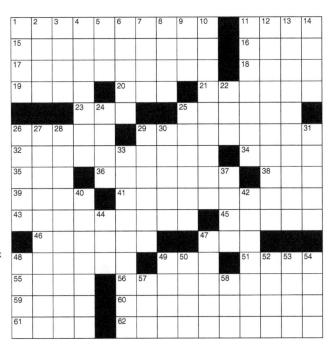

by Brad Wilber and Doug Peterson

124

ACROSS

1 World's tallest building
12 Instagram post
15 One way to cruise along
16 7 a.m. staple, briefly
17 They come out of many mouths
18 Protection from pirates: Abbr.
19 Sets forth thoroughly
20 Trite
22 Guitar maker Fender
23 She's beautiful, per a popular song
24 So-called "weekend pill"
28 Like some liquor stores
29 Like 30-Down
30 Room at the top, maybe
31 Spa treatment, for short
32 Unsurprising outcome
33 Radios, e.g.
34 "Sweet!"
35 Starz alternative
36 Belfast is on its shore
37 Mind
38 Site of the Sibelius Monument
40 Castle's place, initially
41 Took up some of
42 Big time
43 Trepanning targets
44 Some partial appointments
49 Blood
50 Big time
52 It may be cracked or packed
53 "C'est la vie"
54 Co. purchased by Wizards of the Coast
55 Hail Marys, e.g.

DOWN

1 Champion between Holyfield reigns
2 It has "batch" and "patch" commands
3 Not be smooth-talking?
4 Activity with holding and throwing
5 Singer of the 1987 #1 country hit "Do Ya"
6 Buds
7 "I shall not find myself so ___ die": Antony
8 Fictional accounts
9 Text attachment?
10 Bygone yellow-roofed kiosks
11 Forward, back or center
12 Like every Bond film since 1989
13 Virginal
14 Moor

21 Karate trainee in 2010's "The Karate Kid"
23 Agatha Christie's "There Is ___ . . ."
24 Is unable to cut the mustard
25 Form of strength training
26 It'll help you breathe easier
27 Fast flight
28 One in a religious majority
30 Brand on a face
33 Largest river of southern California
34 Norah Jones's "Tell ___ Mama"
36 Not amounting to much
37 "Holy" group in 17th-century literature

39 Something to beg pardon for
40 Ill-paid laborer
42 Something to beg pardon for
44 Not be gratuitous
45 ___ Sant'Gria (wine choice)
46 Servant in the "Discworld" novels
47 Kind of pudding
48 Whole bunch
51 Both Barack and Michelle Obama have them: Abbr.

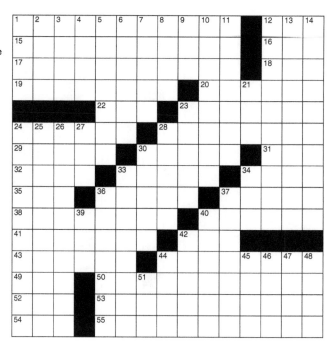

by Julian Lim

ACROSS

1 Holding
9 Way of looking at things
14 Reading light for an audiobook?
16 Detergent component
17 Going nowhere?
18 Pine for
19 Org. always headed by a U.S. general or admiral
20 Baltic native
22 "After ___"
23 Seat cushions?
25 Old airline name
28 Roofing choice
29 "According to reports . . ."
32 Wedded
33 They make a racket
34 Cell alternatives
35 Like each word from this clue
37 Many a time
40 Change places
41 White spread
42 Heavy and clumsy
43 White of the eye
45 The Dom is the third-highest one
46 A whole bunch
49 Blows a fuse
50 Nation with the most Unesco World Heritage Sites
53 Winner over Ohio State in 1935's so-called "Game of the Century"
55 Suez Crisis setting
56 Startling revelation
57 Xerox competitor
58 Buffalo Bill and Calamity Jane wore them

DOWN

1 Hold firmly, as opinions
2 Stuff used to soften baseball mitts
3 Generally
4 Hill house
5 "A whizzing rocket that would emulate a star," per Wordsworth
6 Big name in storage
7 Boortz of talk radio
8 Swinger?
9 Diane Sawyer's employer
10 Land on the Arctic Cir.
11 Most dismal
12 Mouthwash with the patented ingredient Zantrate
13 Shakespearean stage direction
15 Depression creator
21 Crab apple's quality
24 Old-fashioned respirator
26 Not as outgoing
27 Communist bloc news source
30 Experienced
31 Fountain drinks
33 Wrist bones
34 Lamebrain
35 It's not fair
36 Car collectors?
37 Greek salad ingredient
38 They arrive by the truckload
39 Movie trailers, e.g.
40 Carriage with a folding hood
41 Turbine parts
44 Advanced slowly
47 School door sign
48 Amendment to an amendment
51 Southeast Asian language
52 Dark side
54 Ikura or tobiko

by Patrick Berry

ACROSS

1 Where a lot of dough gets thrown around
11 See 51-Across
15 Fuel for a warp drive engine on "Star Trek"
16 Resignation exclamation
17 Sleep aid, for some
18 BMW of North America and others: Abbr.
19 Zip around a field?
20 Makes happen
21 Assistant played by Bruce Lee
22 Wanting for nothing
24 "Celebrity Jeopardy!" show, briefly
25 Took revenge on
26 Broadview ___, O.
29 Become stiff
33 Get by force of will?
37 Punk's cousin
38 Info about a person's education and work history
39 Smooths
40 Follows a military order
41 Their habits give them away
42 Follows a military order
44 Time of long journées
45 Lets go through
46 Brief albums, in brief
48 Needing hand cream, maybe
51 With 11-Across, biblical woman who met a bad end
53 Board
56 "That gives me an idea . . ."
58 First spaceman's first name
59 Setting for "The Misfits"
61 Polo competitor
62 "My bad"

63 Musical production
64 Symbols of sharpness

DOWN

1 One with promotional potential
2 "___ Steps" (Christian best seller)
3 "10" is inscribed on it
4 Temple imperfection
5 Subject of the 2012 book "Circle of Treason"
6 Porter created by Burroughs
7 Winnebago relatives
8 "Incorrect!"
9 Babes in the woods?
10 Smartphone that preceded the Pre
11 Do the impossible, metaphorically
12 Anxious

13 It's never wrong
14 Standard breakup creation
23 Temptation for Luke Skywalker
25 Follow the sun?
27 Sniffs out
28 First capital of the Last Frontier
30 Like some fogs
31 Ham's handoff
32 Name associated with a mobster or a monster
33 Skyscraper component
34 Brief period of darkness?
35 Eager
36 Event with unmarked choices
43 Trial lawyer who wrote "O.J.: The Last Word"

47 Basidium-borne body
49 Adjective on taco truck menus
50 Crumple
51 "Can't Believe Your ___" (1988 Neil Young song)
52 Drink said to have originated on Lesbos
53 Titles for distinguished Indians
54 Main character in "The Paper Chase," e.g.
55 Cousin of a congo eel
57 Blabbers
60 See, in Santiago

by Jeff Chen

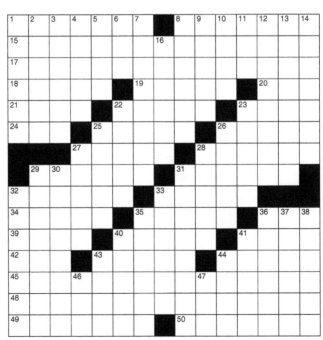

ACROSS

1 Offer to host
8 W.W. II vessels
15 Expressed slight surprise
17 "But really . . ."
18 ___ Empire
19 Deep-seated
20 What you might be overseas?
21 Part of A.M.A.: Abbr.
22 Principal
23 Leave in
24 Rx specification
25 Industry leader
26 Part of a place setting
27 Swelters
28 Absolutely correct
29 Relatives of spoonbills
31 Voyeur
32 Staggered
33 Many chains are found in them
34 Ticked off
35 Works at a museum, say
36 One of the girls
39 Going ___
40 Gnats and mosquitoes
41 Powerful engine
42 Pipe holder?
43 Watch brand once worn by 007
44 One of 24
45 1959 #5 hit with the B-side "I've Cried Before"
48 What a board may be against
49 Euripides tragedy
50 Satyrs, say

DOWN

1 Mountains of ___ (Genesis locale)
2 Strauss opera
3 "Trees" poet
4 Werner of "The Spy Who Came in From the Cold"
5 "In that ___ . . ."
6 Hall-of-Fame outfielder Roush
7 Throws off
8 Flag carried on a knight's lance
9 Blake's "burning bright" cat
10 Pessimist
11 Outmoded: Abbr.
12 Three-time Haitian president
13 Super-wonderful
14 Make more attractive
16 Warriors with supposed powers of invisibility and shapeshifting
22 Ready for an on-air interview
23 "Your mama wears army boots" and such
25 Put a charge into?
26 Leans precariously
27 "L'Arlésienne" composer
28 Workout targets, informally
29 Copycat
30 Long-haired cat breed
31 Simple and serene
32 Fox relative
33 Old arm
35 Pale shades
36 Fought
37 Shot-putter, e.g.
38 Puts in
40 "Positive thinking" pioneer
41 Grounds for a medal
43 Pet
44 Place for a jerk?
46 "Captain Video" figures, for short
47 '50s politico

by Mangesh Ghogre and Doug Peterson

ACROSS

1 They aren't straight
6 "Aarrghh!"
13 Shove off
15 Lures
16 "Oo la la!" jeans, informally
18 Preceder of John Sebastian at Woodstock
19 Scott Joplin's "The Entertainer" and others
21 Chain
22 Heralds
24 Produces lush sounds?
25 Heavily populated areas, informally
26 They adhere to brains
28 Temple inits.
29 Lieutenant colonel's charge
30 Students with outstanding character?
31 See 48-Across
32 Its arms are not solid
35 Difficult journey
36 Gifted trio?
37 Follow the party line?
38 Round trip for one?
40 Direction givers, often
42 Superexcited
43 Delicate needlepoint lace
45 Is so inclined
46 Do some work between parties
47 Brings in for more tests, say
48 Fast parts of 31-Across
49 Meteorological probe

DOWN

1 Like wolves vis-à-vis foxes
2 Not at length
3 Takes up onto the surface
4 Susan's family on "Seinfeld"
5 The Father of the Historical Novel
6 Group of football games played at the beginning of Jan.
7 Dog it
8 Pardons
9 Choose in the end
10 Flawlessly
11 Areas next to bull's-eyes
12 Strongmen of old
14 Remedy for a bad leg
17 Fastballs that drop sharply near the plate
20 Durable cover
23 Wise sort
27 2002 Best Original Screenplay Oscar winner for "Talk to Her"
29 Spotted hybrid house pet
30 1980s Olympic star with the autobiography "Breaking the Surface"
31 Grant
32 Geisha's instrument
33 Expelled
34 Pressure gauge connection
35 Mechanic, say
36 Beyond that
37 Shop keeper?
39 "___ Lucy" (old sitcom)
41 Florida's De ___ National Monument
44 Wii ancestor, briefly

by Tim Croce

ACROSS

1 Begin
10 Donizetti heroine
15 Catches up to
16 Magnetron component
17 Relative of a spouse
19 "Just playin'"
20 Things often dropped in Harvard Yard?
21 Big name in winter vehicles
22 Fixer, perhaps
23 In the way of
24 Phony blazers
25 Birthplace of the Franciscan order
27 "Before My Birth" collagist, 1914
28 __-yo (cold treat, briefly)
29 With 36- and 39-Across, go from 1- to 61-Across
31 10-year-old Best Supporting Actress
33 Robert W. Service's "The Cremation of Sam __"
36 See 29-Across
37 Robert W. Service output
38 Soothing flora
39 See 29-Across
41 Bumped into
42 Bumped into
43 Razor target, maybe
47 Pack into a thick mass
50 Ottoman bigwig
51 Tan in a library
52 Anatomical ring
53 Direction de Paris à Nancy
54 Vegan gelatin substitute
55 Stopgap supervisor's duty
58 __ Montoya, swordsman in "The Princess Bride"
59 Prefixes featured on some maps
60 Baden-Powell of the Girl Guides
61 End

DOWN

1 One known for riding out of gear?
2 Brings out
3 Sends in
4 He'll "talk 'til his voice is hoarse"
5 The Who's "__ Hard"
6 __ Romanova, alter ego of Marvel's Black Widow
7 Landmark anime film of 1988
8 Many pulp heroes, in slang
9 Picking up skill?
10 Cheerful early risers
11 Preposition on a business-hours sign
12 Unit charge
13 "&" or "@," but not "and" or "at"
14 Restricted flight items
18 By yesterday, so to speak
23 Indication of some oxidation
24 Hug or kiss, maybe
26 Drink brand symbolized by a polar bear
27 39th vice president
30 "The Dark Knight Rises" director, 2012
31 Grammy category
32 What's typical
33 "Lordy!" in Lodi
34 Snow job?
35 Been chosen, as for office
40 One-two in the ring?
42 Pavlova portrayed one over 4,000 times
44 Storied place of worship
45 Eastern lodging
46 "2 Fast 2 Furious" co-star Gibson
48 Grand Caravan maker
49 Jumbles
50 One of Jacob's sons
53 Ser, across the Pyrenees
54 Loads
56 Piece of the street
57 __-fi

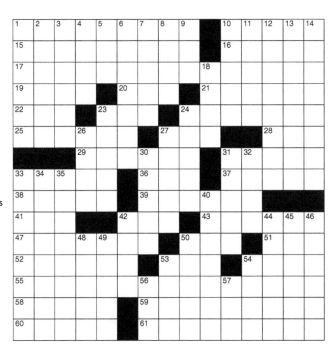

by Peter A. Collins

130

ACROSS

1 Clemson Tigers logo
9 Mistreating
15 Not left hanging, say
16 Draws
17 Mimosas and such
19 Toddler seats?
20 ___ Day (May 1)
21 ___ gratia
22 Become completely absorbed
23 Florida's ___ National Park
25 Rhone feeder
26 It can be found beneath the lower crust
27 "Look ___" (Vince Gill hit)
28 Sauce often served with oysters
32 See 43-Across
33 Beginning of time?
34 Mao's designated successor
35 Snoop Dogg, to Cameron Diaz [fun fact!]
37 Kind of check: Abbr.
38 Coeur ___
39 Capitale européenne
40 Angry Birds or Tetris, e.g.
43 With 32-Across, study of Hesse and Mann, informally
44 W.W. II battle site, for short
45 One might be a couple of years old
46 2013 women's singles champ at Wimbledon
47 Shows levelheadedness
50 Mobile advertising medium?
51 Hardly like the pick of the litter
52 "Oh man, that's bad"
53 Words after "say" or before "bad"

DOWN

1 Ring accompaniers
2 Like stunt pilots' stunts
3 Headed toward bankruptcy
4 Printer rollers
5 Release a claim to, legally
6 What the French think?
7 Marxist Andrés and writer Anaïs
8 Boom source
9 Centennial, e.g.
10 Good at drawing?
11 Continental abbr.
12 Attention-seeking, say
13 Woodenware
14 Davis of Hollywood
18 Put off
23 Occupy opponent
24 Suffix with hex-
26 Eyeshades?
28 Like a customer who may get special notice
29 Plastic that can be made permanently rigid
30 See red?
31 Corroded
33 Braggadocios
36 Inauguration recitation, maybe
37 Confirmed
39 Ones above military heads
40 Lists
41 "Would that it were!"
42 Former Israeli president Katsav
43 Adorned, per menus
46 Something with round parts?
48 Draw
49 Part of 8-Down

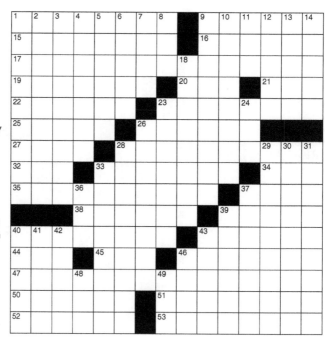

by Joe Krozel

ACROSS

1 Hall-of-Fame rock band or its lead musician
8 It sends out lots of streams
15 Very long European link
16 Rust or combust
17 It flies on demand
18 Skunk, at times
19 Some P.D. personnel
20 One who may be on your case
22 The Spanish I love?
23 What a couple of people can play
25 Stand-out performances
26 Chocolate bar with a long biscuit and caramel
27 Subject of the 2003 book "Power Failure"
29 Without hesitation
30 Subsist on field rations?
31 Its flowers are very short-lived
33 Like a sawhorse's legs
35 Critical
36 Party staple
37 Catered to Windows shoppers?
41 Noodle taxers?
45 Observes
46 Abbr. after 8-Across
48 Last band in the Rock and Roll Hall of Fame, alphabetically
49 "The Hudsucker Proxy" director, 1994
50 Columbia and the like
52 French river or department
53 "___ mentioned . . ."
54 Images on some lab slides
56 Lima-to-Bogotá dir.
57 Frankenstein, e.g.

59 Its passengers were revolting
61 Theodore Roosevelt Island setting
62 Destroyer destroyer
63 Colorful cooler
64 Makeover options

DOWN

1 Like some milk
2 Sashimi staple
3 Changing place
4 Blockbuster?
5 Mediums for dummies, say: Abbr.
6 Where it all comes together?
7 Ex amount?
8 Appointment disappointments
9 Nationals, at one time
10 Flag
11 Tablet banner, say, briefly
12 Reserve
13 Inventory
14 Duped
21 Gradual, in some product names
24 Giant in fantasy
26 Bar that's set very high
28 Physicist Bohr
30 Display on a red carpet
32 Basic solution
34 Without hesitation, in brief
37 Does some outdoor pitching?
38 "Don't joke about that yet"
39 Took away bit by bit
40 Event occasioning 7-Down

41 Cryotherapy choice
42 Artificially small
43 What might take up residence?
44 Truncated trunks?
47 Zero times, in Zwickau
50 Back-pedaler's words
51 About 7% of it is American
54 Vapor: Prefix
55 Apple assistant
58 Lib. arts major
60 Coral ___ (city near Oakland Pk., Fla.)

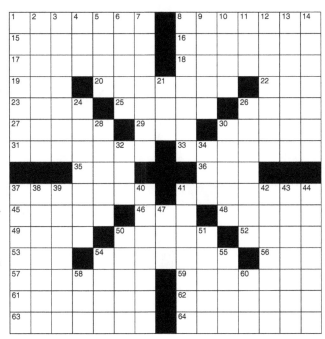

by Bruce R. Sutphin

132

ACROSS

1 It may provide closure in a tragedy
8 Discarded
15 City named for Theodore Roosevelt's vice president
17 Word search technique?
18 Webby Award winner who accepted saying "Please don't recount this vote"
19 With 11-Down, animal called "stubbin" by locals
20 Nascar stat that rises under caution flags
21 Diddly
22 Opening in the computer business?
23 Bad thing to lose
24 Flights
25 Taste makers?
26 Has it bad for, so to speak
27 -i relative
28 Largest city in Moravia
29 Mob member, informally
30 Morale
35 Second in command?
36 Cloverleaf section
37 Flat top
39 Blended dressing?
42 Shutter shutter
43 Literally, "I do not wish to"
44 Sauna exhalations
45 Solomonic
46 Chewed the fat
47 Watson's creator
48 Lowest of the low?
49 Prankery
50 1965 Beach Boys hit
53 Mission

54 Jason Mraz song that spent a record 76 weeks on Billboard's Hot 100
55 Outcries

DOWN

1 Outgoing
2 Lot arrangement
3 Draws
4 Some refrigerants
5 Reinforcement pieces
6 Mantel piece
7 Nissan bumpers?
8 Annual event since 1929, with "the"
9 Hard to pick up
10 Cigarette paper source
11 See 19-Across
12 Author of 1980's "The Annotated Gulliver's Travels"
13 Macedonia's capital
14 "El día que me quieras" and others
16 Large monitors
22 Abandon one's efforts, informally
23 "The Hound of the Baskervilles" backdrop
25 It's around a cup
26 1 Infinite ___ (address of Apple's headquarters)
28 Dover soul
29 Force in red uniforms: Abbr.
31 Course data
32 Palliate
33 Hit hard, as in an accident
34 Tip used for icing
38 They will be missed
39 Lightly hailed?

40 Major report
41 "Yowza!"
42 Hound
43 Dresden decimator of 1945
45 Something beyond the grate divide?
46 Herod's realm
48 1879's Anglo-___ War
49 "Fantastic Mr. Fox" author
51 War on Poverty agcy.
52 Advisory grp. that includes the drug czar

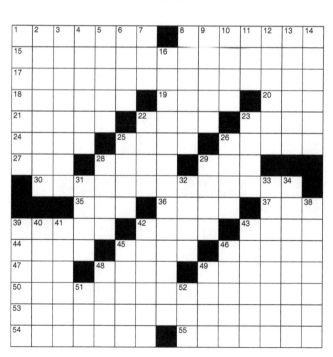

by Byron Walden

ACROSS

1 Forest newcomer
5 Group whose last Top 40 hit was "When All Is Said and Done"
9 To-do list
14 Sound after call waiting?
15 Sense, as a 14-Across
16 Nobel winner Joliot-Curie
17 Turkey sticker
20 "Everybody Is ___" (1970 hit)
21 Response to a threat
22 Old co. with overlapping globes in its logo
23 1960s civil rights leader ___ Brown
25 Katey who portrayed TV's Peg Bundy
27 Benchwarmer's plea
33 Drain
34 Bobby's follower?
35 Fibonacci, notably
36 Hockey Hall of Fame nickname
38 Alternative to ZzzQuil
40 Stat. for Re, La or Ti
41 "___ needed"
43 Papa ___ (Northeast pizza chain)
45 Now in
46 "That subject's off the table!"
49 Luster
50 They have edible shells
51 Whse. sight
53 "Philosophy will clip an angel's wings" writer
56 French class setting
59 Universal query?
62 Uncle Sam, say
63 One featuring a Maltese cross
64 Turkic word for "island"
65 Browser history list
66 Couldn't discard in crazy eights, say
67 Court suspensions

DOWN

1 Relief provider, for short
2 Blasts through
3 "And now?"
4 Sealing worker
5 "Per-r-rfect!"
6 ___-red
7 Alfred H. ___ Jr., founding director of MoMA
8 Like G.I.'s, per recruiting ads
9 Interval
10 Were present?
11 Gets payback
12 Sensed
13 They may be used in veins
18 They may be used around veins
19 All-Star Infante
24 Drone
26 1998 hit from the album "Surfacing"
27 False start?
28 Stockholder?
29 Like some hemoglobin
30 ___-A
31 Plantation habitation
32 Cybermemo
37 Something taken on the stand
39 Ring
42 They're on hunts
44 Revolving feature
47 Revolving features?
48 "Psst . . . buddy"
51 1/20 tons: Abbr.
52 Whence the word "bong"
54 Day of the week of Jul. 4, 1776
55 Wizened up
57 Indiana, e.g., to Lafayette
58 Some use electric organs
60 River Shannon's Lough ___
61 Sudoku segment

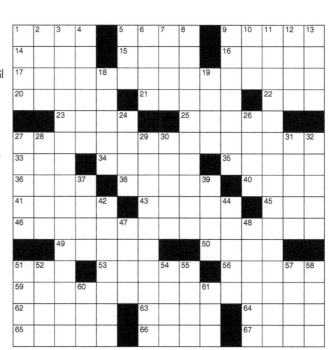

by Peter A. Collins

134

ACROSS

1 Angry missive
10 Body parts often targeted by masseurs
15 Trailing
16 Hatch in the upper house
17 Chutes behind boats
18 Treaty of Sycamore Shoals negotiator, 1775
19 Taking forever
20 Antimissile plan, for short
21 Part of Duchamp's parody of the "Mona Lisa"
22 Octane booster brand
24 San ___, Calif. (border town opposite Tijuana)
26 Discount ticket letters
29 In the main
31 Stuffed bear voiced by Seth MacFarlane
34 Not likely to be a "cheese" lover?
36 Pens for tablets
38 Learn to live with
39 Like the sound holes of a cello
41 1986 Indy 500 champion
42 Champion
44 Venetian mapmaker ___ Mauro
45 Driver's license requirement
47 Portugal's Palácio de ___ Bento
48 What a movie villain often comes to
50 Faced
52 Enter as a mediator
54 Tribe whose sun symbol is on the New Mexico flag
56 Grandson of Abraham
60 Roadster from Japan

61 Sites for shark sightings
63 Gut trouble
64 Group in a star's orbit
65 Disney Hall architect
66 Sci-fi battle site

DOWN

1 Beats at the buzzer, say
2 Like a control freak
3 Houston ballplayer, in sports shorthand
4 Spring events
5 Word spoken 90 times in Molly Bloom's soliloquy
6 Desperately tries to get
7 "Criminal Minds" agent with an I.Q. of 187
8 Singer of the #1 single "Try Again," 2000
9 Half a couple
10 Vacancy clause?
11 Like the crowd at a campaign rally
12 Some mock-ups
13 One in a Kindergarten?
14 Three-time All-Pro guard Chris
21 Owen Wilson's "Midnight in Paris" role
23 Glenda Jackson/Ben Kingsley film scripted by Harold Pinter
25 Cunning one
26 Wolf (down)
27 ___ gun
28 Battle site of June 6, 1944
30 Grand Slam event
32 John Paul's successor
33 Inflicted on

35 Green org.
37 Shade that fades
40 Musical with a cow that's catapulted over a castle
43 Area inside the 20, in football
46 Appetite
49 More likely
51 Sadness symbolized
52 Complacent
53 Plaza square, maybe
55 Least bit
57 Blind strip
58 Morsel for a guppy
59 One with a password, say
61 Street crosser, briefly
62 "You wanna run that by me again?"

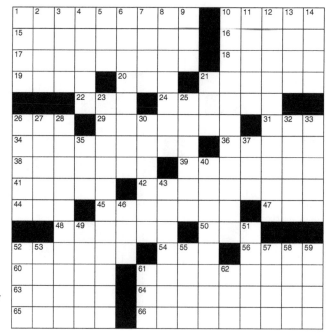

by John Farmer

ACROSS

1 1999 rap hit featuring Snoop Dogg
9 "Sin City" actress
13 Classic TV family
15 Represent
16 45°, for 1
18 Wild things?
19 Puts on eBay again
20 Cuban province where Castro was born
22 Zoological groups
23 Diamond deal
24 Software plug-in
25 Mode of transportation in a 1969 #1 hit
26 Filmdom family name
27 Israel's Sea of __
28 Silence fillers
29 Informal name of the 45th state
30 Softball question
33 Clean, now
34 Songbird Mitchell
35 Turkey __, baseball Hall-of-Famer from the Negro leagues
37 Breaks
38 They get tested
39 __ system, part of the brain that regulates emotion, behavior and long-term memory
40 2000s CBS sitcom
41 Sextet at Woodstock
42 "El Condor __" (1970 Simon & Garfunkel hit)
43 Golda Meir and Yitzhak Rabin led it
45 Division d'une carte
46 Place of outdoor meditation
47 Mock words of understanding
48 Price of an opera?

DOWN

1 Gangster nickname
2 "Carmen" figure
3 Covers
4 Share a secret with
5 From the Forbidden City
6 Bad impressions?
7 Poverty, metaphorically
8 Dutch city ESE of Amsterdam
9 Shape shifters?
10 Try to hear better, maybe
11 Knock-down-drag-out
12 First name in shooting
14 Winter set
17 Didn't make it home, say
21 Arm
23 Email ancestors
25 "Wordplay" vocalist, 2005
27 "In your dreams!"
29 Mary __ (doomed ship)
30 Italian region that's home to Milan
31 Chances that a year ends with any particular digit
32 Florida's Key __
33 Musician who arranged the theme from "2001"
34 Fruit-filled pastry
35 Where to bury the hatchet?
36 Olympic ice dancing gold medalist Virtue and others
37 __ Alley
38 Hypercompetitive
39 About 40–60 beats per minute
41 Volume measure
44 Volume measure

by David Steinberg

136

ACROSS

1 1980 new wave classic
7 1996 hybrid animation/live-action film
15 Cole ___, 2008 World Series M.V.P.
16 "Ahh" sloganeer
17 Juices
18 Hot numbers
19 "Bait Car" channel
20 Some hotels and old cars
21 Lays flat
22 It can precede masochism
23 Kind of mile: Abbr.
24 Location from which the phoenix rose
25 Ulan-___ (city in Siberia)
26 Biographer biographized in "Poison Pen"
29 Wear for Teddy Roosevelt
31 Amt. of copper, say
32 Surmounted
33 Dirty Harry fired them
37 Upstate N.Y. sch.
38 1985 #1 whose video won six MTV Video Music Awards
39 Rhode Island cuisine specialty
43 Rapper with the 2000 single "Party Up (Up in Here)"
44 "___ Story" (2007 Jenna Bush book)
45 Symbols of strength
46 Zales inventory
47 Give some juice
48 Benefits
50 Have thirds, say
51 Jockey competitor
53 Jin dynasty conqueror
54 Female novelist whose given name was Howard

55 Rhyme for "drool" in a Dean Martin classic
56 Something between 49-Downs
57 Out of alignment

DOWN

1 "How's it goin', dawg?"
2 Hobby with Q codes
3 Fresh
4 Gnocchi topper
5 "___ It" (2006 Young Jeezy single)
6 100 metric drops: Abbr.
7 Dirt, in slang
8 Like the Simpson kids' hair
9 Dramatic opening
10 Lewis ___, loser to Zachary Taylor in 1848

11 Prefix with tourism
12 1995–2013 senator from Arizona
13 1985–93 senator from Tennessee
14 Raymond who played Abraham Lincoln
20 Cowboy feature
23 What a leadfoot may do
24 City that's headquarters for Pizza Hut and J. C. Penney
26 Former Australian prime minister Rudd
27 Supposed sighting off the coast of Norway
28 Where faces meet
30 Tight shoe wearer's woe
33 Mercury and Saturn, once

34 Follower of one nation?
35 Soup line
36 Marketing mantra
38 Return service
39 Sci-fi's ___ Binks
40 Many an early tie
41 Safe spots
42 First marketer of Cabbage Patch Kids
46 Outrageously freewheeling
48 ___ concours (unrivaled: Fr.)
49 Way off
50 Bearded mountain dweller
52 Bit of action
53 Deg. from 37-Across

by Peter Wentz

ACROSS

1 Wiped the floor with
16 Use of blockades, say
17 Western daily
18 Lobby
19 Watch things
20 Limited edition?
21 Suffix with electr-
22 Blasting, musically
24 Bay, say . . . or bring to bay
28 Tempest, to Theodor
31 Bellyaches
33 ___ Rose
34 One may be tapped out
37 Brunch orders, briefly
38 McKinley's Ohio birthplace
39 Title priestess of opera
40 Aim
42 Setting of 10, maybe
43 Sony output
44 Bulldogs' sch.
46 Painter ___ della Francesca
48 Certain advertising medium
55 It's not word-for-word
56 Old French epics
57 Idolizes

DOWN

1 1970s–'80s sitcom setting
2 "I'm ___" (Friday declaration)
3 Doctor's orders
4 Passing people
5 What Hamilton called the wealthy
6 "Sure, let's try"
7 ___ Arden Oplev, director of "The Girl With the Dragon Tattoo"
8 Mid third-century year
9 Gershwin biographer David
10 Guarders with droopy ears and pendulous lips
11 Some collectible lithographs
12 It hasn't happened before
13 Sans spice
14 Sought-after rock group?
15 Fun or laugh follower
22 Send quickly, in a way
23 Finders' keepers?
25 What stars may indicate
26 Cause of a class struggle?
27 Allure alternative
28 Sun blocker
29 Pearl Harbor attack initiator
30 Polaris bear
31 Limb-entangling weapon
32 Second-greatest period in the history of something
35 1931 Best Picture
36 Utility bill details
41 Light measures
43 Like much arable land
45 "I ___ Lonely" (1954 hit for the Four Knights)
46 Lead-in to deux or trois
47 Particular paean penner
48 Ozone destroyers, for short
49 "What's Hecuba to him, ___ to Hecuba": Hamlet
50 Sinatra's "Meet ___ the Copa"
51 Biblical miracle setting
52 Police dept. personage
53 Touch
54 Law school newbie

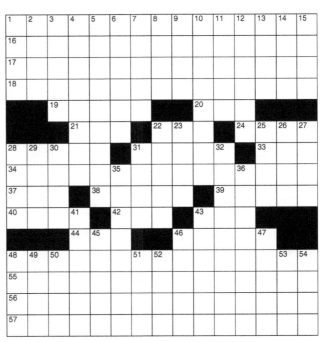

by Martin Ashwood-Smith

138

ACROSS

1 Domino's bottom?
11 Sing
15 Olympic Tower financier
16 Roman marketplaces
17 Lines to be cracked
18 Something to hold down
19 Asian silk center
20 Giving no performances
22 Aid in getting it together?
23 Off-limits
26 Al Bundy's garage, e.g.
28 Spot with a talking bear, maybe: Abbr.
31 XII, perhaps
33 Hailstorm, e.g.
34 Sarah Palin called herself an average one
37 How fresh paint glistens
38 "The Tourist" novelist Steinhauer
39 Best final result
41 Literary character who says "I'll chase him round Good Hope"
42 Kind of horoscope
44 Kids' party game
46 Bell heather and tree heath
48 Topic in a world religions course
49 Follower of Gore?
50 Like some laptop keyboards
52 Minable material
54 Part of un giorno
55 "I'll send for you ___": Othello
57 Record held for decades?
61 Swimmer featured in the 2013 film "Blackfish"

63 Important stud farm visitors
66 Ape's lack
67 Pre-Raphaelite ideal
68 Bad side of literature?
69 Sings

DOWN

1 Spotted South American mammal
2 The white surrounds it
3 99+ things in Alaska?
4 2008 title role for Adam Sandler
5 Buttercup family member
6 See 8-Down
7 Letter string
8 With 6-Down, old wheels
9 When hands are extended straight up and down

10 It may be over a foot
11 Closest bud, briefly
12 Head-turning cry
13 Make a fashionable entrance?
14 Its contents provide juice
21 Apprehended
24 Big name in Hispanic food
25 Juice
27 Sports stud
28 DC transformation location
29 Collection of green panels
30 CH_3COOH
32 Some pleas, briefly
35 Flair
36 Like some colors and cornets
40 Grp. concerned with feeding the kitty

43 Karaoke stand-in?
45 Raiser of dogs?
47 Penalty box, to sports fans
51 Trattoria dessert
53 "32 Flavors" singer Davis, 1998
56 "Barney Miller" Emmy winner Pitlik
58 Armenia's basic monetary unit
59 French suffix with jardin
60 Proposal figs.
62 Draught ___
64 Jubilant cry
65 Trash

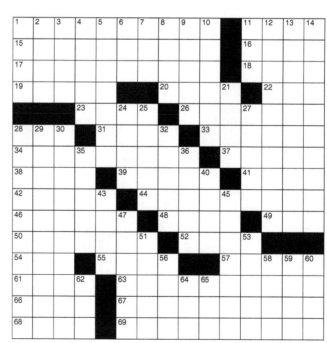

by Barry C. Silk

ACROSS

1 Common catch off the coast of Maryland
9 Light, in a way
15 Crude alternative
16 Jewelry box item
17 Like a bout on an undercard
18 Dickens's Miss Havisham, famously
19 ID clincher
20 Challenge to ambulance chasers
22 Arcade game prize grabber
24 Fiacre, to taxi drivers
27 "___ reminder . . ."
30 Nook occupier
31 Toshiba competitor
32 Some camcorders
33 Besmirch
36 Isaac Bashevis Singer settings
38 Culmination
39 Only proper noun in the Beatles' "Revolution"
41 "Something to Talk About" singer, 1991
42 Golf commentator's subject
43 Classic kitschy wall hanging
46 Slip for a skirt?
47 "Billy Bathgate" novelist
50 Ex-G.I.'s org.
53 Washington State mascot
54 Pre-W.W. I in automotive history
57 "If music be the food of love . . ." speaker in "Twelfth Night"
58 Cry of despair
59 Nothing: It.
60 Periods of warming . . . or cooling off

DOWN

1 M asset
2 Royal Arms of England symbol
3 Bone under a watchband
4 The Orange Bowl is played on it: Abbr.
5 Acupuncturist's concern
6 Croupier's stick material
7 Acknowledges
8 Tab carrier in a bar?
9 Tourist attraction on Texas' Pedernales River
10 Face in a particular direction
11 "Champagne for One" sleuth
12 Shot, informally
13 Serena Williams, often

14 Novel in Joyce Carol Oates's Wonderland Quartet
21 Exasperates
22 Cauldron stirrer
23 "The Avengers" villain, 2012
24 Bit of sachet stuffing
25 Classroom clickers of old
26 Singer who once sang a song to Kramer on "Seinfeld"
27 When "Ave Maria" is sung in "Otello"
28 1970s pact partly negotiated in Helsinki
29 Right hands: Abbr.
32 Arena
34 Orange garnish for a sushi roll
35 Fox hunt cry
37 Bay, for one

40 Prompt a buzzer on "The Price Is Right"
43 Unoccupied
44 Massive, in Metz
45 Block
46 Keep from taking off, as a plane with low visibility
47 Nobel category: Abbr.
48 Loughlin or Petty of Hollywood
49 Italian actress Eleonora
50 Let it all out
51 Unoccupied
52 Rolls of dough
55 One of the Ms. Pac-Man ghosts
56 "There is no ___ except stupidity": Wilde

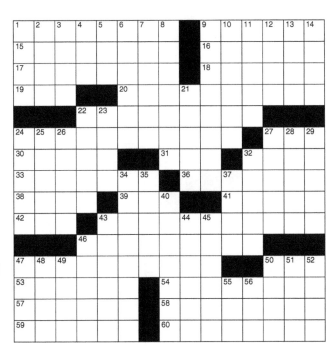

by Brad Wilber

140

ACROSS

1 Insignificant row
9 Traffic reporter's aid
15 Big rush, maybe
16 Twin's rival
17 Offerer of stock advice
18 Grown-up who's not quite grown up
19 No big shot?
20 Nasty intentions
22 Threatening word
23 Overseas rebellion cry
25 One may be played by a geisha
26 Wasn't given a choice
27 "You Be ___" (1986 hip-hop hit)
29 Super German?
31 Pressure
33 Launch site
34 Where many airways are cleared, briefly
35 Antithesis of 32-Down
37 Common sound in Amish country
39 Large amount
42 Classics with 389 engines
44 Scrammed
48 Like Fabergé eggs
51 Schoolyard retort
52 Carry ___
53 So great
55 Paving block
56 Golf lesson topic
57 Goes downhill
59 Troubling post-engagement status, briefly
60 Doctor
62 They were labeled "Breakfast," "Dinner" and "Supper"
64 2002 César winner for Best Film
65 Real rubbish
66 Least significant
67 It really gets under your skin

DOWN

1 Determine the value of freedom?
2 Carp
3 Scandinavia's oldest university
4 Sneeze lead-ins
5 Austrian conductor Karl
6 Recess
7 Be quiet, say
8 Savor the flattery
9 It's bad when nobody gets it
10 "The Guilt Trip" actress Graynor
11 Like some cartilage piercings
12 "Possibly"
13 Dream team member
14 Planet threateners
21 Like a top
24 Stain producers
26 Gallant
28 Result of knuckling down?
30 Hollow
32 Antithesis of 35-Across
36 Pageant judging criterion
38 Ed supporters
39 Park Avenue's ___ Building
40 Radical
41 Shaking
43 Sniffing a lot
45 What a slightly shy person may request
46 1967 Emmy winner for playing Socrates
47 "As you like it" phrase
49 What a bunch of footballers might do
50 Game in which the lowest card is 7
54 Marriott rival
57 Preventer of many bites
58 Bit of action
61 Household name?
63 Soreness

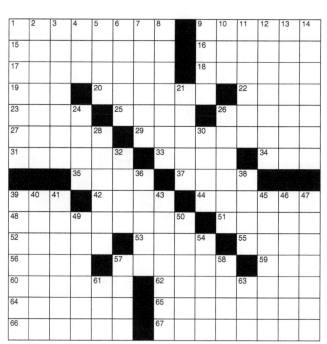

by Tom Heilman

ACROSS

1 African city of 4+ million whose name means, literally, "haven of peace"
12 Seeing things
14 "Why such a fuss?"
16 Start of a Jewish holiday?
17 Put one's two cents in?
18 Arizona's Agua ___ River
19 Not natural for
21 Like Beethoven's Piano Sonata No. 6 or 22
24 Tilting figure: Abbr.
25 ___ Ximénez (dessert sherry)
26 Manipulative health care worker
29 Smash letters
30 Destroy, informally
32 Range ridges
33 Classified
35 Eatery where the Tony Award was born
38 Pitch
39 Juan's "Hey!"
42 Perseveres
44 Some Deco pieces
46 Lead film festival characters?
47 Rhineland Campaign's arena: Abbr.
48 Frito-Lay snack
50 Silver of fivethirtyeight.com
52 California city near Fullerton
54 Author Janowitz
55 Opening line of a 1966 #1 Beatles hit
59 One-hit wonder
60 Events for some antiquers

DOWN

1 Demonstration exhortation
2 A bee might light on it
3 Some N.F.L.'ers
4 Irritate
5 Dopes
6 Restoration notation
7 Even though
8 Polynesian island chain?
9 Lee with an Oscar
10 Home row sequence
11 Kalahari Desert dweller
12 Irritability
13 Femme canonisée
14 Deli menu subheading
15 Foundation for some roofing
20 Silence
22 Verges on
23 Anticipate
27 Mind
28 Irritable state
31 Election surprise
33 What some bombs result in, in brief
34 Fanciful notions
35 Dead
36 Pair of boxers?
37 Give a makeover
39 Pontiac and others
40 "Star Trek" extra
41 It's definitely not the short answer
43 "That's that"
45 Fix a key problem?
49 Kind of yoga
51 Important info for people with connections
53 Clément with two Oscar-winning films
56 Düsseldorf direction
57 La la lead-in
58 Allen of play-by-play

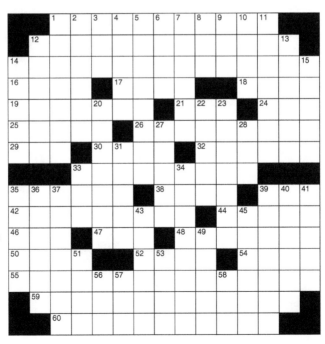

by Alan Arbesfeld

142

ACROSS
1 Made a seat-of-the-pants error?
11 "Your mama wears army boots," e.g.
15 Rioting
16 Popular pizza place, informally
17 Washington, D.C., has a famous one
18 Greets enthusiastically, in a way
19 One working in a corner in an office?
20 Eastern Woodlands native
22 Noted eavesdropper, for short
23 Covenants
25 Splendiferous
27 Bar supply
30 ___ Valley
31 Sulky
32 Tandoori-baked fare
34 "Yes" to an invitation
36 One way to stand
37 They may result when you run into people
40 Hognose snake
41 Of two minds
42 ___ work
43 Lender, legally speaking
45 Lo ___
47 50% nonunion?
48 "Gunsmoke" setting
49 Marina sight
51 Classic Northwest brewski
52 Charlie's land
54 Like a tennis match without a break?
58 Like many a gen.
60 Mother of Andromeda
62 "Iliad" locale
63 Settles in, say
64 Job application info, for short
65 Nootropics, more familiarly

DOWN
1 Internet prowlers
2 Hand or foot
3 Cry frequently made with jazz hands
4 Georg von ___
5 Vice president after whom a U.S. city is thought to have been named
6 Ninny
7 Best Picture of 1960, with "The"
8 ___ Palmas
9 Breastplate of Athena
10 "The High One"
11 Where a canine sits?
12 Whole
13 Winter Olympics sight
14 They use blue books
21 TV show headed by a former writer for "S.N.L."
24 "Mom" and "Mama's Family"
26 Poetic expanses
27 Grumpy
28 They use Blue Books
29 "The Wishing-Chair" series creator
33 Manage
35 Whiner, of a sort
38 Kind of compressor
39 Yankee, once
44 Passes
46 "Uh-uh!"
50 #2 pop
53 Title with an apostrophe
55 Appear stunned
56 Apothecary item
57 Din-din
59 Prefix with peptic
61 2 Tone influence

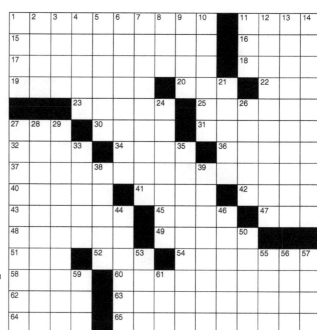

by Michael Ashley

143

ACROSS

1 Their drinks are not on the house
9 Rough limestone regions with sinkholes and caverns
15 Novel title character with a "brief, wondrous life"
16 Hawaii's Forbidden Isle
17 ". . . period!"
19 One buzzing off?
20 Three Stooges display
21 Some lab leaders, for short
22 Like most hall-of-fame inductees: Abbr.
23 Gave belts or socks
24 Swamp
25 Female friends, to Francisco
27 Early-millennium year
28 Jet black
29 Some are soft-shell
30 Spread out
32 He cast the Killing Curse on Dumbledore
33 What the Flying Wallendas refuse to use
34 Powerful Hindu deities
38 That same number of
40 Diner's words of thanks
41 Unlucky accidents, old-style
44 Co. led by Baryshnikov in the 1980s
45 It broke up in the age of dinosaurs
46 Not procrastinating
47 Midday assignation, in slang
49 Stink
50 Olive ___
51 More pointed
52 Give an underhanded hand?

53 Assertion more likely to be correct if 8-Down is given
56 Decision makers
57 Axis, e.g.
58 "Fingers crossed"
59 Whose eyes Puck squeezes magical juice on

DOWN

1 "Well done!"
2 With no dissenters
3 Common result of a slipped disk
4 Foil feature
5 Realty ad abbr.
6 Lies ahead
7 What a vacay provides
8 What an interrogator might administer
9 Bring home, as a run
10 Light as a feather
11 One in a cage
12 Confined
13 Vast historical region controlled by the Mongols
14 Kingdom next to Kent
18 See 24-Down
23 They aid responses, in brief
24 With 18-Down, life today
26 Transcend
30 Speaking of repeatedly, to a Brit
31 1984 award for Elmore Leonard
35 Drifting type
36 Good hand holding in Omaha Hi-Lo
37 It has the densest fur of any animal
39 Alpine skier Julia who won Olympic gold in 2006
41 Still-produced stuff
42 Slangy segue
43 Awful accident
45 Hazards
48 Afresh
51 Film and theater
52 Actor Rickman who played 32-Across
54 Low numero
55 ___ Fáil (Irish coronation stone)

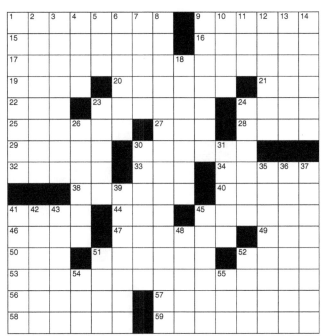

by David Woolf

ACROSS

1. Air protection program?
10. Italian alternative
15. Tight squeeze for a couple?
16. Where Union Pacific is headquartered
17. 1992 chart-topper that mentions "my little turn on the catwalk"
18. Tar
19. 65-Across's title: Abbr.
20. Evian competitor
21. Gun shows?
22. A or O, but not B
24. First name in fashion
26. One going for the big bucks
27. __ Fund Management (investment company)
29. Strike-monitoring org.
30. Contact on Facebook
31. Time reversal?
33. Tore to shreds
35. Diehard sort
38. Dangerous things to go on
39. Long, slender glass for drinking beer
41. River to the North Sea
42. Lowly one
43. Quarterly magazine published by Boeing
45. Norwegian Romanticist
49. Anti
50. Sch. in Madison, N.J.
52. __ Gunn, "Breaking Bad" co-star
53. Killing it
56. Make a touchdown
58. Star opening?
59. Turning blue, maybe
60. Prevent a crash, say
62. Triumphant cry
63. "Buy high and sell low," e.g.
64. Baselines?
65. Case worker

DOWN

1. Springblade producer
2. Marmalade fruit
3. Green piece
4. Wall Street inits.
5. __ Musk, co-founder of Tesla Motors and PayPal
6. Millan who's known as "the Dog Whisperer"
7. Temporarily inactive
8. __ Place (Edmonton Oilers' arena)
9. Frozen food aisle eponym
10. See 11-Down
11. She loves, in 10-Down
12. "G-Funk Classics" rapper
13. Iroquoian tongue
14. Provincials
21. "Holy smokes!"
23. Long Island Rail Road station
25. Old phone trio
28. Spartan gathering place
30. Bakery/cafe chain
32. Schwab rival
34. Rhames of "Mission: Impossible"
35. Pioneering underground publication of the 1960s
36. Early tragedienne Duse
37. 1990s sci-fi series
40. Alternative to die
41. In the direction of
44. Make further advances?
46. Sense
47. Former Italian P.M. Letta
48. Boot covering
51. Open, in a way
54. Kind of threat
55. Certain spirits
57. Frankie Avalon's "__ Dinah"
60. Org. with a top 10 list
61. Shopper's choice

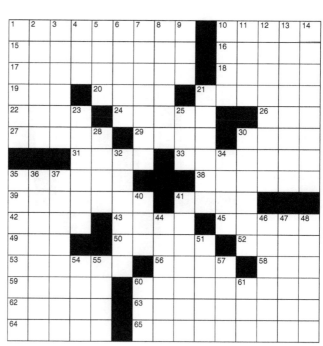

by David Steinberg

ACROSS

1 Milk additive
6 TV actor who lived, appropriately, in Hawaii
14 Hoyt who wrote "Joy to the World"
15 Go-getter on the hunt?
16 Catch
17 Reverse order?
18 "Wrong" way to spell a world leader's name in a New York Times crossword, according to a 1999 episode of "The West Wing"
20 Gets ensconced
21 Altdorf's canton
22 19th-century abbot and scientist
24 Word that begins with an apostrophe
25 Cheese made from the milk of Friesian cows
27 Reposes
28 Relative of a leek
30 Otherworldly
32 Showing irritation
33 On-deck circle?
36 First name in pop
37 Arm bones
38 Charles who was born Angelo Siciliano
39 Reproductive cell
40 Bar in a shower stall
44 Moniker
45 Johns Hopkins program
47 Beat oneself up about
48 Authorized, as to read secrets
51 Paternity prover
53 Dicey issue
55 Light-reflecting shade
56 Deep-fried treat
57 Third-place finisher in 2004 and 2008

58 Unwelcome benchmark?
59 Cygnet's parents

DOWN

1 Language of Navarre
2 City that hosts the California Strawberry Festival
3 Places for races
4 Drapery attachment
5 Wee hour
6 One of the Bushes
7 Makes up (for)
8 Monstrous
9 Modelists' purchases
10 Took a powder
11 Milk additive
12 Stereo system component
13 Showing some wear?

15 Only so-called "Decade Volcano" in the continental U.S.
19 ___ González, longest-serving democratically elected Spanish P.M.
23 Star of Buñuel's "Belle de Jour"
26 Group that offers "protection"
28 Beloved, in Bologna
29 Possible skin test reaction
31 Cinematography choice
32 Scribes
33 Never mind
34 Phone line?
35 Title sort of person in 2008's Best Picture
36 Purina product
39 Officially make

41 Brand in the frozen food aisle
42 "Northanger Abbey" novelist
43 Dwindles to nothing, with "out"
45 ___ dish
46 Begins to develop
49 Each
50 Author Jaffe
52 Détente
54 Shell filler

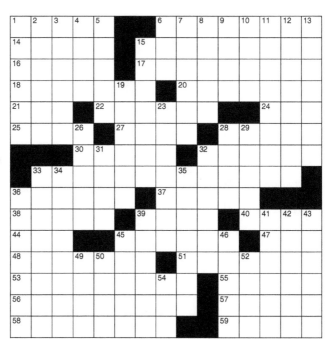

by Patrick Berry

146

ACROSS

1. It includes pinning and throwing
8. "Chicago" setting
15. Rapture
16. Skyrocket
17. Prepare to pull the trigger
18. Couple seen at a baby shower
19. Hard knocks
20. It might hold up a holdup
22. Reason for a semiannual shift: Abbr.
23. Skunk and such
24. Star in Virgo
25. Aid in getting a grip
26. Check spec.
27. Abyss
28. Modern Persian
29. "That's clever!"
31. California's ___ Sea (rift lake)
32. Got a 41-Across on
33. Billy who played the Phantom in "The Phantom"
34. Person with small inventions
37. Slam dunk stat
41. Benchmark mark
42. They have seats
43. Crew's director
44. "Que ___-je?" ("What do I know?": Fr.)
45. "The Great Caruso" title role player
46. Perpetual 10-year-old of TV
47. Wile E. Coyote buy
48. Too, to Thérèse
49. Board game with black and white stones
50. Pupil of Pissarro
52. Like many laptop cameras
54. First name among Italian explorers
55. With ramifications
56. Galls
57. Does some farrier's work on

DOWN

1. One feeling 15-Across after Super Bowl III
2. Title name written "on the door of this legended tomb," in poetry
3. Home of Southeast Asia's largest mosque
4. News briefs
5. Colombian kinfolk
6. "___ see"
7. Like the human genome, before the 1990s
8. "St. John Passion" composer
9. Now, to Nicolás
10. Choice for a long shot
11. Sound in the comic "B.C."
12. Groveled
13. Tepid consent
14. Sitcom pal of Barbarino and Horshack
21. Grammy-nominated Ford
24. No-yeast feast
25. Parking meeter?
27. Cuts up
28. Adder's defense
30. They're off-limits: Var.
31. Pole star?
33. Its main island is Unguja
34. Asset in a drag contest
35. Whence a girl who's "like a samba," in song
36. Member of 31-Down's team
37. Geiger of Geiger counter fame
38. "You're not the only one!"
39. Recess for a joint
40. Reaches
42. Leisurely strolls
45. It's often parried
46. Impolite interruption
48. Indigo source
49. Spinal cord surrounders
51. Rescue vessel?
53. Relative of Aztec

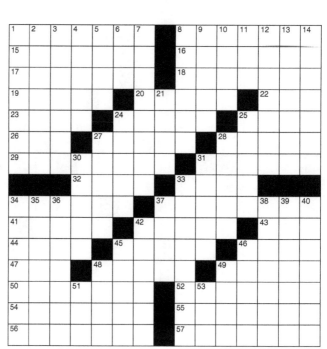

by Frederick J. Healy

ACROSS

1 Cartoon canary's bane
9 Lymph liquid
14 Launch
15 Many a predictable plot
16 Rests
17 One with a game collection, maybe
18 Gate announcement, briefly
19 Longtime model Parkinson of "The Price Is Right"
20 One with a game collection
21 Home to Bar-Ilan Univ.
22 Grp. supported by 17-Acrosses
23 Something groundbreaking
27 Post rival
32 "That is so obvious!"
33 What corned beef is often served on
34 Weights, to a weightlifter
35 Heart-felt thing?
36 Where to take stock?
37 Lamb accompaniment
39 Shade similar to bay
40 One getting into briefs?
41 Least brazen
42 "Eldorado" inits.
43 Forbid
44 Urban phenomenon
48 Coastal diver
49 Sun Devil Stadium's sch.
52 Chill
53 Labor leader?
55 Ray Charles's Georgia birthplace
56 A sprinkling
57 Inc. magazine topic
58 Voice of 1-Across

DOWN

1 Ton
2 Ton, e.g.
3 Quit running
4 Detoxing woe
5 Bagel source?
6 Many a Taiwanese
7 More than bickering
8 It has eight neighbors: Abbr.
9 Stars and stripes, say
10 Tod's sidekick on "Route 66"
11 Court records
12 Hammer and sickle holder, maybe
13 Trivial
15 Delta lead-in
22 Like many holiday letters
23 Jungian principle
24 In favor of the idea
25 Words before know and care
26 Total
27 See 29-Down
28 Sarcastic "I can't wait"
29 With 27-Down, her last film was "High Society"
30 Some food festival fare
31 French body of law?
33 Derby favorite
35 10 or 15 yards, say
38 One shot in a cliffhanger
39 Inner ear?
41 Stall near the stacks
43 Designer Geoffrey
44 Evidence of damage
45 John Paul II, e.g.
46 ___-call
47 Creator of bad apples?
48 Hartmann of talk radio
49 Mont. neighbor
50 Wrapped (up)
51 Grp. with national antidoping rules
54 It might end in "mil"

by Ned White

148

ACROSS

1 1960s sitcom character with the catchphrase "I see nothing!"
11 Kvetch
15 Pitchblende, e.g.
16 Disney title character surnamed Pelekai
17 Singles collection?
18 Hostile
19 Malignant acts
20 "Not serious!"
21 Lose one's place?
22 Itches
23 Places gowns are worn, for short
24 Setting for many reprises
26 Elated outpouring
28 Hercules type
29 Result of some fermentation
33 Ingredient in Worcestershire sauce
35 Still in the 17-Across
37 Still
38 Second baseman in both of the Dodgers' 1980s World Series
40 Like South Carolina vis-à-vis North Carolina, politically
41 Storied abductee
42 Sports mascot who's a popular bobblehead figure
44 Ring
46 Comfort's partner
47 "The X-Files" project, for short
51 Verb in the world's first telegraph message
52 Watergate units: Abbr.
54 Embroidery loop
55 Brand once pitched by Garfield
56 Where filing work is done

58 Relative of aloha or shalom
59 Home of the W.N.B.A.'s Silver Stars
60 Transcendental aesthetic developer
61 Accent for plus fours, often

DOWN

1 Like many drafts
2 Lollipop selection
3 Tarte ___ (French apple dessert)
4 Uncooperative moods
5 What César awards honor
6 Stick close to
7 One paid to make calls
8 Considers
9 "Star Trek: T.N.G." role
10 Literary wife in "Midnight in Paris"
11 Nearly set?
12 Judicious state
13 Minor payment
14 Early riser?
23 Locales that may be well-supplied?
25 Digs on a slope
26 Recognition not sought by Benjamin Franklin
27 Rapper with the 2012 album "Life Is Good"
29 Clear one's way, in a way
30 Latin condenser
31 Cookware that's often hinged
32 Cared
34 Overcome by mud
36 Weir
39 Blue label

43 Lose
45 Medieval merchants' guild
47 Grain elevator components
48 Discount, in combination
49 Vodka ___
50 "There, there"
53 "Up to ___" (1952 game show)
54 Fancy spread
57 Show on Sen. Franken's résumé

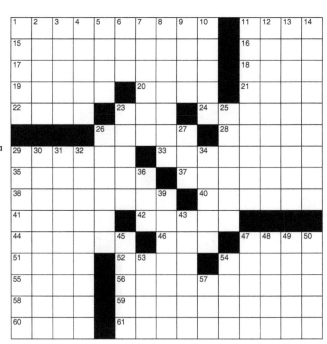

by Byron Walden and Brad Wilber

149

ACROSS

1 Innocent one
6 Short shift?
10 Judgmental clucks
14 Influential style of the 1960s
15 Au courant about
16 Home of Sunset and Paradise
17 Pitching staff work areas
19 Plea opener
20 Coffee order
22 Theology inst.
23 "Praise the Lord!"
26 "Stanley & Iris" director Martin
29 A bit of cheer?
32 "Aw, sorry about that . . ."
33 Here, to Henri
34 B, to scientists
36 Untwisted silk fibers
37 Ganache ingredient
40 Brisbane buddies
41 Country that split in two in 2011
42 22-Across subj.
43 Puts on a pedestal
45 Door sign
46 Combines
47 Cold war defense system
49 Semi part
51 Dancers known for their Japanese street-style wardrobe
57 Water bearer
59 Singer whose first top 10 hit was "Where Does My Heart Beat Now"
60 In Australia her name is Karen
61 1980s Chrysler offering
62 Harper Lee's given name
63 Castaway's spot
64 Amtrak stops: Abbr.
65 "Skyfall" singer

DOWN

1 "The aristocrat of pears"
2 On ___ with
3 Like one end of an electric cord
4 Nursing locale
5 "Hello, ___"
6 Subatomic particle more massive than an electron
7 Many a museum audio guide
8 Chinese menu words
9 Relative of a raspberry
10 Sushi order
11 Plot device?
12 Early "Doctor Who" villain
13 "Nurse Jackie" channel, for short
18 Musket loader
21 Make jokes about
24 Like many turkeys
25 Collectible cars
26 Encircled
27 Producer of cold cuts?
28 Carnival ride since 1927
30 Ones going in circles?
31 [Zzzzz]
34 Get moving
35 Anatomical knot
38 Prevaricate
39 Popular spring break locale
44 They may be offered by way of concessions
46 Withstood
48 Deplane in moments
50 NASA's Gemini rocket
52 ___ Bator
53 Wine-and-cassis drinks
54 Make angry
55 Idle
56 "The Mikado" weapon
57 Penultimate Greek letter
58 Grafton's "___ for Alibi"

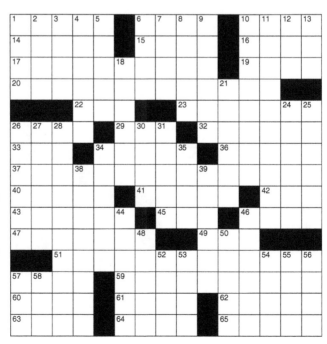

by Elizabeth C. Gorski

150

ACROSS

1. Big name in 25-Across treatment
9. Air piece?
14. Shrugs, maybe
16. Take it as a sign
17. "The Help" co-star, 2011
18. Decorative moldings
19. First of a succession of 13
20. Coot
22. Johnny-jump-up, e.g.
24. Nude medium, often
25. See 1-Across
27. 90° from ouest
28. Really
31. Area map
32. __ d'âme (moods: Fr.)
33. Alternative to 53-Down
34. Secures
37. She's no puritan
40. Farm sounds
41. Station, e.g.
42. Repulsive
43. Get out of practice?
45. Sportscaster Nahan with a star on the Hollywood Walk of Fame
48. Keel extension
49. Unrefined type
50. Key setting
52. Like eggheads
56. Stockholder's group?
57. Universal work
58. Hack, say
60. Nonstop
61. Evidence of having worn thongs
62. Little ones are calves
63. Player of many a tough guy

DOWN

1. Olympian on 2004 and 2012 Wheaties boxes
2. Bach contemporary
3. Onetime pop star who hosted "Pyramid"
4. First name in erotica
5. Fortune subjects: Abbr.
6. Stalin defier
7. Stargazer's focus?
8. Street fair lineup
9. Lodge org.
10. Fryer seen at a cookout?
11. Harvard has an all-male one
12. Creation for many an account
13. Super Mario Bros. runner
15. Backing
21. __ rating (chess skill-level measure)
23. So-far-undiscovered one
26. Name-dropper's abbr.?
29. Aid in making one's move?
30. So-far-undiscovered ones, briefly
32. Like a type B
34. Geishas often draw them
35. Wimp's lack
36. Wrest the reins
37. Crane arm
38. Ace's stat
39. Open love?
41. To the degree that
43. What mops may be made into
44. Feet with rhythm
45. Dealt with
46. Abercrombie design
47. Brought to ruin
51. Kick back
53. Alternative to 33-Across
54. Ripped
55. Drumroll follower
57. Group with family units
59. Actor Penn of "Van Wilder"

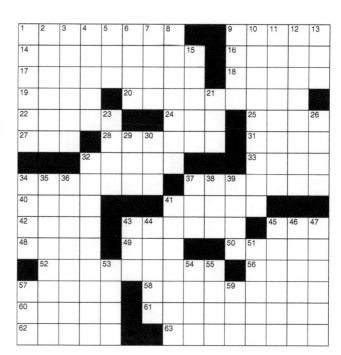

by James Mulhern

The New York Times

SMART PUZZLES

Presented with Style

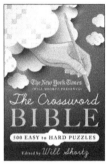
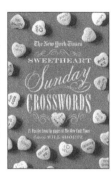

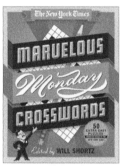
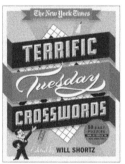
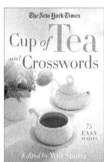

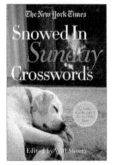
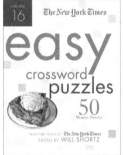

Available at your local bookstore or online at www.nytimes.com/nytstore

ST. MARTIN'S GRIFFIN

fbmacmillan.com/smp/willshortz

ANSWERS

1

P	E	T	I	T	F	O	U	R		Y	A	W	P	S
I	R	O	N	H	O	R	S	E		E	N	I	A	C
D	O	N	N	A	R	E	E	D		S	E	P	I	A
G	I	G	S		E	G	R	E	T		W	E	N	T
I	C	U		W	V	A		E	W	E		O	F	T
N	A	E		Y	E	N		M	I	X	T	U	R	E
			A	C	R	O		S	T	P	E	T	E	R
	M	O	T	H	S			T	E	N	S	E		
G	A	N	N	E	T	T		B	E	D	S			
N	I	C	O	L	A	I		E	R	I		B	A	H
O	N	O		M	M	M		A	V	A		R	A	Y
C	R	U	Z		P	E	N	N	E		C	A	F	E
C	O	R	E	S		L	I	B	R	A	R	I	A	N
H	A	S	T	Y		A	N	A	S	T	A	S	I	A
I	D	E	A	L		G	O	G	E	T	T	E	R	S

2

A	S	I	A	N			D	J	P	A	U	L	Y	D
C	O	N	D	O		G	R	E	A	T	B	E	A	R
T	U	T	O	R		L	A	T	C	H	O	N	T	O
U	S	E	R		M	I	N	S	K		A	D	E	N
P	A	R	K	R	A	N	G	E	R		T	A	S	E
		V	A	U	L	T		T	A	B				
C	R	A	B	B	I	E	R		T	I	P	P	L	E
P	O	L	L	O		D	O	S		G	R	A	I	N
R	O	S	E	U	P		T	E	E	T	E	R	E	D
			T	A	C		A	L	O	F	T			
A	R	C	S		T	H	E	C	A	P	I	T	O	L
M	O	O	T		D	I	X	O	N		G	I	V	E
A	U	D	I	T	O	R	I	A		L	U	M	E	N
S	T	O	N	E	W	A	L	L		A	R	E	N	T
S	E	N	T	E	N	C	E		V	E	R	S	O	

3

A	C	C	E	N	T				K	A	S	D	A	N
T	R	A	L	E	E			T	R	I	P	O	L	I
M	U	R	D	E	R		C	H	I	L	L	O	U	T
S	I	D	E	D	I	S	H	E	S		A	R	M	S
	S	P	R	Y		C	E	N	S	U	S			
W	E	L	L		C	R	A	C	K	S	H	O	T	
I	S	A	Y		O	A	T	E	R	S		N	A	G
S	H	Y		O	P	T	S	F	O	R		E	L	M
P	I	E		M	A	C	H	O	S		H	I	K	E
	P	R	E	A	C	H	E	R	S		E	D	E	N
		I	N	A	P	E	T		D	E	A	D	
E	G	G	S		B	A	T	H	P	I	L	L	O	W
P	R	I	N	T	A	D	S		O	C	T	A	V	E
P	I	G	E	O	N	S			S	T	A	K	E	D
S	P	A	R	T	A				T	A	P	E	R	S

4

C	A	N	A	D	A	B	L	U	E	G	R	A	S	S
T	R	A	D	I	T	I	O	N	A	L	I	R	A	S
N	A	V	A	L	E	N	G	A	G	E	M	E	N	T
S	T	E	M	L	E	S	S	G	L	A	S	S	E	S
	L	A	Y		H	I	E	S					
C	D	R		S	K	I		S	O	S	P	A	D
R	A	I	D		R	A	P	S		N	E	A	L	E
I	N	N	O	W	A	Y		I	T	S	A	L	O	T
S	I	G	M	A		O	R	Z	O		R	E	N	O
P	O	S	S	U	M		O	E	R		S	E	X
		K	E	R	T		S	A	T	
O	B	S	C	E	N	E	G	E	S	T	U	R	E	S
P	O	T	A	S	S	I	U	M	I	O	D	I	D	E
E	L	E	P	H	A	N	T	T	R	A	I	N	E	R
D	E	N	T	A	L	A	S	S	I	S	T	A	N	T

5

S	H	O	R	E	■	H	O	T	E	L	B	A	R	S
M	O	P	E	D	■	A	N	I	M	A	L	F	A	T
O	N	E	L	S	■	S	A	N	I	T	A	R	I	A
G	E	N	I	E	■	A	S	I	R	E	C	A	L	L
G	Y	M	C	L	A	S	S	E	S	■	K	I	E	L
I	B	I	S	■	M	E	I	R	■	T	O	D	D	S
E	E	K	■	B	O	A	S	■	F	O	P	■	■	■
R	E	E	N	A	C	T	■	L	I	S	S	O	M	E
■	■	■	O	T	O	■	M	A	N	S	■	P	A	Y
S	A	A	B	S	■	L	E	V	I	■	J	A	K	E
A	R	G	O	■	D	I	M	E	S	T	O	R	E	S
B	E	E	T	H	O	V	E	N	■	R	A	T	S	O
O	N	T	H	E	M	E	N	D	■	A	N	I	O	N
T	O	W	E	L	E	T	T	E	■	I	N	S	U	M
S	T	O	R	M	D	O	O	R	■	L	A	T	T	E

6

B	A	N	A	N	A	G	R	A	M	S	■	U	S	M
A	D	O	B	E	R	E	A	D	E	R	■	G	E	E
T	I	J	U	A	N	A	T	A	X	I	■	G	A	G
E	D	I	T	■	E	R	A	■	■	S	A	B	R	A
S	A	V	■	C	L	U	T	C	H	■	S	O	O	N
■	S	E	T	H	■	P	A	L	O	■	P	O	U	F
■	■	A	E	C	■	T	E	R	Z	E	T	T	O	■
I	L	O	V	E	L	A	■	F	A	I	R	S	E	X
F	A	C	E	P	A	L	M	■	E	N	S	■	■	■
I	V	A	R	■	R	E	U	P	■	G	E	E	Z	■
D	A	R	N	■	A	C	R	O	S	S	■	R	A	G
I	T	I	S	I	■	■	D	I	P	■	W	A	N	E
D	O	N	■	T	A	X	O	N	O	M	I	S	T	S
I	R	A	■	E	J	E	C	T	O	R	S	E	A	T
T	Y	S	■	S	A	S	H	A	F	I	E	R	C	E

7

A	R	C	T	I	C		W	H	O	S	T	H	A	T
W	A	H	I	N	E		H	O	W	A	R	E	Y	A
S	T	A	N	C	E		A	M	E	N	A	M	E	N
	P	L	E	A		R	T	E	S		D	A	R	K
A	O	K		S	M	O	T	E		H	E	N	S	
M	I	L	E	H	I	G	H	C	L	U	B			
I	S	I	S		S	U	E		S	T	O	P	I	T
C	O	N	C	I	S	E		Y	E	S	O	R	N	O
O	N	E	A	R	M		S	U	V		K	O	O	K
			P	E	E	R	P	R	E	S	S	U	R	E
	T	R	E	S		A	E	T	N	A		D	D	S
H	E	I	R		A	W	E	S		L	I	M	E	
E	S	P	O	U	S	E	D		S	I	T	A	R	S
P	L	E	A	S	E	G	O		A	V	E	R	T	S
S	A	N	D	B	A	G	S		C	A	N	Y	O	N

8

Z	O	M	B	I	E			S	W	A	M	P	E	D
A	N	O	M	A	L	Y		S	O	S	U	E	M	E
G	E	T	I	N	T	O		W	R	I	T	E	I	N
A	T	O		S	O	D	A		D	A	I	N	T	Y
T	O	R	A		N	E	W	T	O	N	S			
R	O	C	C	O		L	O	A	F		M	S	G	S
A	M	Y	T	A	N		L	P	G	A		U	L	U
T	A	C	I	T	U	S		S	O	B	E	R	U	P
E	N	L		S	M	O	G		D	E	L	E	T	E
D	Y	E	S		B	O	O	B		S	H	E	E	R
			T	E	S	T	B	A	N		I	N	N	S
U	N	L	O	C	K		S	N	E	E		O	F	T
R	A	I	N	O	U	T		D	R	L	A	U	R	A
N	U	T	E	L	L	A		S	T	I	N	G	E	R
S	T	E	R	I	L	E		S	A	S	H	E	S

9

L	E	T	S	D	O	T	H	I	S	T	H	I	N	G
A	N	I	M	A	T	I	O	N	S	T	U	D	I	O
H	A	D	A	L	O	N	G	W	A	Y	T	O	G	O
A	M	I	C	I	■	S	T	A	■	L	U	N	G	S
B	E	E	K	■	B	E	I	N	G	■	S	O	L	E
A	L	S	■	V	A	L	E	T	E	D	■	T	E	D
N	E	U	T	E	R	■	D	O	T	E	S	■	■	■
A	D	P	A	G	E	S	■	F	E	L	T	T	I	P
■	■	X	A	X	I	S	■	V	O	Y	A	G	E	
A	M	A	■	S	A	M	I	S	E	N	■	C	O	T
R	A	N	D	■	M	U	L	A	N	■	N	O	T	E
A	R	A	I	L	■	L	E	U	■	G	A	B	O	R
B	A	N	D	E	D	A	N	T	E	A	T	E	R	S
I	C	A	N	N	O	T	T	E	L	L	A	L	I	E
C	A	S	T	O	N	E	S	S	P	E	L	L	O	N

10

B	A	R	B	A	R	A	B	U	S	H	■	B	E	E
E	Q	U	I	V	A	L	E	N	C	E	■	R	R	R
F	A	S	C	I	N	A	T	I	O	N	■	O	I	L
O	B	E	S	■	D	R	A	F	T	■	W	A	K	E
G	A	S	■	M	O	M	M	Y	■	L	E	D	S	■
■	■	■	M	A	M	B	A	■	M	A	D	C	A	P
A	H	E	A	D	■	E	X	F	O	L	I	A	T	E
C	A	R	R	O	L	L	■	L	E	A	D	S	I	N
E	M	I	L	N	O	L	D	E	■	K	I	T	E	S
D	O	C	E	N	T	■	E	X	M	E	T	■	■	■
■	M	A	N	A	■	F	S	T	A	R	■	M	E	W
Z	E	K	E	■	K	L	E	I	N	■	P	I	S	A
A	L	A	■	Y	O	U	R	M	A	J	E	S	T	Y
G	E	N	■	O	L	I	V	E	G	A	R	D	E	N
S	T	E	■	U	N	D	E	R	E	X	P	O	S	E

11

```
  P R E S E N T A R M S
  D O O B E D O O B E D O O
G I M M E G I M M E G I M M E
A S P   R O T   C S I   E E L
S M A R T   M T A   S H O R T
P A N E   T E A T S   O N T O
S L O P P I N G   A E G E A N
      U S A U S A U S A
K E V L A R   A R C T U R U S
E L I S   A P L E Y   G A N T
B U R E N   U E Y   B E T T E
A D A   O E R   O S E   T R I
B E G S T H E Q U E S T I O N
  D O U B L E B O G E Y E D
  S P E E D S K A T E R
```

12

```
B A S   F L I P O N E S L I D
A C H   J U K E B O X H E R O
T R A   O R E G O N T R A I L
H O M B R E   W I E   I S N T
S P E E D   D O S   Y M H A
H O L E   P H O T O O P
E L E C   O L D S A W   H E R
B I S H O P     S L E A Z Y
A S S   D O G S I T   M I R A
    R E V O L T S   B R A N
  C B E R   K O S   T E M P O
P A R I   L A V   H E R E O N
O R A N G E P E K O E   T U E
S O V I E T U N I O N   A N A
T B O N E S T E A K S   L D L
```

13

A	R	M	Y	C	A	M	P	■	■	U	R	G	E	S
R	E	A	D	A	B	O	O	K	■	T	A	U	N	T
P	I	N	S	T	R	I	P	E	■	T	H	E	D	A
E	N	E	■	■	A	R	S	E	N	E	■	S	L	Y
L	A	D	Y	S	■	A	T	P	A	R	■	T	E	C
■	■	O	P	A	■	H	I	P	■	E	S	S	O	
■	L	A	K	E	P	O	E	T	■	F	A	T	S	O
L	O	V	E	C	O	N	Q	U	E	R	S	A	L	L
I	D	O	L	S	■	P	U	P	P	E	T	R	Y	■
L	E	I	S	■	R	A	E	■	I	T	O	■		
L	S	D	■	N	U	T	S	O	■	S	N	O	U	T
I	T	A	■	Y	E	R	T	L	E	■	V	S	O	
P	O	N	T	E	■	O	I	L	T	Y	C	O	O	N
U	N	C	U	T	■	L	O	I	T	E	R	I	N	G
T	E	E	N	S	■	■	N	E	A	T	I	D	E	A

14

K	A	M	A	S	U	T	R	A	■	L	O	N	G	S
E	G	O	M	A	N	I	A	C	■	E	N	E	R	O
P	E	N	N	Y	A	N	T	E	■	L	E	G	A	L
T	R	O	I	S	■	T	E	R	R	A	N	O	V	A
■	■	O	A	S	■	E	N	O	T	E	S			
S	W	M	■	H	O	U	S	E	M	D	■	I	S	T
T	H	I	S	■	U	S	E	R	S	■	K	A	T	Y
B	A	L	L	■	P	A	X	I	L	■	O	T	O	E
O	L	I	O	■	N	I	E	C	E	■	P	E	N	A
N	E	T	■	M	A	R	S	H	E	S	■	D	E	R
I	B	A	N	E	Z	■	■	P	O	M	■			
F	O	R	E	L	I	M	B	S	■	N	A	R	C	S
A	N	I	L	L	■	R	A	T	I	O	N	O	U	T
C	E	E	L	O	■	A	L	A	N	M	O	O	R	E
E	S	S	E	N	■	Z	E	N	G	A	R	D	E	N

T	R	A	M	P	■	C	A	B	S	■	S	P	O	T
R	E	B	A	R	■	Y	O	R	E	■	P	E	N	H
I	N	I	G	O	■	C	L	O	G	D	A	N	C	E
O	E	D	I	P	A	L	■	W	E	I	R	D	E	R
S	E	E	■	C	L	O	D	■	R	E	S	U	M	E
■	■	J	O	L	T	E	D	■	■	■	L	O	S	
■	C	A	M	E	R	A	O	B	S	C	U	R	A	
■	G	O	B	I	G	O	R	G	O	H	O	M	E	■
C	R	E	S	C	E	N	T	M	O	O	N	S	■	■
H	E	D	■	■	S	H	A	K	E	S	■	■	■	■
R	E	D	C	A	P	■	S	T	E	M	■	M	B	A
I	N	O	R	D	E	R	■	I	D	A	H	O	A	N
S	T	R	E	A	K	E	R	S	■	K	I	O	S	K
T	E	M	P	■	E	D	I	T	■	E	D	S	E	L
O	A	S	T	■	S	O	B	S	■	R	E	E	S	E

A	L	C	H	E	M	I	S	T	S	■	B	A	S	E
P	I	R	A	T	E	S	H	I	P	■	O	M	A	R
S	T	A	Y	A	T	H	O	M	E	■	S	E	M	I
E	R	N	S	■	H	O	W	■	D	V	O	R	A	K
S	E	E	T	O	■	T	D	S	■	E	M	I	R	S
■	■	■	A	A	A	■	O	L	A	Y	■	C	I	A
B	L	A	C	K	M	A	G	I	C	■	W	A	T	T
R	I	S	K	S	I	T	■	M	T	S	I	N	A	I
O	P	T	S	■	C	O	M	E	U	N	D	O	N	E
A	R	R	■	J	I	M	I	■	P	E	E	■	■	■
D	E	O	R	O	■	S	N	L	■	E	R	A	S	E
B	A	D	E	G	G	■	I	A	N	■	I	R	A	S
A	D	O	S	■	A	R	C	H	A	N	G	E	L	S
N	E	M	O	■	W	H	A	T	A	S	H	A	M	E
D	R	E	W	■	D	O	M	I	N	A	T	R	I	X

I	R	A	Q		C	A	V	E	R	S		O	D	S
R	A	C	E		A	D	I	D	A	S		J	O	T
I	D	I	D		L	I	V	I	N	G	W	A	G	E
S	I	N		A	L	E	R	T		T	H	Y	M	E
H	I	G	H	N	O	T	E	S		A	S	A	P	
			A	T	P			A	F	T				
T	R	A	D	I	T	I	O	N	A	L	I	R	A	S
M	A	L	A	R	I	A	P	A	R	A	S	I	T	E
E	M	O	T	I	O	N	A	L	O	U	T	L	E	T
N	A	T	I	O	N	A	L	A	N	T	H	E	M	S
			N	T	S			C	I	I				
A	B	B	E		T	E	X	A	S	S	I	Z	E	
T	O	R	A	H		O	V	E	R	T		V	I	A
S	T	O	R	E	F	R	O	N	T		W	A	L	T
I	O	N		R	O	C	K	I	E		O	N	C	E
X	X	X		R	E	H	E	A	R		K	A	H	N

L	A	B	A	M	B	A		A	T	A	V	I	S	T
I	P	A	D	A	I	R		S	I	S	E	N	O	R
R	E	T	W	E	E	T		K	T	H	X	B	Y	E
A	S	E	A		N	E	B	U	L	A				
			R	E	V		O	P	E	N	T	O	P	
S	U	P	E	R	E	G	O			T	A	B	L	E
N	N	E		S	N	A	K	E	B	I	T	T	E	N
A	C	R	E		U	N	C	L	E		S	A	D	D
G	O	O	G	L	E	G	L	A	S	S		I	T	O
S	I	N	G	E			U	N	T	I	L	N	O	W
	L	I	O	N	C	U	B		D	R	E			
			S	E	N	S	O	R		F	O	W	L	
P	A	J	A	M	A	S		P	A	D	T	H	A	I
D	V	D	C	A	S	E		T	M	O	B	I	L	E
F	I	S	H	N	E	T		S	A	M	E	O	L	D

I	C	K	I	N	E	S	S	■	F	L	A	G	O	N
T	H	E	N	A	N	N	Y	■	T	A	T	A	M	I
C	I	T	A	T	I	O	N	■	C	I	T	R	I	C
H	A	T	S	■	S	W	E	E	■	D	E	A	T	H
■	■	■	T	A	L	I	■	A	M	O	N	G	S	T
S	C	H	A	D	E	N	F	R	E	U	D	E	■	■
E	R	A	T	O	■	■	R	E	N	T	■	D	E	A
M	A	Z	E	■	S	P	A	D	E	■	L	O	S	T
I	B	M	■	C	H	A	N	■	■	R	O	O	S	T
■	A	L	L	M	Y	C	H	I	L	D	R	E	N	■
A	C	T	A	E	O	N	■	E	R	S	E	■	■	■
R	A	S	T	A	■	E	C	T	O	■	S	E	A	S
B	R	U	I	N	S	■	R	E	B	O	T	T	L	E
O	V	I	N	E	S	■	A	R	O	M	A	T	I	C
R	E	T	O	R	T	■	N	O	T	G	R	E	A	T

J	A	I	L	B	R	E	A	K	■	M	E	C	C	A
A	P	O	L	L	O	X	I	I	■	S	T	O	L	I
C	A	N	D	Y	S	H	O	P	■	D	A	K	A	R
O	T	I	S	■	S	A	L	■	A	O	L	E	R	S
B	O	Z	■	B	I	L	I	O	U	S	■	Z	I	P
S	W	E	A	R	■	E	S	P	N	■	M	E	T	A
■	■	■	T	I	C	S	■	■	S	T	E	A	R	I	C
M	O	J	I	T	O	■	■	I	N	T	O	N	E
O	P	U	L	E	N	T	■	B	E	E	T	■	■
N	E	S	T	■	D	R	E	I	■	M	E	S	A	S
A	N	T	■	G	O	I	N	G	B	Y	■	E	R	E
R	A	D	N	E	R	■	C	H	A	■	L	A	I	T
C	R	O	O	N	■	G	O	O	G	L	E	B	O	T
H	E	I	S	T	■	A	R	A	G	O	N	E	S	E
Y	A	T	E	S	■	S	E	X	Y	S	A	D	I	E

21

G	O	T	A	B	■	S	O	B	S	■	■	C	P	R
S	A	H	I	B	■	E	N	E	M	Y	■	O	H	O
U	S	E	D	C	A	R	S	A	L	E	S	M	A	N
I	I	N	■	R	I	V	E	T	■	S	A	P	S	■
T	S	O	■	A	M	I	C	I	■	E	L	L	I	E
■	■	O	K	D	■	C	O	N	E	S	■	E	N	D
S	I	N	A	I	■	E	N	G	R	■	E	X	G	I
A	N	D	R	O	M	E	D	A	S	T	R	A	I	N
I	T	A	L	■	E	N	T	R	■	H	A	N	N	A
T	H	Y	■	L	A	T	H	E	■	E	T	A	■	■
H	E	D	G	E	■	R	O	T	O	S	■	L	C	D
■	W	E	R	E	■	A	U	R	A	L	■	Y	E	R
L	I	V	E	D	A	N	G	E	R	O	U	S	L	Y
A	L	I	■	S	A	C	H	A	■	T	R	I	L	L
M	D	L	■	S	E	T	T	■	S	I	S	S	Y	

22

H	O	L	M	E	S	I	A	N	■	T	B	A	R	S
A	T	A	G	L	A	N	C	E	■	A	R	P	E	L
K	I	S	S	Y	F	A	C	E	■	M	A	P	L	E
E	S	T	■	S	E	N	T	■	H	A	I	L	E	D
■	■	■	T	I	L	E	■	H	O	R	N	E	T	S
S	U	B	W	A	Y	■	S	E	R	I	F	S	■	■
A	L	A	I	N	■	H	U	M	A	N	R	A	C	E
C	E	N	T	■	W	A	R	P	S	■	E	U	R	O
S	E	A	T	M	A	T	E	S	■	P	E	C	A	N
■	■	N	E	U	T	E	R	■	D	O	Z	E	N	S
S	M	A	R	T	E	D	■	A	A	R	E	■	■	■
T	I	P	J	A	R	■	B	U	M	S	■	C	R	U
P	A	E	A	N	■	B	O	D	A	C	I	O	U	S
A	T	E	I	T	■	I	R	I	S	H	M	O	S	S
T	A	L	L	S	■	B	E	E	K	E	E	P	E	R

23

T	O	W	E	L	S		B	E	S	S	E	M	E	R
I	N	A	P	E	T		E	X	I	T	L	A	N	E
M	E	N	A	G	E		T	E	X	A	S	T	E	A
E	S	T		S	N	O	W	D	E	N		H	R	S
L	I	E	V		O	N	E	R	S		L	E	G	O
A	D	D	I	N		K	E	A		C	A	R	Y	N
G	E	T	S	O	P	E	N		P	U	N			
	D	O	I	T	B	Y	T	H	E	B	O	O	K	
			T	A	J		W	O	R	E	T	H	I	N
A	S	C	O	T		R	O	O		S	T	I	N	E
T	B	A	R		G	A	F	F	S		E	D	D	A
T	A	S		S	I	Z	E	S	U	P		U	L	T
A	R	T	M	A	J	O	R		M	I	N	N	I	E
C	R	U	M	H	O	R	N		A	T	O	N	E	S
H	O	P	E	L	E	S	S		C	A	V	O	R	T

24

F	L	E	W	B	Y		G	E	S	T	A	T	E	S
R	E	D	H	O	T		A	L	T	E	R	A	N	T
I	N	W	A	R	D		Z	I	P	D	R	I	V	E
E	N	O	L	A		T	E	X	A	S		L	I	T
Z	O	O	E	X	H	I	B	I	T		T	O	S	S
E	N	D	S		O	D	O	R		M	A	R	I	O
			P	R	E	S		S	E	X	T	O	N	
H	E	R	A	L	D	S		L	E	G	I	O	N	S
O	P	A	Q	U	E		L	E	E	S				
M	I	N	U	S		T	E	A	M		S	A	S	S
E	S	A	I		G	R	A	P	E	J	E	L	L	Y
P	O	L		G	R	I	F	T		U	P	P	E	D
O	D	O	N	N	E	L	L		O	M	A	H	A	N
R	E	N	T	A	B	L	E		A	B	L	A	Z	E
T	I	G	H	T	E	S	T		F	O	S	S	E	Y

25

C	A	B	B	I	E	S	■	B	U	M	M	E	R	S
O	R	L	A	N	D	O	S	E	N	T	I	N	E	L
S	O	U	R	C	E	S	O	F	I	N	C	O	M	E
A	W	E	D	■	N	O	M	O	■	S	E	T	U	P
■	C	O	D	S	■	A	R	A	■	E	S	T		
M	E	H	T	A	■	K	L	E	B	A	N	■		
A	L	I	■	M	M	I	I	■	B	L	I	M	E	Y
C	A	P	T	A	I	N	P	H	I	L	L	I	P	S
E	N	S	I	G	N	■	I	R	E	S	■	S	E	E
■		M	E	S	S	R	S	■	E	T	H	E	R	
S	A	G	■	K	E	A	■	A	T	R	A	■		
C	L	E	A	T	■	E	T	A	S	■	I	N	G	E
A	L	E	X	A	N	D	E	R	C	A	L	D	E	R
L	O	S	E	O	N	E	S	M	A	R	B	L	E	S
P	R	E	S	S	E	D	■	S	P	R	Y	E	S	T

26

C	O	R	N	C	O	B	P	I	P	E	■	T	A	M
O	N	A	C	A	R	O	U	S	E	L	■	A	L	E
R	A	N	A	N	E	R	R	A	N	D	■	K	T	S
G	I	G	A	■	■	D	R	O	N	E	B	E	E	S
I	R	E	■	A	W	E	■	A	R	E	A	R	■	
■		S	T	A	R	D	O	M	■	T	I	N	S	
S	P	H	I	N	X	L	I	K	E	■	A	M	A	H
Y	O	U	D	O	■	I	C	E	■	O	R	A	T	E
N	O	D	E	■	I	N	T	E	G	R	A	T	E	D
E	L	S	A	■	T	E	A	C	O	Z	Y	■		
■	T	O	R	T	E	■	H	B	O	■	S	U	B	
S	A	N	M	A	R	I	N	O	■	C	A	S	E	
E	B	B	■	D	A	N	U	B	E	R	I	V	E	R
A	L	A	■	A	N	C	I	E	N	T	R	O	M	E
U	E	Y	■	S	T	A	T	E	S	E	C	R	E	T

S	A	T	E	L	L	I	T	E	S	T	A	T	E	S
A	D	E	L	A	I	D	E	S	L	A	M	E	N	T
M	A	R	I	N	E	I	N	S	U	R	A	N	C	E
S	I	N	G	I	N	G	T	O	G	E	T	H	E	R
■	R	E	I	■	S	I	E	■	I	D	I	O	■	■
■	■	S	B	A	■	T	R	O	T	■	S	U	M	O
■	■	■	L	I	S	■	■	R	O	Z	■	R	A	H
S	N	E	E	R	A	T	■	G	U	E	S	S	S	O
H	E	X	■	E	M	I	■	■	T	A	C	■	■	■
A	Z	O	V	■	M	A	P	A	■	L	A	S	■	■
■	■	R	I	M	Y	■	A	R	M	■	R	T	S	■
S	A	C	R	I	F	I	C	I	A	L	L	A	M	B
A	M	I	G	L	A	D	T	O	S	E	E	Y	O	U
G	A	S	O	L	I	N	E	S	T	A	T	I	O	N
A	N	T	S	I	N	O	N	E	S	P	A	N	T	S

W	H	O	A	■	P	R	I	M	A	L	U	R	G	E
H	A	R	M	■	L	E	G	A	L	I	Z	E	I	T
A	B	A	B	■	I	D	O	B	E	L	I	E	V	E
T	A	L	E	S	E	■	T	E	X	T	■	F	E	R
I	N	E	R	T	■	A	Y	L	A	■	R	E	I	N
S	E	X	S	Y	M	B	O	L	■	L	O	R	N	E
I	R	A	■	L	U	L	U	■	C	U	T	■	■	■
T	O	M	K	I	T	E	■	D	U	C	H	A	M	P
■	■	I	S	T	■	P	O	R	K	■	N	A	E	■
D	E	A	T	H	■	P	A	T	T	Y	C	A	K	E
O	N	E	S	■	K	E	N	S	■	M	O	T	E	L
O	R	R	■	T	H	E	O	■	K	E	N	O	B	I
F	I	O	N	A	A	P	P	L	E	■	E	L	A	N
U	C	B	E	R	K	E	L	E	Y	■	Y	I	N	G
S	H	E	S	A	I	D	Y	E	S	■	S	A	K	S

M	O	V	E	B	A	C	K	■	B	B	K	I	N	G
I	R	E	A	L	I	Z	E	■	L	I	E	S	O	N
D	E	L	T	A	R	A	Y	■	U	G	A	N	D	A
■	V	A	D	E	R	■	P	E	G	■	T	E	T	■
S	P	E	W	E	D	■	R	A	J	A	H	■	■	■
I	O	T	A	S	■	F	A	C	E	M	A	S	K	S
G	O	R	Y	■	K	A	F	K	A	E	S	Q	U	E
H	B	O	■	K	I	T	T	E	N	S	■	U	R	L
T	A	P	D	A	N	C	E	R	S	■	N	A	T	E
S	H	E	D	T	E	A	R	S	■	D	O	R	I	C
■	■	T	E	S	T	S	■	D	I	V	E	S	T	■
A	N	N	■	M	C	S	■	C	U	R	E	D	■	■
T	O	O	T	O	O	■	P	O	P	E	L	E	O	X
T	H	E	A	S	P	■	I	D	E	C	L	A	R	E
N	O	L	O	S	E	■	T	E	D	T	A	L	K	S

C	O	L	B	E	R	T	B	U	M	P	■	C	H	E
E	V	E	R	S	O	S	O	R	R	Y	■	O	A	R
L	E	G	I	S	L	A	T	U	R	E	■	N	I	N
T	R	O	T	■	A	R	S	■	O	D	I	S	T	S
■	■	■	I	N	S	■	M	A	O	S	U	I	T	■
A	S	G	A	R	D	■	V	I	R	G	I	L	■	■
H	E	E	L	S	■	D	A	R	K	S	T	A	R	S
A	L	O	E	■	H	A	S	T	E	■	A	T	O	I
B	A	C	K	B	E	N	C	H	■	F	R	E	O	N
■	A	S	I	A	G	O	■	S	E	T	S	T	O	■
D	O	C	E	N	T	S	■	B	A	Y	■	■	■	■
O	N	H	I	G	H	■	O	A	F	■	A	W	E	S
L	I	I	■	H	E	A	T	S	E	N	S	O	R	S
C	O	N	■	A	R	C	T	I	C	O	C	E	A	N
E	N	G	■	M	Y	C	O	L	O	G	I	S	T	S

F	O	S	H	I	Z	Z	L	E	■	C	A	N	S	T
A	T	H	E	N	A	E	U	M	■	E	P	O	C	H
S	T	A	N	D	I	N	G	O	■	L	I	T	H	E
T	O	R	■	O	R	I	G	■	G	L	A	M	O	R
O	M	I	T	■	E	T	A	L	I	I	■	U	L	E
N	A	N	A	S	■	H	G	T	V	■	S	C	A	T
E	N	G	I	N	E	■	E	Y	E	■	T	H	R	O
■	■	I	N	L	A	W	■	R	U	N	A	T	■	■
M	A	S	T	■	T	A	B	■	P	A	Y	O	L	A
A	R	C	S	■	S	N	U	B	■	P	A	L	I	N
N	E	A	■	P	A	S	C	A	L	■	T	O	O	T
M	A	R	M	O	T	■	O	M	A	R	■	O	N	O
A	R	I	A	L	■	A	L	A	N	A	R	K	I	N
D	U	N	N	O	■	L	I	K	E	C	R	A	Z	Y
E	G	G	O	S	■	■	E	C	O	S	Y	S	T	E	M

L	E	S	S	C	O	M	P	L	I	C	A	T	E	D
O	N	E	A	F	T	E	R	A	N	O	T	H	E	R
T	H	E	G	O	B	L	E	T	O	F	F	I	R	E
H	A	T	E	S	■	D	W	A	R	F	■	E	I	S
A	N	O	S	■	D	I	R	K	■	E	L	V	E	S
I	C	I	■	K	E	N	A	I	■	R	E	E	S	E
R	E	T	■	E	G	G	P	A	N	■	E	S	T	D
■	■	I	G	A	■	■	U	A	R	■	■	■	■	■
S	N	C	C	■	S	O	M	B	E	R	■	I	C	E
C	O	L	O	R	■	S	I	E	V	E	■	N	A	Y
A	T	O	N	E	■	M	A	J	A	■	H	A	M	E
C	A	S	■	S	P	O	S	E	■	B	A	S	E	L
C	L	E	A	N	A	S	A	W	H	I	S	T	L	E
H	O	S	T	I	L	E	R	E	A	C	T	I	O	N
I	T	T	A	K	E	S	A	L	L	S	O	R	T	S

33

C	H	I	L	L	A	X	■	G	A	G	A	R	I	N
H	A	V	E	A	G	O	■	A	D	R	I	A	N	A
U	V	I	N	D	E	X	■	T	E	R	R	I	F	Y
M	R	E	D	■	S	O	P	H	S	■	E	S	O	S
P	E	D	A	L	■	X	K	E	■	I	D	E	M	■
■	■	H	O	L	O	G	R	A	M	■	H	A	D	■
D	E	J	A	V	U	■	S	E	X	S	C	E	N	E
E	X	E	N	E	M	Y	■	R	I	T	A	L	I	N
B	A	L	D	S	P	O	T	■	O	U	T	L	A	Y
S	M	L	■	E	S	U	R	A	N	C	E	■	■	■
■	P	O	E	T	■	L	I	D	■	K	R	A	U	T
F	A	S	T	■	G	L	O	A	T	■	W	N	B	A
I	P	H	O	N	E	S	■	P	A	R	A	D	O	X
L	E	O	N	I	N	E	■	T	R	O	U	B	L	E
A	R	T	S	A	L	E	■	S	T	Y	L	E	T	S

34

C	A	M	P	■	H	O	W	D	A	R	E	Y	O	U
E	V	E	R	■	I	N	A	U	G	U	R	A	L	S
D	I	D	O	■	M	E	L	O	N	B	A	L	L	S
A	L	I	T	O	■	A	T	S	E	A	■	E	A	R
R	A	C	E	C	A	R	D	■	W	T	S	■	■	■
■	■	■	S	U	M	M	I	T	■	O	K	B	U	T
E	A	S	T	L	A	■	S	E	W	■	Y	O	K	E
C	A	L	V	I	N	A	N	D	H	O	B	B	E	S
O	R	E	O	■	A	C	E	■	A	T	O	A	S	T
N	E	W	T	O	■	H	Y	D	R	O	X	■	■	■
■	■	■	E	R	N	■	W	I	F	E	S	W	A	P
A	R	T	■	L	I	M	O	S	■	S	E	E	M	E
R	E	T	R	O	V	I	R	U	S	■	A	W	A	R
A	N	Y	O	N	E	E	L	S	E	■	T	O	T	O
B	E	L	T	S	A	N	D	E	R	■	S	N	I	T

35

C	L	I	C	K	B	A	I	T	■	A	N	G	S	T
H	E	N	R	I	E	T	T	A	■	N	O	R	A	H
I	N	S	O	M	N	I	A	C	■	D	R	I	V	E
R	A	P	S	■	M	L	K	J	R	■	N	A	B	
A	P	O	S	T	L	E	■	■	L	E	A	N	N	E
C	E	T	E	R	A	■	A	G	O	■	N	I	N	A
■	■	■	D	O	T	T	I	E	■	J	O	N	A	S
F	I	V	E	T	H	I	R	T	Y	E	I	G	H	T
A	D	A	Y	S	■	R	E	S	E	W	N	■	■	■
C	O	R	E	■	R	E	D	■	L	E	T	S	A	T
E	N	D	S	I	T	■	A	L	L	E	N	D	E	
S	T	A	■	K	E	L	P	S	■	D	A	V	E	
O	L	L	I	E	■	O	U	T	S	P	O	K	E	N
F	I	O	N	A	■	S	T	R	A	I	N	E	R	S
F	E	S	T	S	■	S	T	O	P	P	E	D	B	Y

36

M	A	K	E	S	A	M	E	S	S	■	A	T	A	D
O	P	E	R	A	M	U	S	I	C	■	B	O	B	O
B	O	Y	S	O	P	R	A	N	O	■	S	P	O	T
I	S	E	E	■	■	D	I	E	T	Z	■	H	U	H
L	E	D	■	M	M	E	■	W	I	I	M	O	T	E
■	■	■	T	I	A	R	A	■	A	G	E	N	T	J
■	P	S	A	L	M	I	S	T	■	C	O	H	O	
A	L	A	S	K	A	N	K	I	N	G	C	R	A	B
L	A	Y	S	■	C	O	M	E	L	A	S	T	■	
P	C	H	E	L	P	■	F	E	T	U	S	■	■	
H	E	E	L	E	R	S	■	S	H	E	■	F	C	C
A	N	Y	■	G	O	T	A	T	■	K	A	R	L	
S	A	K	E	■	B	A	B	A	O	R	I	L	E	Y
I	M	I	T	■	S	L	A	M	D	A	N	C	E	D
G	E	D	S	■	T	E	A	P	O	T	D	O	M	E

37

L	C	H	A	I	M			K	R	U	G	M	A	N
L	E	A	D	T	O		D	I	E	T	R	I	T	E
A	T	M	O	S	T		A	B	N	O	R	M	A	L
M	U	M	B	O	J	U	M	B	O			E	N	L
A	S	Y	E		U	T	I	L	I	Z	E			
			S	H	E	E	R	A	G	O	N	Y		
U	N	B	E	A	T	E	N		I	G	L	O	O	
S	C	U	L	L	E	R		C	A	R	E	E	N	S
M	A	N	E	T		T	U	N	E	D	O	U	T	
C	A	T	C	H	A	C	O	L	D					
	T	O	W	R	O	P	E		A	N	I	L		
H	E	S		N	O	H	A	R	M	D	O	N	E	
A	L	P	A	C	I	N	O		S	I	Z	E	U	P
C	L	A	R	I	N	E	T		O	R	E	L	S	E
K	E	Y	T	A	G	S		N	A	S	S	E	R	

38

B	A	N	J	O		M	C	M	A	N	S	I	O	N
O	L	E	I	C		C	R	A	Z	Y	B	O	N	E
T	O	W	N	S		D	O	N	T	P	A	N	I	C
C	H	E	X		C	U	E	D		I	N	T		
H	A	R	E	M		S	H	A	K		M	A	Y	A
	S	E	Q	U	E	L		M	I	N	E	R		
D	S	O		R	U	N	T		B	O	N	S	A	I
R	A	R	E	G	A	S		L	A	N	T	E	R	N
E	L	A	T	E	D		W	O	R	K		A	S	E
A	L	L	E	S		H	E	B	R	E	W			
M	I	E	S		B	A	B	E		Y	A	L	T	A
L	E	X		H	E	R	S		P	O	O	R		
A	M	A	R	Y	L	L	I	S		Z	I	P	P	O
N	A	M	E	P	L	A	T	E		A	T	E	A	M
D	E	S	M	O	I	N	E	S		P	I	Z	Z	A

39

Z	A	C	H		M	A	M	A		A	M	A	Z	E
I	L	I	E		O	V	I	D		P	U	T	O	N
N	O	G	S		L	E	T	I	T	B	L	E	E	D
C	O	A	S	T	T	O	C	O	A	S	T			
	F	R	E	R	E		H	S	T		I	R	R	
		A	N	S				S	P	E	E			
H	O	S	T	I	L	E	T	A	K	E	O	V	E	R
A	T	E	E	N	A	G	E	R	I	N	L	O	V	E
W	H	A	T	E	V	E	R	I	T	T	A	K	E	S
G	E	N	E	R	A	L	I	N	T	E	R	E	S	T
	R	C	A	S				G	E	N				
	S	E	T		S	A	G		N	C	A	A	S	
		E	N	T	R	A	N	C	E	F	E	E	S	
L	A	S	T	H	U	R	R	A	H		I	S	N	T
A	S	N	E	R		O	T	T	O		R	O	S	Y
X	H	O	S	A		W	H	E	W		E	P	E	E

40

F	A	S	T	P	A	C	E		W	E	B	B	S
A	U	T	O	L	O	A	N		S	A	T	U	R	N
U	P	I	N	A	R	M	S		P	R	A	G	U	E
L	A	F	I	T	T	E		C	R	Y		B	C	E
T	I	L	T		A	L	M	A	Y		D	E	E	R
	R	E	E	F		C	O	M		K	O	A	L	A
			T	R	A	D	E	S	E	C	R	E	T	
	P	A	O	L	O	V	E	R	O	N	E	S	E	
L	U	C	K	B	E	A	L	A	D	Y				
A	R	E	A	S		L	E	T		A	D	A	M	
W	I	R	Y		D	R	D	R	E		O	R	E	M
O	T	B		B	A	Y		I	M	P	L	O	R	E
M	A	I	T	A	I		A	P	P	L	A	U	S	E
A	N	T	O	N	S		G	O	T	U	P	S	E	T
N	S	Y	N	C			O	D	Y	S	S	E	Y	S

41

C	A	R	O	U	S	E	S	■	■	P	E	R	F
O	V	E	R	S	T	A	T	E	■	O	V	A	L
L	A	T	E	A	U	T	U	M	N	■	S	E	G	A
A	I	R	G	U	N	S	■	B	O	D	E	R	E	K
N	L	E	A	S	T	■	D	E	G	A	U	S	S	■
D	I	A	N	A	■	P	I	Z	A	R	R	O		
E	N	T	O	■	G	U	Z	Z	L	E	S	■		
R	G	S	■	D	A	Z	Z	L	E	D	■	M	P	S
		T	I	Z	Z	I	E	S	■	W	E	R	E	
		F	O	O	Z	L	E	R	■	M	I	X	E	R
	H	E	N	N	A	E	D	■	V	I	S	I	N	E
M	O	N	T	E	R	O	■	S	E	N	E	C	A	N
O	M	N	I	■	A	U	N	T	I	E	M	A	M	E
P	E	E	N	■	T	O	L	D	T	A	L	E	S	
E	R	L	E	■	B	O	T	A	N	I	S	T		

42

R	A	M	B	L	E	O	N	■	L	I	E	T	O
A	N	A	L	O	G	U	E	■	B	A	N	Y	A	N
N	I	C	E	W	O	R	K	■	U	P	N	E	X	T
I	S	A	A	C	■	S	O	M	M	E	■	S	F	O
N	E	W	T	O	Y	■	E	S	L	■	F	R	A	
■	■	M	O	T	H	S	■	B	R	A	S			
	T	H	E	W	H	O	S	E	L	L	O	U	T	
	N	O	O	D	L	E	D	A	R	O	U	N	D	■
J	I	M	M	Y	S	W	A	G	G	A	R	T		
E	C	H	O	■	O	D	E	O	N	■				
T	K	O	■	S	A	M	■	T	S	K	T	S	K	
S	N	O	■	C	U	B	I	C	■	H	A	I	T	I
K	A	P	L	A	N	■	G	O	T	A	H	E	A	D
I	M	E	A	N	T	■	O	V	E	R	L	O	R	D
S	E	R	B	S	■	R	E	C	K	O	N	S	O	

43

B	E	A	T	P	O	E	T			H	I	F	I	S
L	A	D	I	E	S	M	A	N		A	M	I	N	O
O	V	E	R	S	H	A	R	E		H	I	N	D	U
T	E	L	E		K	I	P	S		A	T	E	I	T
S	S	E		L	O	L	I	T	A		P	A	H	
		M	I	S	S	T	E	P		G	R	A	B	
J	U	D	I	T	H		S	A	P	P	H	I	R	E
A	N	I	S	E				R	A	N	I	N		
M	U	S	T	R	E	A	D		M	I	N	T	E	D
E	S	P	Y		G	R	E	N	A	D	A			
S	U	E		G	A	L	O	R	E		A	C	U	
D	A	R	L	A		F	I	J	I		A	L	E	S
E	L	S	I	E		A	L	O	N	G	S	I	D	E
A	L	A	M	O		T	A	K	E	A	S	T	A	B
N	Y	L	O	N		H	E	R	S	T	O	R	Y	

44

S	T	R	E	E	T	F	A	I	R		C	O	G	S
P	O	O	L	N	O	O	D	L	E		A	N	O	N
R	O	U	G	H	R	I	D	E	R		N	E	B	O
E	N	T	R	A	I	L	S		O	U	T	L	A	W
E	S	S	E	N	E	S		S	O	L	O	I	N	G
			C	C	S		P	A	T	E	R	N	A	L
S	T	J	O	E		M	E	L	E	E		E	N	O
M	I	E	S		L	I	K	E	D		G	R	A	B
A	G	R		S	O	N	E	S		P	O	S	S	E
R	E	S	E	R	V	E	S		D	A	S			
T	R	E	A	T	E	D		P	A	S	S	I	N	G
A	M	Y	T	A	N		C	O	N	T	I	N	U	E
L	O	I	S		E	M	A	N	C	I	P	A	T	E
E	T	T	A		S	E	N	T	I	M	E	N	T	S
C	H	E	T		T	R	A	I	N	E	D	E	Y	E

R	I	S	K	■	F	I	V	E	K	■	A	C	S
A	R	C	A	D	E	F	I	R	E	■	S	N	A	P
M	A	R	T	I	N	A	M	I	S	■	P	I	P	E
S	T	U	R	M	■	■	C	H	A	I	T	E	A
■	E	M	I	■	A	B	S	■	A	T	T	A	C	K
■	■	N	A	R	U	T	O	■	T	A	H	O	E
J	A	V	A	S	C	R	I	P	T	■	L	I	R	A
A	N	A	■	H	E	I	N	I	E	S	■	L	A	S
C	A	P	S	■	D	A	K	A	R	R	A	L	L	Y
O	B	I	T	S	■	L	E	T	S	O	N	■
B	I	D	I	N	G	■	R	E	E	■	T	S	K	■
Z	O	N	E	O	U	T	■	■	O	N	E	A	L
U	S	E	R	■	T	Y	L	E	R	P	E	R	R	Y
M	I	S	S	■	S	P	E	C	I	E	S	I	S	M
A	S	S	■	Y	O	Y	O	S	■	T	A	T	E

S	P	A	M	B	O	T	■	W	A	L	K	O	F	F
M	A	N	C	A	V	E	■	A	S	A	R	U	L	E
I	R	A	Q	W	A	R	■	B	E	R	A	T	E	S
L	A	C	■	L	L	A	M	A	■	D	U	C	A	T
E	D	I	T	■	S	W	I	S	H	■	T	O	B	E
S	E	N	O	R	■	A	S	H	O	T	■	M	A	R
■	■	R	E	N	T	S	■	M	A	X	E	N	E
F	E	A	R	N	O	T	■	D	E	B	A	S	E	D
O	U	T	E	A	T	■	X	E	R	O	X	■
O	P	T	■	L	E	G	O	S	■	R	I	F	T	S
S	H	E	A	■	S	E	X	E	S	■	S	A	R	I
B	O	S	C	O	■	T	O	R	C	H	■	K	I	N
A	R	T	E	M	I	S	■	T	H	E	B	E	S	T
L	I	T	I	N	T	O	■	E	M	E	R	I	T	A
L	A	O	T	I	A	N	■	R	O	L	O	D	E	X

47

```
M A D E M A N █ N E T W O R K
C H O C O L A T E C O O K I E
I S H O T T H E S H E R I F F
█ █ C L O S E T O █ D E L I █
A D R I E N █ █ █ █ M I S E R
B R O D Y █ O N E S I E █ █ █
Z A N E █ S K I N N E R B O X
U N C █ C O A L G A S █ L E D
G O O G O L P L E X █ P A S O
█ █ R A D I A L █ █ B A N T U
R O G E T █ █ █ █ R A C K E T
O D O M █ S I E N E S E █ █ █
S O U L J A B O Y T E L L E M
A U D I O V I S U A L A I D S
S L A N T E D █ K R Y P T O N
```

48

```
J O A N B A E Z █ P A C K O N
I N N U E N D O █ E N H A L O
L E T S D O W N █ N E A T E R
T I L █ S T A K I N G █ M A T
E D E R █ E R O D E █ G A S H
D A R E S █ D U I █ M O N T E
█ █ █ P O I N T O F O R D E R
S C H E R Z O █ S O J O U R N
C R A N B E R R Y B O G █ █ █
H O S T S █ T O N █ S U E R S
A N T S █ T O S C A █ E L E C
E K E █ D E N A R I I █ I V O
F I N I A L █ L A S T E X I T
E T E R N E █ I S L A M I S T
R E D S O X █ E Y E S O R E S
```

C	L	E	A	R	O	N	E	S	T	H	R	O	A	T
R	E	S	T	O	R	E	T	O	H	E	A	L	T	H
A	T	S	O	M	E	O	T	H	E	R	T	I	M	E
S	T	E	P	S	O	N	O	N	E	S	T	O	E	S
S	S	N			T	R	E		H	E	S			
		A	W	G	E	E		J	E	D				
R	A	I	N	H	A	T		D	A	Y		E	L	M
A	M	A	T	E	U	R		I	N	B	O	X	E	S
J	O	N		N	S	A		N	I	A	L	O	N	G
		H	I	S		S	N	E	R	D				
	C	A	M		S	T	E				C	A	B	
O	R	A	N	G	E	M	A	R	M	A	L	A	D	E
W	I	S	D	O	M	O	F	S	O	L	O	M	O	N
A	S	C	E	N	T	O	F	E	V	E	R	E	S	T
R	E	A	L	E	S	T	A	T	E	S	A	L	E	S

C	A	B	O	O	S	E		S	H	A	S	T	A
A	S	S	U	R	E	D		C	H	E	R	O	O	T
S	K	I	T	E	A	M		P	I	N	E	N	U	T
T	A	D	L	I	N	C	O	L	N		A	G	R	A
S	N	E	A	D		B	L	U	E	S		C	D	C
			N	A	I	A	D	S		K	A	Y	A	K
S	H	E	D		R	I	S		S	A	N	C	T	A
T	O	L	E	D	A	N		N	E	T	T	L	E	D
A	V	E	R	Y	S		M	A	R		H	E	S	S
L	E	A	S	E		R	E	D	F	I	R			
I	R	R		D	I	O	N	E		C	A	D	I	Z
N	O	N	I		S	O	U	R	C	E	C	O	D	E
E	V	I	N	C	E	D		I	O	D	I	Z	E	S
R	E	N	D	E	R	S		T	A	U	T	E	S	T
A	R	G	Y	L	E		E	X	P	E	R	T	S

51

O	N	B	A	S	E		B	U	M	S		D	R	S
M	O	O	R	E	D		A	G	E	N	C	I	E	S
I	R	O	N	E	D		R	A	N	A	L	O	N	G
T	A	K	E	M	Y	W	O	R	D	F	O	R	I	T
		R	T	S		A	N	T	E	U	P			
M	E	E	T		G	I	M	E	L		P	S	A	T
A	L	T		E	T	T	U		P	E	T	R	A	
D	O	U	B	L	E	E	N	T	E	N	D	R	E	S
A	R	R	A	Y		C	R	O	C		I	N	T	
T	O	N	S		I	T	H	A	S		O	K	A	Y
		S	A	M	O	A	N		O	N	E			
H	O	T	A	S	B	L	U	E	B	L	A	Z	E	S
A	P	P	L	A	U	D	S		I	M	P	O	R	T
N	A	K	E	D	E	Y	E		B	E	A	N	I	E
S	H	E		A	S	A	N		S	C	R	E	E	N

52

A	P	R	I	C	O	T	J	A	M		E	X	A	M
G	U	I	T	A	R	S	O	L	O		T	R	I	O
A	Z	E	R	B	A	I	J	A	N		C	A	R	T
S	O	N	Y	A		N	O	M	E		H	Y	P	O
			N	A	G		O	Y	S		V	A	R	
B	A	D	S	A	N	T	A		E	L	V	I	S	H
F	R	E	E		T	A	B		D	O	E	S	S	O
L	E	T	G	O		O	C	T		P	R	I	A	M
A	Y	E	A	Y	E		T	E	E		D	O	G	E
T	O	R	R	E	Y		V	A	C	C	I	N	E	S
M	U	M		Z	E	D		M	O	D				
A	S	I	F		M	E	O	W		C	H	I	L	I
J	U	N	E		A	L	L	O	S	A	U	R	U	S
O	R	E	S		S	T	A	R	T	S	M	A	L	L
R	E	D	S		K	A	F	K	A	E	S	Q	U	E

53

T	A	K	E	S	T	O			B	O	A	T	E	R
O	N	A	L	E	A	S	H		I	M	B	U	S	Y
A	G	R	I	C	O	L	A		P	I	E	R	C	E
D	E	M	O		S	O	V	I	E	T		N	A	B
S	L	A	T	E			E	N	D		P	E	R	E
				N	O	V	A	S		F	U	D	G	E
	M	A	R	G	I	N	O	F	E	R	R	O	R	
	B	E	F	O	R	E	I	F	O	R	G	E	T	
B	A	T	T	L	E	S	C	A	R	R	E	D		
E	T	H	E	L		F	E	R	M	I				
S	T	A	R		P	O	T		S	A	L	M	A	
T	E	D		F	U	R	R	O	W		S	A	A	B
I	R	O	B	O	T		I	R	I	S	H	P	U	B
R	U	N	O	U	T		P	E	T	P	E	E	V	E
S	P	E	A	R	S		S	T	A	N	L	E	Y	

54

S	C	A	R	F	R	I	N	G		B	O	M	B	E
T	O	L	E	R	A	N	C	E		A	V	A	I	L
R	O	L	L	I	N	G	O	N		D	I	N	K	S
A	L	S	A	T	I	A		D	R	A	F	T	E	E
P	H	O	T	O	N		G	E	A	R	O	I	L	
P	E	R	E	S		B	A	R	T	E	R	S		
E	A	T	S		J	I	M	B	E	A	M			
D	D	S		F	A	K	E	I	D	S		B	A	H
			D	I	V	E	B	A	R		M	I	R	O
	B	O	L	E	R	O	S		C	A	N	S	T	
	N	O	M	E	R	C	Y		S	U	N	G	O	D
C	O	R	I	N	T	H		G	A	R	D	E	N	A
A	R	E	N	A		I	C	A	L	L	E	D	I	T
S	T	R	O	M		C	E	L	L	U	L	O	S	E
H	E	S	S	E		K	N	E	E	P	A	N	T	S

T	A	S	T	E	S	B	A	D	█	D	O	D	G	E
S	E	W	E	R	L	I	N	E	█	O	N	E	A	M
E	N	E	R	G	Y	B	A	R	█	G	U	M	U	P
T	E	A	M	O	█	█	K	I	N	G	S	I	Z	E
S	I	T	S	█	F	R	I	D	A	Y	█	J	E	R
E	D	Y	█	R	O	O	N	E	Y	█	P	O	P	O
█	█	B	U	T	T	S	█	█	L	E	H	A	R	█
F	A	C	E	B	O	O	K	F	R	I	E	N	D	S
L	I	O	N	S	█	Y	E	A	R	N	█	█	█	█
A	R	N	E	█	T	O	W	A	G	E	█	J	A	Y
P	F	C	█	C	E	D	A	R	S	█	M	E	R	E
J	O	E	C	A	M	E	L	█	█	B	A	R	C	A
A	R	D	O	R	█	S	K	I	P	A	R	K	A	S
C	C	E	L	L	█	S	E	V	E	N	C	E	N	T
K	E	S	E	Y	█	A	R	E	A	C	O	D	E	S

C	P	L	█	S	C	O	W	L	E	D	█	B	R	O
U	R	I	█	E	A	R	H	O	L	E	█	O	E	R
T	A	P	P	A	N	Z	E	E	B	R	I	D	G	E
L	I	B	A	T	I	O	N	B	E	A	R	E	R	S
E	R	A	T	O	█	█	█	T	U	G	A	T	█	█
T	I	L	T	█	S	N	O	O	P	█	L	A	D	E
S	E	M	I	S	O	F	T	C	H	E	E	S	E	S
█	█	█	A	L	L	H	A	I	L	█	█	█	█	█
I	D	O	N	T	F	E	E	L	L	I	K	E	I	T
N	E	V	A	█	A	R	R	A	S	█	E	L	M	O
S	P	A	N	G	█	█	█	█	C	R	A	I	G	█
E	A	R	T	H	S	H	A	T	T	E	R	I	N	G
A	R	I	Z	O	N	A	C	A	R	D	I	N	A	L
M	T	A	█	S	O	L	A	R	I	A	█	E	W	E
S	S	N	█	T	W	O	D	O	O	R	█	S	E	D

Y	A	H	E	A	R	D	■	F	R	A	I	D	S	O
O	P	E	N	B	A	R	■	T	E	R	R	E	L	L
G	E	L	C	A	P	S	■	C	A	C	K	L	E	D
I	S	L	A	■	G	E	O	■	C	O	S	T	A	S
■	■	S	C	R	U	N	C	H	■	■	A	Z	O	
F	I	R	E	H	O	S	E	S	■	A	A	H	E	D
A	G	O	■	R	U	S	S	I	A	N	M	O	B	■
B	E	D	H	O	P	■	■	S	I	O	U	A	N	
■	T	E	A	M	S	P	O	R	T	S	■	S	L	Y
D	I	O	D	E	■	T	H	E	R	E	B	E	L	S
E	T	D	■	S	A	N	J	O	S	E	■	■	■	
B	O	R	A	G	E	■	O	O	N	■	N	A	P	E
A	K	I	H	I	T	O	■	I	A	S	I	M	O	V
S	A	V	A	L	A	S	■	N	U	T	C	A	S	E
E	Y	E	B	A	T	H	■	S	T	P	E	T	E	R

C	O	S	M	O	S	■	A	G	T	■	E	L	B	A
S	C	H	U	S	S	■	G	O	A	L	L	O	U	T
H	U	R	L	E	R	■	A	T	T	I	T	U	D	E
A	L	O	T	■	W	R	O	T	E	O	N	■	■	
R	A	V	I	O	L	I	■	Y	O	U	N	G	E	R
P	R	E	T	Z	E	L	L	O	O	P	■	E	S	A
■	■	A	M	A	D	E	U	S	■	C	R	A	M	
E	L	I	S	A	■	C	A	R	■	G	A	S	U	P
L	A	R	K	■	W	A	R	R	I	O	R	■	■	
A	M	I	■	F	O	R	Y	O	U	R	L	O	V	E
L	A	S	S	O	E	D	■	O	D	E	S	S	A	N
■	■	H	O	T	I	T	E	M	■	A	M	I	D	
I	M	A	L	O	S	E	R	■	B	E	G	O	N	E
T	A	L	I	S	M	A	N	■	E	R	A	S	E	R
S	P	E	D	■	E	M	O	■	D	I	N	E	R	S

M	A	Y	O	■	A	S	T	I	■	S	W	E	P	T
E	L	A	M	■	C	H	I	N	C	H	I	L	L	A
D	O	W	N	G	O	E	S	F	R	A	Z	I	E	R
S	E	N	I	O	R	S	■	A	U	G	■	Z	A	P
■	■	P	U	N	■	O	L	D	G	O	A	T	S	■
S	T	A	R	R	■	B	O	L	E	Y	N	■	■	■
T	O	L	E	D	O	O	H	I	O	■	C	O	S	A
D	I	S	S	E	N	T	■	B	I	A	L	I	E	S
S	L	O	E	■	A	T	A	L	L	C	O	S	T	S
■	■	N	E	L	L	I	E	■	C	U	E	I	N	■
A	S	H	T	R	E	E	S	■	T	O	D	■	■	■
T	E	A	■	O	A	S	■	T	U	R	N	S	T	O
B	R	I	T	I	S	H	S	O	L	D	I	E	R	S
A	R	T	I	C	H	O	K	E	S	■	N	A	I	L
R	A	I	T	A	■	P	A	S	A	■	E	L	M	O

G	E	T	S	R	E	A	L	■	■	M	O	V	I	E
A	L	I	T	A	L	I	A	■	W	I	N	O	N	A
S	T	M	O	R	I	T	Z	■	O	C	U	L	A	R
J	O	E	P	E	S	C	I	■	W	A	S	A	B	I
E	R	L	■	■	■	H	O	O	F	■	■	T	I	N
T	O	Y	O	T	A	■	■	P	A	U	S	I	N	G
■	■	■	P	O	S	T	E	R	C	H	I	L	D	■
■	■	S	E	A	C	R	E	A	T	U	R	E	■	■
■	■	J	E	R	S	E	Y	S	H	O	R	E	■	■
M	U	L	A	T	T	O	■	■	R	U	N	D	M	C
I	L	E	■	■	I	N	S	T	■	■	O	O	O	■
R	I	C	R	A	C	■	T	E	N	S	P	O	T	S
R	A	T	E	D	A	■	A	T	O	M	I	Z	E	S
O	N	E	N	I	L	■	L	O	V	E	B	I	T	E
R	A	D	O	N	■	■	K	N	O	W	B	E	S	T

61

A	C	I	D	I	C	■	C	H	A	C	H	I	N	G
S	U	N	O	C	O	■	A	I	W	E	I	W	E	I
P	L	A	N	A	R	■	B	E	A	N	T	O	W	N
■	W	E	N	D	■	B	R	I	T	■	J	A	G	■
A	R	O	A	R	■	R	I	O	T	■	T	I	G	E
C	A	R	N	E	G	I	E	■	T	A	M	E	R	■
T	O	D	D	L	E	S	■	S	I	R	K	A	Y	■
■	■	D	A	N	K	■	C	L	U	E	■	■	■	■
■	K	N	O	T	T	Y	■	R	E	S	T	A	T	E
K	R	O	N	E	■	S	I	X	T	H	M	A	N	■
O	I	S	E	■	A	S	A	P	■	N	E	R	D	S
W	S	W	■	S	E	T	I	■	S	O	F	A	■	■
T	H	E	C	L	O	U	D	■	L	O	A	D	E	D
O	N	A	H	U	N	C	H	■	I	N	L	I	N	E
W	A	T	E	R	S	K	I	■	M	E	L	O	D	Y

62

M	A	N	E	N	O	U	G	H	■	B	A	N	G	S
O	N	O	N	E	K	N	E	E	■	U	R	I	A	H
V	E	A	L	O	S	C	A	R	■	T	I	E	T	O
E	T	H	A	N	■	R	E	N	T	A	C	O	P	■
■	■	R	S	V	P	■	E	N	D	E	R	S	■	■
S	M	O	G	■	A	R	T	I	S	A	N	■	■	■
O	R	W	E	L	L	I	A	N	■	K	E	B	A	B
T	S	E	■	U	S	E	R	F	E	E	■	R	C	A
S	C	R	U	B	■	R	O	A	L	D	D	A	H	L
■	■	T	R	U	S	T	M	E	■	E	Y	E	D	■
S	A	V	O	I	R	■	Y	E	S	T	■	■	■	■
C	L	I	P	C	L	O	P	■	O	E	S	T	E	■
A	T	R	I	A	■	T	U	R	D	U	C	K	E	N
R	E	G	A	N	■	B	L	U	E	S	T	A	T	E
F	R	O	N	T	■	S	P	Y	M	A	S	T	E	R

G	A	N	G	N	A	M		L	E	A	P	S	A	T
A	M	E	R	I	C	A		O	I	L	R	I	C	H
S	O	M	E	T	H	I	N	G	S	F	I	S	H	Y
O	R	E		E	D	Y	S		A	S	T	E	R	
H	O	S			E	S	O	S		M	I	S	O	
O	S	I	S		O	N	E	U	P	S		N	O	I
L	O	S	E	R	S			T	A	I	L	E	N	D
			R	O	C			N	G	O				
A	L	L	T	H	A	T		S	O	N	N	E	T	S
L	E	E		E	R	I	T	U		I	N	R	E	
A	T	A	N		S	T	A	N			C	A	D	
M	I	N	E	D		R	U	B	E		A	L	I	A
O	N	T	H	E	W	A	T	E	R	F	R	O	N	T
D	O	O	R	M	A	T		L	O	O	K	S	E	E
E	N	S	U	I	T	E		T	O	P	S	E	E	D

K	F	C		D	E	L	S			S	W	A	M	P
N	A	U	T	I	L	U	S		S	H	A	V	E	S
A	L	B	A	N	I	A	N		P	I	T	O	N	S
P	L	A	T	E	A	U		P	I	N	E	N	U	T
S	A	N	T	A	S		D	E	T	E	R			
A	S	C	O	T		G	I	N	S	B	E	R	G	
C	L	I	O		V	O	O	D	O	O	D	O	L	L
K	E	G		L	A	S	C	A	U	X		B	A	A
S	E	A	S	E	R	P	E	N	T		H	E	S	S
	P	R	I	C	I	E	S	T		F	I	R	S	T
		S	T	A	L	E		C	A	N	T	O	S	
H	O	T	T	U	B	S		T	A	N	G	E	N	T
A	W	H	I	R	L		C	O	R	D	E	L	I	A
R	O	O	N	E	Y		I	M	P	O	S	E	O	N
M	E	M	E	S		D	E	E	M		E	N	D	

Z	A	Z	U		P	C	B	S		B	A	B	K	A
S	L	I	M		E	R	L	E		A	P	L	A	N
A	P	P	L	E	P	I	E	S		N	O	U	R	I
	C	A	R	I	B	B	E	A	N	S	E	A		
A	M	O	U	N	T	S			R	E	T	T	O	N
R	E	D	T	E	A		H	A	I	R	L	I	K	E
C	H	E	S	S		M	O	C	S		E	T	E	S
			T	I	R	A	D	E	S					
A	T	M	S		M	E	R	C		H	A	J	J	I
R	H	A	P	S	O	D	Y		A	I	L	E	E	N
R	E	L	I	E	F		R	A	N	L	A	T	E	
	P	A	C	I	F	I	C	O	C	E	A	N		
T	I	R	E	S		S	U	P	E	R	G	L	U	E
I	L	I	U	M		A	B	E	L		E	U	R	O
C	L	A	P	S		K	A	R	L		S	C	I	S

G	Y	P	S	Y	J	A	Z	Z		E	P	C	O	T
N	O	T	Y	O	U	T	O	O		P	L	U	T	O
A	H	A	M	O	M	E	N	T		O	A	T	E	S
T	E	R	M		P	A	K		U	N	S	U	R	E
S	A	M	E	S		M	S	O	L	Y	M	P	I	A
	V	I	T	U	S		G	U	M	S				
D	E	G	R	E	E	M	I	L	L	S		M	C	S
S	H	A	Y		M	E	D	E	A		S	A	H	L
T	O	N		D	I	D	I	S	T	U	T	T	E	R
		M	E	T	A		E	N	A	T	E			
B	E	E	R	B	E	L	L	Y		D	R	D	R	E
A	I	R	B	U	S		I	A	N		W	A	I	L
H	E	A	L	S		W	A	R	C	R	I	M	E	S
T	I	T	U	S		I	N	D	I	S	P	O	S	E
S	O	O	E	Y		M	E	S	S	T	E	N	T	S

B	B	Q	S	A	N	D	W	I	C	H		H	E	H
S	A	U	D	I	A	R	A	B	I	A		I	N	O
T	R	A	I	N	S	I	G	N	A	L		B	A	M
A	H	I		G	A	V	E			T	E	A	M	O
R	O	L	L	E		E	W	E	S		D	C	O	N
S	P	A	Y		F	R	A	N	K	G	E	H	R	Y
	S	T	E	A	L		R	O	Y	A	L	I	S	M
			M	I	L		S	L	R					
I	T	S	M	A	G	I	C		I	P	A	D	S	
D	E	E	P	T	H	R	O	A	T		A	R	T	Y
C	A	T	E		T	R	A	P		P	H	Y	L	A
A	M	I	G	A		R	A	G	A		F	U	N	
R	U	N		B	L	I	S	T	E	R	P	A	C	K
D	S	T		L	A	K	E	O	N	T	A	R	I	O
S	A	O		E	Z	E	R	W	E	I	Z	M	A	N

A	M	B	I	T		F	O	U	L		B	E	D	S
P	E	A	C	E		A	D	Z	E		A	R	I	A
E	A	C	H	C	L	U	E	I	N		P	S	S	T
X	T	C		S	A	C			T	A	T	A	M	I
	F	A	D		P	E	P	S		S	I	T	A	R
E	R	R	O	L		T	H	E	P	U	Z	Z	L	E
S	E	A	G	O	D		A	T	O	N	E			
P	E	T		S	U	L	L	I	E	D		S	T	Y
			M	E	D	E	A		T	E	M	P	E	R
I	S	M	I	S	S	I	N	G		R	O	L	E	S
Q	U	A	S	I		A	X	O	N		B	I	T	
T	I	N	C	T	S			A	A	A		T	E	A
E	T	T	U		T	H	E	L	E	T	T	E	R	N
S	O	R	E		A	U	D	I		O	W	N	E	D
T	R	A	S		T	R	U	E		P	A	D	D	Y

69

C	R	O	W	D	S	O	U	R	C	E		A	L	E
H	O	N	O	R	S	Y	S	T	E	M		L	A	X
I	N	A	N	U	T	S	H	E	L	L		O	R	C
R	E	G		M	A	T	E		L	E	B	E	A	U
P	L	E	B		R	E	R	I		N	E	V	I	S
S	Y	R	U	P		R	I	C	O		B	E	D	E
		C	A	P		N	E	D	R	O	R	E	M
R	A	C	H	A	E	L		T	O	S	P	A	R	E
E	D	H	A	R	R	I	S		M	V	P			
A	D	E	N		M	A	C	Y		P	E	T	I	T
R	I	C	A	N		T	H	A	R		D	A	M	E
E	T	H	N	O	S		M	M	I	V		I	G	A
X	I	N		M	A	R	I	A	C	A	L	L	A	S
I	V	Y		A	N	D	T	H	E	N	S	O	M	E
T	E	A		R	E	S	T	A	S	S	U	R	E	D

70

L	O	M	B	A	R	D		G	O	G	O	B	A	R
A	Z	O	B	L	U	E		O	V	E	R	A	T	E
Z	Z	Z	Q	U	I	L		G	A	N	G	S	T	A
A	F	I		I	N	T	E	G	R	A		S	I	D
R	E	L	Y		G	O	L	L	Y		M	A	M	E
U	S	L	A	W		I	K	E		B	A	L	E	R
S	T	A	S	H	E	D		S	E	E	R	E	S	S
		M	I	X				D	I	Y				
F	I	T	I	N	T	O		J	U	N	K	A	R	T
U	P	O	N	E		N	A	E		G	A	T	O	R
J	A	N	E		P	A	P	A	S		Y	O	G	I
I	D	E		A	L	D	E	N	T	E		M	A	P
T	A	L	A	R	I	A		A	O	L	M	A	I	L
S	P	O	N	G	E	R		R	O	S	A	N	N	E
U	P	C	C	O	D	E		P	L	A	Y	T	E	X

O	L	D	A	G	E	P	E	N	S	I	O	N	E	R
R	E	E	D	U	C	A	T	I	O	N	C	A	M	P
R	A	C	E	T	O	T	H	E	B	O	T	T	O	M
■	V	O	S	S	■	■	K	E	N	S	■	■	■	■
W	E	N	T	■	F	E	A	R	■	■	H	M	O	
A	S	S	E	T	A	L	L	O	C	A	T	I	O	N
I	T	T	■	O	Z	M	A	■	I	S	O	L	D	E
T	O	R	I	N	O	■	■	C	A	P	L	E	T	
I	D	U	N	N	O	■	R	O	A	M	■	B	R	O
N	I	C	K	E	L	A	N	D	D	I	M	I	N	G
G	E	T	■	■	D	A	D	A	■	A	L	D	O	
■	■	C	H	A	W	■	■	P	O	L	A	■		
P	A	T	R	O	N	A	G	E	H	I	R	I	N	G
G	R	E	A	T	G	R	A	N	D	N	I	E	C	E
S	T	E	M	L	E	S	S	G	L	A	S	S	E	S

C	H	I	C	K	F	I	L	A	■	M	Y	O	P	E
R	A	D	I	O	E	D	I	T	■	A	E	R	I	E
O	N	E	A	N	D	A	L	L	■	G	A	S	S	Y
A	G	E	■	Y	E	H	■	■	E	N	R	I	C	O
K	O	F	I	■	R	O	A	D	R	U	N	N	E	R
E	V	I	N	C	E	■	L	O	O	M	■	O	S	E
D	E	X	T	E	R	■	A	S	S	O	C	■		
■	R	E	E	L	■	G	M	T	■	P	I	N	G	■
		R	E	T	R	O	■	P	U	R	E	E	S	
O	T	O	■	R	E	E	D	■	E	S	C	O	R	T
P	I	N	K	Y	S	W	E	A	R	■	A	L	T	A
E	N	L	I	S	T	■	■	B	S	A	■	O	R	I
R	H	I	N	E	■	S	Q	U	I	R	T	G	U	N
A	A	N	D	E	■	P	U	T	S	A	S	I	D	E
S	T	E	A	D	■	F	A	S	T	P	A	C	E	D

S	T	A	D	I	U	M	R	O	C	K	■	D	I	R
I	M	O	U	T	T	A	H	E	R	E	■	E	N	O
T	A	K	E	S	T	H	E	R	A	P	■	A	D	M
U	N	I	■	C	E	R	A	■	Y	T	T	R	I	A
■	■	B	O	R	E	■	G	O	F	I	R	S	T	■
P	H	O	T	O	S	■	B	E	N	I	C	E	T	O
H	O	V	E	L	■	M	A	N	E	T	■	A	I	M
O	W	E	N	■	N	A	K	E	D	■	E	D	N	A
N	O	R	■	B	O	X	E	S	■	E	L	E	C	T
E	N	S	N	A	R	E	D	■	Q	U	A	R	T	O
D	E	T	E	C	T	S	■	F	U	R	L	■	■	■
H	A	R	R	A	H	■	C	L	I	O	■	D	V	D
O	R	E	■	R	E	T	A	I	L	P	R	I	C	E
M	T	S	■	D	R	I	V	E	T	O	W	O	R	K
E	H	S	■	I	N	T	E	R	S	P	E	R	S	E

A	D	E	P	T	■	C	O	L	U	M	N	I	S	T
T	O	S	E	A	■	P	R	O	N	O	U	N	C	E
T	W	O	A	M	■	L	E	T	T	E	R	B	O	X
A	N	T	H	E	M	■	■	I	N	S	E	R	T	■
C	H	E	E	S	E	B	A	L	L	■	I	T	E	M
K	E	R	N	■	S	I	N	E	■	S	N	A	R	E
E	R	I	S	■	C	O	A	T	I	N	G	■	■	■
D	E	C	■	B	A	D	G	I	R	L	■	C	A	T
■	■	C	O	L	O	R	T	V	■	C	H	I	A	■
I	M	H	I	P	■	M	A	G	I	■	B	E	R	G
N	O	U	N	■	L	E	M	O	N	G	R	A	S	S
C	O	M	E	L	Y	■	■	G	R	A	P	P	A	■
I	N	A	M	O	R	A	T	A	■	I	D	E	A	L
T	E	N	A	C	I	O	U	S	■	M	I	N	C	E
E	Y	E	S	O	C	K	E	T	■	M	O	S	E	S

H	U	M	B	L	E	B	R	A	G		A	R	C	S
I	N	A	D	E	Q	U	A	T	E		T	E	L	E
L	E	N	A	D	U	N	H	A	M		E	L	E	A
L	A	D	Y		A	D	M	S		P	I	L	A	F
T	R	A		I	L	L		L	L	A	N	E	R	O
O	T	T	E	R		E	M	A	I	L		N	E	O
P	H	E	N	O	M		O	N	R	E	C	O	R	D
			O	N	E	P	O	T	A	T	O			
P	O	L	L	S	T	E	R		S	T	E	E	P	S
A	R	A		I	R	I	S	H		E	N	T	R	E
S	L	U	M	D	O	G		O	B	S		V	O	X
S	A	T	I	E		N	A	M	E		B	O	O	P
I	N	N	S		S	O	C	I	A	L	L	I	F	E
O	D	E	S		W	I	N	E	C	O	O	L	E	R
N	O	R	M		F	R	E	S	H	S	T	A	R	T

S	T	R	E	A	K	S			L	E	A	D	U	P
Q	U	I	R	R	E	L	L		A	N	G	I	N	A
U	N	D	E	R	D	O	G		S	T	R	E	W	N
A	N	D		A	S	P	E	C	T	R	A	T	I	O
D	E	L	T	S		L	O	S	E		S	E	P	
S	L	E	W		A	P	E	X		P	O	L	L	
			O	P	T	I	C		S	O	D	D	Y	
	P	R	O	J	E	C	T	R	U	N	W	A	Y	
C	L	A	U	S		R	I	F	L	E				
L	A	I	T		C	O	M	O		R	A	V	E	
A	Y	N		S	H	U	N		A	S	T	I	N	
M	A	G	I	C	T	R	I	C	K	S		H	O	F
A	R	E	N	O	T		C	O	C	A	C	O	L	A
T	E	A	R	U	P		S	T	U	N	T	M	A	N
O	A	R	E	R	S			S	P	A	R	E	S	T

P	A	R	I	S		S	H	A	G		S	A	A	B
A	G	E	N	T		P	I	P	E		T	R	I	O
B	I	N	G	O	N	I	G	H	T		A	G	R	A
S	L	E	E	P	E	R	H	I	T		B	O	H	R
T	E	E		W	I	S	D	O	M		N	O	D	
	B	U	S	T				O	H	A	R	E		
	B	U	M	M	I	N	G	A	R	O	U	N	D	
C	A	R	P	E	N	T	E	R	A	N	T	S		
R	O	C	K	I	N	G	H	O	R	S	E	S		
O	A	K	E	N			L	A	S	S				
B	L	T		G	I	B	S	O	N		P	J	S	
O	M	A	N		D	R	A	G	G	E	D	O	U	T
T	I	L	E		L	O	U	I	E	L	O	U	I	E
I	N	K	S		E	O	N	S		S	I	N	C	E
C	E	S	T		S	K	A	T	E	N	D	E	D	

I	B	E	F	O	R	E	E		F	L	U	K	E
D	E	L	A	W	A	R	E		J	O	I	N	E	D
S	E	A	L	S	K	I	N		O	U	T	I	N	G
A	B	B	A		E	C	I	G	A	R	E	T	T	E
Y	E	O		K	E	E	N							
	R	E	B	S		T	R	U		M	B	A	
I	C	A	L	L	E	M	A	S	I	S	E	E	E	M
N	A	T	I	O	N	A	L	A	V	E	R	A	G	E
B	R	E	A	K	E	R	O	N	E	N	I	N	E	R
I	N	O	N	E	S	S	P	A	R	E	T	I	M	E
G	E	N		S	C	H		S	T	U	N			
	E	A	S	T			G	P	S					
T	O	P	T	E	N	L	I	S	T		P	L	I	E
A	R	A	B	I	C		E	A	R	P	I	E	C	E
W	E	C	A	R	E		G	R	O	A	N	S	A	T
S	N	A	R	E		E	S	P	R	E	S	S	O	

A	R	S	O	N	I	S	T	S	■	D	C	C	A	B
N	O	T	S	O	F	A	S	T	■	E	A	R	L	E
G	O	A	T	R	O	D	E	O	■	A	L	A	R	M
L	T	D	■	I	L	L	T	R	A	D	E	Y	O	U
E	R	I	N	■	D	O	S	E	S	■	B	O	S	S
R	O	U	E	N	■	T	E	S	T	Y	■	L	E	E
S	T	M	A	R	K	■	S	U	R	E	H	A	N	D
■	■	M	O	H	S	■	P	O	N	E	■	■		
D	I	M	E	T	A	P	P	■	S	T	A	S	I	S
U	N	O	■	C	L	A	R	O	■	E	R	N	S	T
N	A	P	A	■	I	C	O	N	S	■	T	A	D	A
A	L	P	H	A	F	E	M	A	L	E	■	R	U	S
W	I	E	S	T	■	B	O	J	A	N	G	L	E	S
A	N	T	I	C	■	A	T	A	N	Y	R	A	T	E
Y	E	S	N	O	■	R	E	G	G	A	E	T	O	N

B	R	O	M	A	N	C	E	■	R	I	B	A	L	D
E	A	S	Y	P	O	U	R	■	E	C	O	C	A	R
N	T	H	P	O	W	E	R	■	L	A	O	T	Z	U
T	E	A	R	G	A	S	■	D	I	N	K	I	E	R
■	■	E	E	R	■	D	U	G	■	I	D	Y		
S	A	U	C	E	■	V	A	R	I	E	D	■	■	
A	G	N	I	■	M	A	R	I	O	N	E	T	T	E
G	O	T	O	R	A	C	K	A	N	D	R	U	I	N
A	B	O	U	T	T	U	R	N	S	■	N	E	M	O
■	■	S	E	R	I	E	S	■	W	I	S	E	S	
R	I	B	■	I	T	D	■	S	H	E	■	■		
A	S	A	G	R	A	Y	■	S	T	I	R	R	E	R
M	I	D	A	I	R	■	D	I	E	T	C	O	K	E
B	A	L	Z	A	C	■	A	N	N	E	R	I	C	E
O	H	Y	E	A	H	■	G	E	T	R	I	D	O	F

81

```
. F R E E W A Y . . D E A D
. P L E A S E D O . P A N T Y
T R O U S S E A U . A R I S E
R O A S T E D . C R U I S E R
O P T I O N . C H O C U L A .
U M I N N . C H E M I S E . .
P A N G . . C H I A N T I . .
E N G . . C H A N T E Y . R D S
. . . C H U T N E Y . B E E T
. . C H A R T E D . P R I M A
. C H A R R E D . M O A N E D
W A R R I O R . B A L I H A I
A P O L O . B A R C E L O N A
C O M E T . O V E R A L L S .
O N E S . X E R O X E D .
```

82

```
A T W H O L E S A L E . S O D
B R E A K I N G B A D . E P A
B A B Y S I T T E R S . M E W
E V E S . . E S T E E M I N G
Y E R . W A R . D L I S T .
. . . S O C . E C O . S W A B
A F T E R M A T H . S H E B A
G R E A S E T H E W H E E L S
H O R S E . M A T U R A T E S
A G R A . T E N . S E R . .
. M A L T A . . T S K . K I P
B A R T E N D E R . T A R A
A R I . A D I M E A D O Z E N
I C U . K E V I N D U R A N T
O H M . S M A R T P H O N E S
```

M	O	B	I	L	E	A	P	P	■	W	A	I	T	E
O	N	O	N	E	S	W	A	Y	■	A	M	A	H	L
S	E	E	N	I	T	A	L	L	■	D	O	M	E	D
T	A	R	■	A	G	E	E	■	■	D	R	A	K	E
■	■	B	A	T	■	■	S	A	L	A	M	I	S	■
S	T	R	O	B	E	S	■	R	E	L	E	N	T	■
T	H	I	N	A	S	A	R	E	E	D	■	R	G	S
R	E	T	D	■	M	A	R	■	F	I	D	O	■
U	M	A	■	F	A	S	H	I	O	N	I	C	O	N
C	O	M	S	A	T	■	S	T	R	E	A	M	S
K	N	O	T	T	E	D	■	R	A	F	■	■	■
D	I	R	A	C	■	Y	O	G	A	■	D	D	T
U	T	E	R	I	■	A	L	A	N	M	O	O	R	E
M	O	N	E	T	■	D	I	E	T	S	O	D	A	S
B	R	O	D	Y	■	S	O	L	O	S	H	O	T	S

M	E	S	S	K	I	T	S	■	C	R	O	T	C	H
A	G	E	L	I	M	I	T	■	L	A	U	R	I	E
N	O	S	E	C	O	N	E	■	A	S	T	U	T	E
■	S	E	E	K	■	A	P	P	S	■	S	T	E	P
■	■	■	P	S	Y	C	H	O	P	A	T	H	■	■
A	W	L	■	T	U	T	E	E	■	U	R	I	A	H
V	I	A	■	A	M	I	N	■	S	T	I	N	G	O
A	L	S	O	R	A	N	■	C	O	O	P	E	R	S
S	C	E	N	T	S	■	C	A	L	C	■	S	E	E
T	O	R	T	E	■	R	O	L	E	O	■	S	E	A
■	D	I	R	T	Y	H	A	R	R	Y	■	■
C	R	I	P	■	T	E	E	M	■	R	A	F	A
H	U	S	T	L	E	■	R	A	R	E	B	I	R	D
A	S	C	O	T	S	■	E	R	I	C	B	A	N	A
D	E	S	E	R	T	■	D	I	C	T	A	T	E	D

O	R	A	L	E	X	A	M	S	■	C	R	A	S	S
R	E	D	C	A	R	P	E	T	■	Z	I	P	U	P
G	R	A	D	U	A	T	E	D	■	A	T	A	R	I
C	O	M	S	■	Y	E	T	■	X	R	A	T	E	D
H	U	B	■	A	S	S	E	N	T	S	■	H	O	E
A	T	E	S	T	■	T	R	E	E	■	S	Y	F	Y
R	E	D	E	E	M	■	S	E	R	T	A	■	■	■
T	S	E	L	I	O	T	■	T	R	O	U	P	E	S
■	■	E	N	N	I	S	■	A	N	D	A	L	E	■
J	A	W	S	■	I	N	K	S	■	T	I	M	I	D
U	Z	O	■	L	E	T	I	T	G	O	■	P	T	A
L	A	N	C	E	S	■	S	E	A	■	F	L	I	T
E	L	T	O	N	■	T	U	R	N	L	O	O	S	E
P	E	O	N	Y	■	G	I	N	J	O	I	N	T	S
S	A	N	K	A	■	I	T	S	A	B	L	A	S	T

T	R	A	P	■	M	M	X	L	■	X	T	I	N	A
R	A	R	E	■	A	I	D	E	■	M	O	R	E	S
I	N	T	R	A	N	S	I	T	■	A	M	E	N	S
X	I	S	■	L	I	O	N	S	■	R	E	N	E	E
■	■	■	C	P	A	S	■	P	O	K	I	E	S	T
S	T	R	O	H	S	■	O	A	T	S	■	■	■	■
K	U	A	L	A	■	I	R	R	I	T	A	T	E	S
I	D	I	D	N	T	C	A	T	C	H	T	H	A	T
S	E	N	S	U	A	L	L	Y	■	E	R	A	S	E
■	■	■	M	O	A	B	■	B	S	I	D	E	S	■
P	I	E	J	E	S	U	■	P	E	P	A	■	■	■
A	N	D	O	R	■	D	R	A	N	O	■	O	E	R
R	A	D	I	I	■	I	O	N	S	T	O	R	M	S
E	P	I	S	C	■	U	P	D	O	■	A	C	T	V
S	T	E	T	S	■	S	E	A	N	■	R	A	S	P

R	O	C	K	B	A	N	D	S	■	■	J	A	C	K
W	H	A	L	E	B	O	A	T	■	T	O	P	O	L
A	D	V	I	S	A	B	L	E	■	S	E	P	I	A
N	E	O	N	S	■	R	A	W	T	A	L	E	N	T
D	A	R	K	■	R	A	I	S	E	■	■	T	A	C
A	R	T	■	L	E	I	■	■	A	W	E	I	G	H
■	■	■	C	O	G	N	O	S	C	E	N	T	E	■
■	■	B	U	R	I	E	D	A	L	I	V	E	■	■
■	H	O	R	R	O	R	S	T	O	R	Y	■	■	■
L	O	O	S	E	N	■	E	T	S	■	C	D	S	■
A	P	B	■	A	M	I	S	H	■	T	R	E	E	■
M	E	T	A	L	L	I	C	A	■	K	O	A	L	A
O	F	U	S	E	■	M	O	U	S	E	O	V	E	R
N	O	B	I	S	■	I	N	C	A	R	N	A	T	E
T	R	E	S	■	■	C	O	E	X	I	S	T	E	D

E	L	A	T	E	■	S	C	I	F	I	■	C	O	L	O	R
L	E	T	O	N	■	A	A	R	O	N	■	I	N	A	N	E
B	A	T	T	L	E	F	I	E	L	D	■	C	O	S	T	S
O	P	I	E	■	R	E	M	■	D	E	L	E	■	H	O	T
W	A	R	■	L	A	R	A	M	■	P	U	R	E	■	■	■
S	T	E	N	O	S	■	N	E	U	T	R	O	G	E	N	A
■	■	■	E	L	E	M	■	A	S	H	E	■	O	V	E	R
M	A	R	T	I	■	T	A	T	A	■	R	E	T	I	L	E
I	D	E	S	T	■	M	R	B	I	G	■	V	I	L	L	A
N	O	M	A	A	M	■	M	A	N	Y	■	E	S	S	E	S
O	R	A	L	■	O	N	E	L	■	P	E	R	T	■	■	■
R	E	P	E	A	T	E	D	L	Y	■	A	L	S	A	C	E
■	■	S	N	O	W	■	S	A	L	T	Y	■	R	A	D	■
S	P	F	■	G	R	A	F	■	S	O	U	■	C	A	N	I
P	L	A	C	E	■	G	R	O	S	S	P	R	O	F	I	T
R	I	V	A	L	■	E	E	R	I	E	■	B	E	A	N	O
Y	E	A	R	S	■	R	E	A	R	S	■	I	N	T	E	R

89

A	N	G	S	T	■	D	E	M	O	B	■	F	D	A
L	E	A	C	H	■	E	M	B	A	R	G	O	E	S
K	U	M	A	R	■	S	T	A	K	E	O	U	T	S
A	R	M	R	E	S	T	■	■	L	A	B	R	E	A
L	O	O	S	E	L	I	M	B	E	D	■	D	R	Y
I	N	N	■	F	I	N	E	L	Y	■	C	O	R	E
■	■	S	O	M	A	L	I	■	M	O	O	E	D	
■	B	U	L	L	E	T	I	N	B	O	A	R	D	■
W	I	P	E	D	■	I	N	D	E	N	T	■		
E	G	A	D	■	T	O	D	A	T	E	■	C	B	S
B	B	C	■	P	E	N	A	L	T	Y	S	H	O	T
F	U	R	M	A	N	■	■	L	E	C	T	U	R	E
O	C	E	A	N	S	I	D	E	■	L	O	R	N	E
O	K	E	Y	D	O	K	E	Y	■	I	N	N	E	R
T	S	K	■	A	R	E	A	S	■	P	E	S	O	S

90

E	A	R	T	H	R	I	S	E	■	B	A	L	S	A
B	I	O	W	E	A	P	O	N	■	A	M	A	T	I
B	L	O	O	M	B	E	R	G	■	S	O	B	E	R
T	E	T	■	P	A	C	T	■	■	R	A	P	T	
I	R	O	N	■	T	A	I	L	■	G	A	M	M	A
D	O	U	S	E	■	C	E	R	E	A	L	B	O	X
E	N	T	E	R	S	■	S	O	L	S	■	A	M	I
■	C	O	M	B	■	N	A	T	S	■				
O	R	S	■	T	O	O	L	■	L	A	H	O	R	E
B	A	T	S	I	G	N	A	L	■	X	E	N	O	N
L	Y	R	I	C	■	Y	S	E	R	■	B	E	A	M
I	G	E	R	■	S	N	O	W	■	I	D	A		
Q	U	A	R	K	■	P	O	O	L	R	O	O	M	S
U	N	M	E	T	■	P	E	R	F	E	C	T	A	S
E	S	S	E	S	■	G	R	E	E	N	T	A	P	E

91

A	P	P			S	C	I	F	I			J	E	B
T	O	O		R	O	A	M	O	F	F		A	R	R
A	W	L		E	N	D	P	O	S	T		M	E	A
L	E	O	V	I	I	I		T	A	C	T	I	C	S
E	R	T	E		A	L	L	B	Y		W	E	T	S
	P	E	S	T		L	O	A		S	I	L	O	
	C	A	P	I	T	A	L	L	E	T	T	E	R	
	M	U	S	I	C	A	L	N	O	T	E			
	C	H	E	S	S	M	O	V	E					
	D	E	C	A	D	E		A	L	E	R	T	S	
N	O	T	I		V	I	S			S	H	A	H	
E	G	O		P	R	I	N	C	E	S		A	V	E
G	E	N	E	R	A	L	H	O	S	P	I	T	A	L
R	A	I	S	E	D	L	E	T	T	E	R	I	N	G
O	R	C	A	S		E	R	S		C	E	S	T	A

92

S	O	T	H	A	T	S	I	T		I	B	M	P	C
K	N	E	E	P	A	T	C	H		N	O	O	I	L
A	P	P	L	E	T	R	E	E		F	R	O	Z	E
T	O	I	L	S		A	F	F	L	U	E	N	Z	A
E	T	D		P	I	L	E	O	N		W	A	N	
		S	E	A	G	O	D	S		T	A	P	S	
	W	H	A	T	T	H	E		Y	A	L	I	E	
T	O	O	F	A	S	T		C	L	O	C	K	E	D
A	R	L	E	S		B	O	O	H	I	S	S		
X	K	E	S		T	S	E	L	I	O	T			
C	H	I		M	U	T	T	O	N			G	M	C
H	O	N	E	Y	B	E	A	R		M	A	R	I	O
E	R	O	D	E		E	M	I	L	E	Z	O	L	A
A	S	N	E	R		L	A	S	T	M	O	V	E	S
T	E	E	N	S		E	X	T	R	O	V	E	R	T

93

J	O	N	E	S	I	N	G	■	A	I	R	B	U	S
E	M	O	T	I	C	O	N	■	P	R	O	U	S	T
R	E	D	S	A	U	C	E	■	E	A	S	T	E	R
K	A	S	E	M	■	L	I	P	■	N	I	T	R	E
I	R	A	Q	■	B	A	S	A	L	■	E	D	N	A
N	A	T	■	P	A	S	S	I	O	N	■	I	A	M
■	■	F	A	Y	S	■	N	B	A	G	A	M	E	■
H	E	L	E	N	A	■	■	S	C	A	L	E	D	■
O	P	E	N	E	R	A	■	A	T	R	Y	■	■	■
W	I	T	■	D	E	S	I	R	E	E	■	S	O	R
S	P	E	C	■	A	S	T	I	R	■	N	A	P	E
T	H	R	O	E	■	T	A	Z	■	M	A	X	E	S
H	A	R	A	S	S	■	L	O	C	A	V	O	R	E
A	N	I	T	A	S	■	I	N	D	I	A	N	A	N
T	Y	P	I	S	T	■	C	A	T	A	L	Y	S	T

94

F	O	S	H	I	Z	Z	L	E	■	K	N	O	W	S
E	X	C	U	S	E	Y	O	U	■	E	O	S	I	N
W	A	R	M	O	N	G	E	R	■	S	U	S	I	E
E	L	I	E	■	D	O	S	■	G	E	N	O	M	E
R	I	B	■	P	A	T	S	D	R	Y	■	B	O	Z
■	C	E	C	E	■	E	E	R	O	■	M	U	T	E
■	■	R	R	R	■	R	E	P	L	A	C	E	D	■
■	F	R	A	C	A	S	■	D	E	I	M	O	S	■
B	R	E	Z	H	N	E	V	■	S	T	E	■	■	■
A	I	D	E	■	C	R	A	N	■	H	T	T	P	■
R	E	D	■	R	I	O	L	O	B	O	■	A	F	B
S	N	I	P	E	D	■	E	S	L	■	T	R	I	O
E	D	W	I	N	■	D	R	O	I	D	R	A	Z	R
A	L	I	K	E	■	M	I	A	M	I	A	R	E	A
T	Y	P	E	E	■	Z	E	P	P	O	M	A	R	X

95

Grid 95:

M	A	W	■	■	S	T	E	A	M	S	■	S	E	T
A	D	O	S	■	H	A	R	L	E	Y	■	P	R	E
J	E	R	U	SALE	M	C	R	O	S	S	■	R	I	A
O	L	D	P	R	O	■	H	O	T	L	I	C	K	■
R	E	S	I	N	■	I	V	A	N	■	O	N	C	E
■	■	■	N	O	S	H	E	S	■	B	E	G	A	T
R	A	T	E	■	T	O	T	■	N	E	W	SALE	R	T
O	D	E	■	C	A	P	E	C	O	D	■	A	L	L
SALE	M	S	L	O	T	■	R	O	I	■	S	K	E	E
E	I	L	A	T	■	B	A	R	D	O	T	■	■	■
P	S	A	T	■	B	I	N	D	■	M	Y	L	A	R
A	S	C	E	T	I	C	■	■	R	A	M	A	D	A
R	I	O	■	B	L	A	C	K	F	R	I	D	A	Y
K	O	I	■	A	B	R	O	A	D	■	E	L	M	O
S	N	L	■	R	O	B	O	T	S	■	E	SALE	N	■

96

Grid 96:

A	D	M	I	R	E	S	■	H	O	G	W	A	S	H
D	E	I	C	E	R	S	■	A	G	R	E	E	T	O
M	A	L	A	Y	A	N	■	G	R	E	E	N	E	R
I	L	L	N	E	S	S	■	S	E	E	K	E	R	S
T	W	I	T	S	■	■	■	■	D	E	A	N	E	■
S	I	B	S	■	P	A	A	R	■	I	N	S	O	■
I	T	A	L	■	I	M	S	A	V	E	D	■	■	■
T	H	R	E	E	L	E	T	T	E	R	W	O	R	D
■	■	■	E	V	E	B	E	S	T	■	A	B	E	R
■	M	O	P	E	■	A	R	O	O	■	R	A	G	E
D	U	R	A	N	■	■	■	■	E	R	M	A	S	■
R	E	D	W	O	O	D	■	M	E	N	I	A	L	S
I	S	A	I	D	N	O	■	A	N	S	O	N	I	A
B	L	I	N	D	E	R	■	S	T	O	R	I	N	G
S	I	N	K	S	I	N	■	C	O	R	S	A	G	E

G	O	D	I	H	O	P	E	N	O	T		D	A	D
I	T	U	N	E	S	S	T	O	R	E		I	C	E
S	T	E	V	E	C	A	R	E	L	L		V	I	M
T	E	T	E		I	T	E		Y	E	S	I	D	O
	R	O	S	I	N	S			X	E	S	I	N	
		T	R	E		J	A	W		W	I	F	E	
	S	T	I	R		B	O	R	I	C		B	I	S
T	U	R	N	E	D	T	H	E	T	A	B	L	E	S
E	N	E		G	O	W	N	S		M	R	E	D	
A	T	E	N		C	O	Q		B	E	E			
D	A	R	I	N			O	B	L	A	S	T		
A	N	I	M	A	L		M	S	G		T	H	E	O
N	O	N		D	I	E	L	A	U	G	H	I	N	G
C	I	G		E	V	E	L	K	N	I	E	V	E	L
E	L	S		R	E	L	E	A	S	E	D	A	T	E

H	M	S	B	O	U	N	T	Y			S	L	I	M
E	Y	E	O	F	N	E	W	T		T	W	I	N	E
P	L	A	N	T	F	O	O	D		H	A	N	D	M
T	O	L	D		A	C	T		H	A	N	K	I	E
A	V	I	S		Z	O	O	L	A	N	D	E	R	
D	E	N		M	E	N	N	E	N		I	D	E	S
		G	O	D	S	E	N	D		V	I	C	K	
A	L	A	R	M					V	E	N	T	I	
S	O	S	O		B	L	E	S	S	E	S			
P	O	P	O		B	I	G	C	A	T		J	A	B
	K	I	M	J	O	N	G	I	L		R	O	M	E
J	E	R	S	E	Y		W	E	T		A	V	E	R
A	D	A	M	S		C	A	N	T	A	B	I	L	E
M	A	T	E	S		O	S	C	A	R	B	A	I	T
B	T	E	N			T	H	E	X	F	I	L	E	S

A	B	B	E	S	S			A	M	P	E	D	U	P
C	O	O	L	A	I	R		C	O	L	G	A	T	E
T	O	S	T	A	D	A		C	R	O	O	N	E	R
O	K	T	O	B	E	R	F	E	S	T				
N	E	O	N			K	E	E	P	I	T	R	E	A	L
E	R	N			F	I	G	H	T		W	I	L	C	O
			V	I	C	A	R		J	I	C	A	M	A
H	I	J	I	N	K	S		B	A	S	E	M	E	N
A	D	O	N	I	S		S	E	C	T	S			
Z	O	N	E	S		M	I	L	K	S		C	A	P
E	L	I	S	H	A	O	T	I	S		Y	U	L	E
				L	E	D	Z	E	P	P	E	L	I	N
T	H	E	W	I	R	E		F	R	A	N	K	E	N
R	E	T	I	N	O	L		S	A	L	T	I	N	E
E	Y	E	T	E	S	T			T	E	E	N	S	Y

100

B	U	T	T	O	C	K	S		A	C	R	O	S	S
O	N	E	O	N	O	N	E		N	O	H	O	P	E
L	I	Q	U	O	R	U	P		T	O	O	H	O	T
S	T	U	S		A	R	T	I	S	T		L	I	L
H	A	I	L			L	E	N	O		C	A	L	I
O	R	L	E	S	S		T	A	N		A	L	E	S
I	D	A		L	T	D		W	A	L	M	A	R	T
			M	O	R	E		A	L	O	E			
S	H	O	O	T	E	R		Y	O	N		B	A	D
W	I	F	E		E	A	U		G	I	J	A	N	E
E	T	A	T		T	I	N	A		A	L	T	S
E	M	S		I	M	L	A	T	E		B	L	O	C
P	E	O	P	L	E		B	R	I	S	B	A	N	E
E	U	R	E	K	A		L	I	N	K	E	D	I	N
A	P	T	E	S	T		E	A	S	Y	R	E	A	D

101

S	P	A	■	O	L	I	V	E	R	T	W	I	S	T
T	O	N	■	P	I	R	A	T	E	R	A	D	I	O
E	L	K	■	S	T	A	N	D	S	A	L	O	N	E
N	O	L	O	■	E	N	E	■	T	U	L	L	E	S
O	P	E	N	M	R	I	S	■	A	M	O	■		
P	O	S	E	A	S	■	T	R	A	W	L	S	■	
A	N	T	S	Y	■	A	C	R	E	■	S	E	E	R
D	I	R	■	O	J	T	R	I	A	L	■	A	N	I
S	E	A	L	■	O	R	Y	X	■	A	D	D	I	N
	S	P	I	R	E	A	■		B	R	A	V	O	S
		N	E	C	■	T	O	Y	S	T	O	R	E	
P	E	S	E	T	A	■	A	F	R	■	A	C	I	D
D	R	A	C	O	M	A	L	F	O	Y	■	A	T	O
F	I	G	U	R	E	S	K	A	T	E	■	L	I	U
S	E	A	T	T	L	E	S	L	E	W	■	S	S	T

102

P	O	T	F	A	R	M	S	■	W	A	M	P	U	M
A	F	R	O	B	E	A	T	■	I	G	U	A	N	A
S	T	A	R	B	A	S	E	■	C	A	L	L	O	N
T	E	N	T	A	C	L	E	■	C	R	E	E	D	S
A	N	K	H	■	H	I	L	D	A	■	S	O	U	L
■				M	I	N	E	O	■		D	E	A	
P	O	P	G	U	N	■	D	O	C	I	L	I	T	Y
A	P	L	E	N	T	Y	■	M	O	L	I	E	R	E
R	E	A	L	G	O	O	D	■	U	L	S	T	E	R
T	R	Y	■		W	A	S	P	S	■				
Y	A	M	S	■	C	L	U	E	D	■	M	E	M	E
T	R	A	C	E	R	■	P	R	E	N	A	T	A	L
R	O	T	A	T	E	■	H	A	T	E	M	A	I	L
A	L	E	R	T	S	■	I	P	A	D	M	I	N	I
Y	E	S	Y	E	S	■	N	E	T	S	A	L	E	S

103

A	C	T	■	S	T	U	N	G	■	■	S	W	E	P	T
S	O	R	E	L	O	S	E	R	■	■	C	I	G	A	R
I	N	A	M	O	R	A	T	A	■	■	A	N	G	I	E
A	K	I	M	B	O	■	■	M	R	D	E	E	D	S	■
G	E	N	A	■	■	S	H	O	E	S	■	D	O	S	■
O	R	E	■	S	L	O	O	P	S	■	M	O	U	E	■
■	S	E	A	T	O	F	T	H	E	P	A	N	T	S	■
■	■	R	E	N	T	M	O	N	E	Y	■	■	■	■	■
S	A	V	I	N	G	S	A	N	D	L	O	A	N	■	■
O	P	E	D	■	I	C	I	E	S	T	■	N	O	W	■
A	P	T	■	V	E	I	L	S	■	■	F	I	V	E	■
P	R	E	C	I	S	E	■	■	H	E	R	M	E	S	■
B	O	R	A	X	■	N	A	V	Y	S	E	A	L	S	■
O	V	A	T	E	■	C	H	A	P	P	E	L	L	E	■
X	E	N	O	N	■	E	A	T	E	N	■	S	A	X	■

104

H	E	S	B	A	C	K	■	M	A	L	T	H	U	S
E	T	E	R	N	A	L	■	A	M	O	R	O	S	O
M	A	R	I	A	N	O	■	P	I	N	A	T	A	S
P	I	T	C	H	E	S	■	L	E	G	I	T	■	■
S	L	A	K	E	■	S	H	E	■	B	L	O	K	E
■	■	O	I	L	■	E	L	M	O	■	T	I	S	■
■	M	T	V	M	O	V	I	E	A	W	A	R	D	S
T	O	R	E	■	F	E	R	A	L	■	D	O	D	O
G	R	A	N	D	T	H	E	F	T	A	U	T	O	■
I	I	I	■	A	Y	E	S	■	A	T	L	■	■	■
F	A	N	C	Y	■	M	S	S	■	A	T	O	M	S
■	■	F	O	S	S	E	■	L	A	R	S	S	O	N
I	T	A	L	I	A	N	■	A	D	A	W	A	R	E
M	O	R	O	N	I	C	■	M	A	X	I	M	A	L
S	T	E	R	N	L	Y	■	S	K	Y	M	A	L	L

W	A	S	A	T	C	H	■	K	I	D	N	A	P	S
A	R	T	S	A	L	E	■	S	H	O	O	F	L	Y
S	O	A	P	B	O	X	■	T	R	I	S	T	A	N
A	M	I	■	O	D	A	M	A	E	■	T	E	S	S
B	A	N	C	O	■	G	A	R	■	T	E	R	M	■
I	S	S	O	■	D	R	T	■	Y	A	P	S	A	T
■	■	■	T	H	E	A	T	E	A	M	■	I	T	O
J	U	L	Y	I	V	M	D	C	C	L	X	X	V	I
A	B	O	■	H	A	S	A	C	H	A	T	■	■	■
M	E	S	I	A	L	■	M	E	T	■	R	O	M	A
■	R	E	N	T	■	J	O	N	■	S	A	T	A	N
A	G	F	A	■	S	U	N	T	A	N	■	T	U	G
B	E	A	R	C	A	T	■	R	C	A	D	O	M	E
R	E	C	U	R	V	E	■	I	N	I	T	I	A	L
I	K	E	T	T	E	S	■	C	E	L	S	I	U	S

A	S	C	H	■	C	U	B	A	■	B	O	S	N	S
S	H	A	Q	■	O	P	E	N	M	A	R	K	E	T
T	O	N	S	■	L	E	N	T	I	L	S	O	U	P
R	E	V	■	S	A	N	J	O	S	E	■	A	R	A
O	S	A	M	A	■	D	I	N	G	■	C	L	O	T
■	■	S	A	Y	I	■	■	■	O	M	A	■	■	■
N	A	T	I	O	N	A	L	A	V	E	R	A	G	E
I	W	A	N	N	A	B	E	S	E	D	A	T	E	D
P	E	R	M	A	N	E	N	T	R	E	C	O	R	D
S	E	P	A	R	A	T	E	I	N	C	O	M	E	S
■	■	■	S	A	S	■	■	S	A	L	E	■	■	■
J	O	L	T	■	Y	E	G	G	■	D	E	G	A	S
E	X	E	■	E	L	N	O	R	T	E	■	O	B	E
T	I	N	A	T	U	R	N	E	R	■	R	Y	A	N
E	D	D	I	E	M	O	N	E	Y	■	F	A	T	S
R	E	S	T	S	■	N	A	D	A	■	K	N	E	E

107

J	U	S	T	A	D	R	O	P	■	S	T	A	R	K
A	N	T	O	N	I	O	N	I	■	R	E	G	A	L
C	R	A	N	K	C	A	S	E	■	S	M	O	T	E
K	E	Y	■	H	O	N	E	S	T	■	P	U	R	E
P	A	S	S	■	T	S	R	■	R	A	T	T	A	N
O	D	I	O	U	S	■	V	E	I	L	■	I	C	E
T	Y	N	A	N	■	G	E	N	T	L	E	S	E	X
■	■	R	U	S	E	■	D	E	B	S	■	■	■	■
S	W	I	S	S	A	L	P	S	■	U	N	D	E	R
H	A	S	■	E	L	S	E	■	E	T	E	R	N	E
O	R	E	I	D	A	■	R	N	A	■	S	I	C	S
O	W	E	D	■	D	E	S	O	T	O	■	V	A	T
T	O	Y	E	D	■	M	O	D	E	L	L	E	R	S
A	R	O	S	E	■	I	N	O	R	D	E	R	T	O
T	N	U	T	S	■	L	A	Z	Y	S	U	S	A	N

108

R	E	M	A	N	D	■	S	Q	U	I	D	I	N	K
E	X	E	T	E	R	■	P	U	N	T	E	D	O	N
D	E	S	T	R	Y	■	L	I	M	O	R	I	D	E
C	R	O	W	D	S	C	E	N	E	■	B	O	R	E
A	T	N	O	■	E	R	E	C	T	■	I	T	A	L
P	O	I	■	C	A	I	N	E	■	A	N	I	M	A
E	N	C	L	O	S	E	S	■	B	I	G	C	A	T
■	■	■	I	Z	O	D	■	F	A	L	L	■	■	■
H	A	P	P	E	N	■	R	E	D	E	E	M	E	R
A	D	O	R	N	■	B	E	A	D	Y	■	A	P	O
M	U	L	E	■	L	U	C	R	E	■	P	R	I	I
P	L	E	A	■	D	R	E	S	S	S	U	I	T	S
T	A	N	D	O	O	R	I	■	I	A	M	N	O	T
O	T	T	E	R	P	O	P	■	G	R	A	E	M	E
N	E	A	R	E	A	S	T	■	N	A	S	S	E	R

109

A	S	S	E	T	■	T	E	S	T	M	A	T	C	H
S	T	A	L	E	■	A	P	P	I	A	N	W	A	Y
Q	A	N	D	A	■	R	A	I	N	S	T	O	R	M
U	N	D	E	R	■	H	U	T	C	H	I	S	O	N
I	D	B	R	A	C	E	L	E	T	■	L	O	L	A
T	E	A	■	T	R	E	E	S	■	C	A	M	E	L
H	E	R	B	■	A	L	T	■	S	O	B	E	R	S
■	■	E	A	T	S	■	S	H	O	O	■	■	■	■
A	C	H	E	B	E	■	S	E	E	■	R	O	S	E
B	R	A	T	S	■	B	I	T	E	S	■	W	P	A
R	U	S	H	■	L	A	N	A	T	U	R	N	E	R
E	M	B	O	W	E	R	E	D	■	R	E	G	A	L
A	B	E	V	I	G	O	D	A	■	E	V	O	K	E
S	L	E	E	P	O	N	I	T	■	L	U	A	U	S
T	E	N	N	E	S	S	E	E	■	Y	E	L	P	S

110

H	E	Y	M	R	D	J	■	A	S	C	R	I	B	E
I	C	K	Y	P	O	O	■	M	A	R	I	N	E	S
T	O	N	S	I	L	S	■	A	D	E	P	T	A	T
C	L	O	T	■	L	E	G	■	A	T	T	E	N	D
H	E	W	E	D	■	P	E	T	H	A	I	R	■	■
■	■	■	R	I	G	H	T	H	A	N	D	M	A	N
S	A	W	Y	E	R	■	A	I	R	■	E	S	T	E
P	E	A	■	T	E	A	R	S	U	P	■	O	W	E
E	R	R	S	■	C	S	A	■	O	U	T	F	O	R
C	O	M	E	G	O	W	I	T	H	M	E	■	■	■
■	■	■	H	E	I	R	E	S	S	■	A	A	R	G	H
G	H	E	T	T	O	■	E	G	O	■	B	O	S	E
M	I	A	H	A	M	M	■	A	N	N	A	S	U	I
A	D	R	E	N	A	L	■	R	E	E	L	S	I	N
J	E	T	S	O	N	S	■	P	R	B	L	I	T	Z

T	H	E	W	H	O	■	S	N	A	P	■	J	E	T
R	E	N	A	I	L	■	T	O	B	E	S	U	R	E
A	N	G	L	E	D	■	A	M	B	R	O	S	I	A
Y	I	E	L	D	S	■	S	E	A	O	T	T	E	R
S	E	L	A	■	A	S	H	■	E	T	H	I	C	■
■	■	C	O	W	H	E	R	B	■	A	F	A	R	■
A	L	T	E	R	■	O	S	H	A	■	T	I	N	O
L	O	E	S	S	E	R	■	I	N	A	H	E	A	P
A	S	S	T	■	V	T	E	N	■	L	A	D	L	E
S	A	T	E	■	E	U	R	O	P	O	P	■	■	■
■	L	A	V	I	N	■	O	S	H	■	P	O	G	S
P	A	T	E	N	T	E	D	■	O	N	E	S	E	T
I	M	O	N	F	I	R	E	■	B	A	N	K	S	Y
N	O	R	S	E	M	A	N	■	I	D	E	A	T	E
E	S	S	■	R	E	S	T	■	C	A	D	R	E	S

M	A	T	T	D	A	M	O	N	■	P	A	S	S	E
S	P	E	E	D	D	A	T	E	■	I	N	A	L	L
R	E	L	A	T	E	S	T	O	■	E	N	I	A	C
P	R	E	K	■	N	C	O	S	■	C	E	N	T	I
■	■	■	R	O	O	M	■	S	E	X	T	E	D	■
G	E	S	S	O	■	T	A	B	O	O	■	■	■	■
I	T	H	A	C	A	■	N	U	F	F	S	A	I	D
S	T	A	R	K	L	Y	■	B	T	W	E	L	V	E
H	U	G	I	T	O	U	T	■	C	O	R	D	O	N
■	■	■	H	E	M	E	N	■	R	E	A	R	S	■
G	N	O	M	E	S	■	D	U	C	K	■	■	■	■
S	A	W	I	V	■	I	T	C	H	■	D	U	P	E
P	I	N	T	O	■	M	A	L	E	N	U	R	S	E
O	V	E	T	T	■	P	L	E	A	S	E	S	I	R
T	E	R	S	E	■	S	K	I	P	C	L	A	S	S

113

```
K I D N E Y B E A N █ L A T E
A N Y O N E E L S E █ E R I S
T R E N C H C O A T █ G E N T
Z E D █ █ A I R F R A N C E
█ █ L U L U █ U L U L A T E
S H I I T E S █ L I S T █ █
W A R G A M E █ E X T E N D S
U H O H █ █ █ N C A A
M A N T R A S █ B R A D A W L
█ █ S U V A █ R E V E R S E
S E V E N A M █ U B E R █ █
P L E C T R U M S █ █ G W B
L E G O █ I R A Q I D I N A R
I V A N █ C A Y U G A L A K E
T E N D █ E I S E N H O W E R
```

114

```
S O T █ H A B E R D A S H E R
W H O █ O N C L O U D N I N E
E P A █ R I C K Y N E L S O N
E L F M A N █ H A N S █ M R T
T E A R S █ B A L E █ K A M A
S A R I █ W O R F █ A N S E L
O S E █ W A X T A B L E T █
P E T M I C E █ M A E W E S T
█ H I T O R M I S S █ R P I
G O E T H █ B A L K █ M S R P
A R E A █ O R L Y █ T I V O S
S S W █ G A I L █ W O N O U T
L I E D E T E C T O R █ I T E
O N L I N E F O R U M █ C U R
G O L D E N S P I K E █ E P S
```

115

O	M	A	H	A		E	L	M	S		S	E	R	F
H	E	L	E	N		K	I	C	K	B	O	X	E	R
C	A	P	R	I		G	E	R	A	L	D	I	N	E
A	T	H	O	M	E		S	I	T	U	A	T	E	D
L	E	A	N	E	R	S		B	E	E	P			
C	A	B	S		R	E	F		B	O	O	S	T	
U	T	E		N	A	I	L	C	L	I	P	P	E	R
T	E	T		A	N	N	U	L	A	R		E	L	I
T	R	I	B	U	T	E	B	A	N	D		N	F	C
A	S	C	O	T		S	I	C		P	E	S	O	
		A	I	R	S		R	E	O	R	D	E	R	
S	C	O	T	L	A	N	D		T	H	E	F	E	D
A	R	T	M	U	S	E	U	M		A	L	I	K	E
K	A	T	E	S	P	A	D	E		R	A	R	E	R
E	B	O	N		S	K	E	W		E	W	E	R	S

116

G	O	D	E	L	E	S	C	H	E	R	B	A	C	H
P	R	I	V	A	T	E	A	U	D	I	E	N	C	E
S	U	M	A	N	D	S	U	B	S	T	A	N	C	E
		D	E	S		G	R	E	A	T				
P	A	N	E	S		P	H	I	L		I	N	D	S
O	R	O	S		B	E	T	S		A	F	O	O	T
T	A	K		Z	O	R	A		C	R	I	N	G	E
S	P	O	K	E	O	F	F	T	H	E	C	U	F	F
D	A	M	A	S	K		E	R	O	S		S	O	A
A	H	I	N	T		Z	W	E	I		L	E	O	N
M	O	S	S		D	E	W	Y		P	A	R	D	O
		A	T	A	R	I		A	I	M				
O	N	E	S	E	C	O	N	D	P	L	E	A	S	E
P	U	T	S	T	H	E	K	I	B	O	S	H	O	N
S	T	A	T	E	A	S	S	I	S	T	A	N	C	E

117

A	T	W	A	R		F	L	E	E		S	A	P	S
B	U	R	M	A		R	A	I	L		C	L	A	W
O	N	I	O	N	R	I	N	G	S		R	E	N	E
D	E	S	K		O	N	T	H	E	L	E	V	E	L
E	S	T		P	U	G	E	T		E	W	E	L	L
		B	A	L	L	E	R	I	N	A	S			
P	R	A	G	U	E		N	E	E	D		P	B	S
D	Y	N	A	S	T	S		S	A	F	A	R	I	S
Q	E	D		S	T	E	P		R	O	D	E	O	S
			P	I	E	A	L	A	M	O	D	E		
G	E	O	R	G		T	A	C	I	T		M	A	P
E	R	G	O	N	O	M	I	C	S		L	P	G	A
I	R	I	S		B	A	T	E	S	M	O	T	E	L
C	O	V	E		I	T	E	S		I	R	E	N	E
O	R	E	S		T	E	D	S		L	E	D	T	O

118

A	B	L	E		M	S	N	B	C		A	B	R	A
N	A	A	N		I	L	I	E	D		M	E	A	N
T	Y	P	E	W	R	I	T	E	R	S	T	A	N	D
F	A	D		H	O	T	S	P	O	T		R	D	A
A	R	E	N	A	S			M	E	C	C	A	N	
R	E	S	E	T		A	N	N		P	O	U	L	T
M	A	K	E	M	I	N	E	A	D	O	U	B	L	E
		D	E	L	I	C	I	O	U	S				
S	I	D	E	W	A	L	K	A	R	T	I	S	T	S
O	T	E	R	O		L	S	D		S	N	A	R	E
M	E	S	S	R	S			M	I	S	L	E	D	
E	M	E		R	A	D	I	O	A	D		T	V	A
S	O	R	R	Y	F	O	R	T	H	E	W	A	I	T
A	N	T	I		E	L	A	T	E		E	I	N	E
Y	E	S	M		S	E	N	O	R		T	R	O	D

119

P	E	D	I	C	A	B	█	B	R	A	P	A	D	S
A	R	I	G	A	T	O	█	E	A	T	E	N	U	P
P	A	N	A	R	A	B	█	R	I	H	A	N	N	A
A	S	K	█	L	L	B	█	T	S	A	R	I	S	M
█	█	█	T	O	O	L	S	█	I	N	L	E	T	S
J	U	S	T	A	S	E	C	O	N	D	█	█	█	█
U	N	I	O	N	S	H	O	P	S	█	M	O	E	T
B	U	R	P	S	█	E	N	E	█	W	E	L	S	H
A	M	I	S	█	M	A	C	N	C	H	E	E	S	E
█	█	█	R	I	D	E	S	H	O	T	G	U	N	
S	T	R	A	W	S	█	S	E	A	L	S	█	█	█
W	E	E	L	A	S	S	█	C	L	E	█	I	R	E
A	P	L	E	N	T	Y	█	R	U	B	S	O	U	T
B	E	A	R	D	E	N	█	E	P	I	C	W	I	N
S	E	X	T	A	P	E	█	T	A	T	I	A	N	A

120

X	E	N	O	█	A	L	I	S	T	█	G	R	A	F
A	T	O	N	█	L	E	N	T	O	█	H	A	L	O
C	H	O	C	O	L	A	T	E	S	H	A	K	E	S
T	A	K	E	N	O	P	R	I	S	O	N	E	R	S
O	N	S	█	C	U	T	A	N	D	P	A	S	T	E
█	█	G	U	T	█	M	O	T	█	█	█	█	█	█
Z	A	I	R	E	█	S	E	A	W	O	R	T	H	Y
A	R	N	O	█	S	P	U	R	N	█	A	S	I	A
K	I	C	K	S	T	A	R	T	█	O	N	K	E	Y
█	█	█	P	E	R	█	M	F	G	█	█	█	█	█
I	M	A	G	I	N	E	T	H	A	T	█	S	A	M
C	O	M	E	T	O	T	H	E	R	E	S	C	U	E
A	P	P	L	E	P	I	E	A	L	A	M	O	D	E
R	U	L	E	█	A	R	U	D	E	█	U	N	I	T
E	P	E	E	█	D	E	N	S	E	█	G	E	T	S

121

M	I	C	H	E	L	E	B	A	C	H	M	A	N	N
S	T	R	A	T	E	G	I	C	R	O	U	T	E	S
T	H	E	L	A	T	E	L	A	T	E	S	H	O	W
■	A	T	T	S	■	R	I	P	■	S	E	E	N	■
N	C	I	S	■	S	I	O	U	X	■	D	I	A	Z
C	A	N	■	E	P	A	U	L	E	T	■	S	T	E
O	N	S	T	A	R	■	S	C	R	A	M	M	E	D
■	■	A	S	I	F	■	O	O	P	S	■	■	■	■
A	F	L	U	T	T	E	R	■	X	E	S	O	U	T
D	O	E	■	S	E	R	A	P	E	S	■	V	S	O
O	R	A	L	■	S	R	T	A	S	■	B	E	B	E
■	S	V	E	N	■	A	R	I	■	T	E	R	P	■
H	U	E	V	O	S	R	A	N	C	H	E	R	O	S
U	R	B	A	N	D	I	C	T	I	O	N	A	R	Y
P	E	E	R	A	S	S	E	S	S	M	E	N	T	S

122

J	I	M	M	Y	F	A	L	L	O	N	■	P	B	J
A	R	E	Y	O	U	R	E	A	D	Y	■	A	L	A
K	I	N	G	S	R	A	N	S	O	M	■	R	O	C
E	S	S	O	■	L	B	S	■	R	E	R	A	C	K
S	H	A	D	S	■	I	C	K	■	T	I	C	K	S
■	■	■	O	S	C	A	R	S	■	S	H	A	Q	■
T	I	S	S	U	E	■	P	I	E	■	K	U	D	U
O	T	H	E	L	L	O	■	S	A	G	E	T	E	A
G	A	O	L	■	M	A	C	■	M	O	D	E	S	T
A	L	O	E	■	A	T	O	A	S	T	■	■	■	■
P	I	T	C	H	■	S	N	L	■	O	M	E	G	A
A	C	E	T	I	C	■	S	A	W	■	A	L	U	M
R	I	M	■	M	A	G	I	N	O	T	L	I	N	E
T	Z	U	■	O	R	I	G	I	N	A	L	S	I	N
Y	E	P	■	M	E	A	N	S	T	R	E	E	T	S

123

P	O	V	E	R	T	Y	R	O	W	■	G	A	R	R
U	R	A	N	I	U	M	O	R	E	■	E	P	E	E
C	A	R	R	O	T	C	A	K	E	■	L	P	G	A
E	N	Y	A	■	U	A	R	■	D	I	A	L	U	P
■	■	■	G	A	S	■	P	E	N	T	E	L	■	■
E	S	T	E	R	■	S	T	E	A	D	I	C	A	M
W	A	R	S	A	W	P	A	C	T	■	N	I	T	E
O	N	E	■	B	O	L	S	T	E	R	■	D	I	A
K	T	E	L	■	R	E	T	I	R	E	M	E	N	T
S	A	G	E	G	R	E	E	N	■	B	E	R	G	S
■	C	U	T	S	I	N	■	F	A	N	■	■	■	■
B	L	A	S	T	S	■	O	N	O	■	D	I	S	K
C	A	R	O	■	O	T	H	E	R	W	O	M	A	N
U	R	D	U	■	M	S	M	A	G	A	Z	I	N	E
P	A	S	T	■	E	A	S	T	O	R	A	N	G	E

124

B	U	R	J	K	H	A	L	I	F	A	■	P	I	C
O	N	A	U	T	O	P	I	L	O	T	■	G	M	A
W	I	S	D	O	M	T	E	E	T	H	■	T	M	S
E	X	P	O	S	I	T	S	■	O	L	D	H	A	T
■	■	■	■	L	E	O	■	A	M	E	R	I	C	A
C	I	A	L	I	S	■	S	T	A	T	E	R	U	N
A	S	I	A	N	■	S	U	I	T	E	■	T	L	C
N	O	R	M	■	S	E	N	D	S	■	Y	E	A	H
T	M	C	■	M	A	I	N	E	■	S	E	E	T	O
H	E	L	S	I	N	K	I	■	C	O	R	N	E	R
A	T	E	I	N	T	O	■	E	O	N	■	■	■	■
C	R	A	N	I	A	■	C	R	O	N	Y	I	S	M
K	I	N	■	M	A	J	O	R	L	E	A	G	U	E
I	C	E	■	A	N	D	S	O	I	T	G	O	E	S
T	S	R	■	L	A	S	T	R	E	S	O	R	T	S

125

C	L	A	S	P	I	N	G	■	■	A	N	G	L	E
L	A	S	E	R	B	E	A	M	■	B	O	R	A	X
I	N	A	N	I	M	A	T	E	■	C	R	A	V	E
N	O	R	A	D	■	L	E	T	T	■	Y	O	U	■
G	L	U	T	E	I	■	■	E	A	S	T	E	R	N
T	I	L	E	■	R	U	M	O	R	H	A	S	I	T
O	N	E	■	C	O	N	A	R	T	I	S	T	S	■
■	■	L	A	N	D	L	I	N	E	S	■	■	■	■
■	F	O	U	R	L	E	T	T	E	R	■	O	F	T
C	O	I	N	P	U	R	S	E	S	■	B	R	I	E
H	U	L	K	I	N	G	■	■	S	C	L	E	R	A
A	L	P	■	G	O	B	S	■	R	A	G	E	S	■
I	T	A	L	Y	■	N	O	T	R	E	D	A	M	E
S	I	N	A	I	■	E	Y	E	O	P	E	N	E	R
E	P	S	O	N	■	■	S	T	E	T	S	O	N	S

126

P	I	Z	Z	A	J	O	I	N	T	■	W	I	F	E
A	N	T	I	M	A	T	T	E	R	■	A	L	A	S
W	H	I	T	E	N	O	I	S	E	■	L	L	C	S
N	I	L	■	S	E	E	S	T	O	■	K	A	T	O
■	S	E	T	■	S	N	L	■	G	O	T	■	■	■
■	■	H	T	S	■	T	I	E	O	N	E	O	N	■
I	N	H	E	R	I	T	■	N	E	W	W	A	V	E
B	I	O	D	A	T	A	■	G	R	E	A	S	E	S
A	T	T	A	C	K	S	■	S	I	S	T	E	R	S
R	E	T	R	E	A	T	S	■	E	T	E	■	■	■
■	O	K	S	■	E	P	S	■	■	R	A	W	■	■
L	O	T	S	■	S	T	E	P	O	N	■	S	A	Y
Y	U	R	I	■	R	E	N	O	N	E	V	A	D	A
I	Z	O	D	■	I	S	C	R	E	W	E	D	U	P
N	O	T	E	■	S	T	E	E	L	T	R	A	P	S

A	S	K	O	V	E	R	■	P	T	B	O	A	T	S
R	A	I	S	E	D	A	N	E	Y	E	B	R	O	W
A	L	L	K	I	D	D	I	N	G	A	S	I	D	E
R	O	M	A	N	■	I	N	N	E	R	■	S	I	E
A	M	E	R	■	M	A	J	O	R	■	S	T	E	T
T	E	R	■	T	I	T	A	N	■	K	N	I	F	E
■	■	B	A	K	E	S	■	D	E	A	D	O	N	■
■	I	B	I	S	E	S	■	P	E	E	P	E	R	■
A	M	A	Z	E	D	■	M	A	L	L	S	■	■	■
R	I	L	E	D	■	B	U	S	T	S	■	S	H	E
A	T	I	T	■	P	E	S	T	S	■	V	T	E	N
P	A	N	■	S	E	I	K	O	■	K	A	R	A	T
A	T	E	E	N	A	G	E	R	I	N	L	O	V	E
H	O	S	T	I	L	E	T	A	K	E	O	V	E	R
O	R	E	S	T	E	S	■	L	E	E	R	E	R	S

L	I	A	R	S	■	■	B	L	A	S	T	I	T
U	N	D	O	C	K	■	C	O	M	E	O	N	S
S	A	S	S	O	N	S	■	S	A	N	T	A	N	A
T	W	O	S	T	E	P	S	■	F	E	T	T	E	R
F	O	R	E	T	E	L	L	S	■	S	L	U	R	S
U	R	B	S	■	P	I	A	M	A	T	E	R	S	■
L	D	S	■	B	A	T	T	A	L	I	O	N	■	■
■	■	L	E	T	T	E	R	M	E	N	■	■	■
■	C	O	N	C	E	R	T	O	S	■	S	E	A
■	T	O	U	G	H	R	O	A	D	■	M	A	G	I
C	O	N	G	A	■	S	O	L	O	H	O	M	E	R
L	O	C	A	L	S	■	F	E	V	E	R	I	S	H
A	L	E	N	C	O	N	■	C	A	R	E	S	T	O
M	E	D	I	A	T	E	■	R	E	S	E	E	S
P	R	E	S	T	O	S	■	S	O	N	D	E

129

G	E	R	M	I	N	A	T	E	■	L	U	C	I	A
O	V	E	R	T	A	K	E	S	■	A	N	O	D	E
D	O	M	E	S	T	I	C	P	A	R	T	N	E	R
I	K	I	D	■	A	R	S	■	S	K	I	D	O	O
V	E	T	■	A	L	A	■	G	A	S	L	O	G	S
A	S	S	I	S	I	■	A	R	P	■	■	F	R	O
■	■	■	C	H	A	N	G	E	■	O	N	E	A	L
M	C	G	E	E	■	O	N	E	■	P	O	E	M	S
A	L	O	E	S	■	L	E	T	T	E	R	■	■	■
M	E	T	■	■	S	A	W	■	A	R	M	P	I	T
M	A	T	D	O	W	N	■	A	G	A	■	A	M	Y
A	R	E	O	L	A	■	E	S	T	■	A	G	A	R
M	I	N	D	I	N	G	T	H	E	S	T	O	R	E
I	N	I	G	O	■	A	R	E	A	C	O	D	E	S
A	G	N	E	S	■	T	E	R	M	I	N	A	T	E

130

P	A	W	P	R	I	N	T	■	M	E	A	N	T	O
R	E	E	L	E	D	I	N	■	I	N	F	E	R	S
O	R	N	A	M	E	N	T	A	L	T	R	E	E	S
P	O	T	T	I	E	S	■	L	E	I	■	D	E	I
O	B	S	E	S	S	■	B	I	S	C	A	Y	N	E
S	A	O	N	E	■	P	I	E	T	I	N	■	■	■
A	T	U	S	■	M	I	G	N	O	N	E	T	T	E
L	I	T	■	B	I	G	B	A	N	G	■	H	U	A
S	C	H	O	O	L	M	A	T	E	■	C	E	R	T
■	■	■	D	A	L	E	N	E	■	B	E	R	N	E
T	I	M	E	S	I	N	K	■	G	E	R	M	A	N
I	W	O	■	T	O	T	■	B	A	R	T	O	L	I
L	I	S	T	E	N	S	T	O	R	E	A	S	O	N
T	S	H	I	R	T	■	R	U	N	T	I	E	S	T
S	H	E	E	S	H	■	I	T	I	S	N	T	S	O

131

S	A	N	T	A	N	A	■	N	E	T	F	L	I	X
C	H	U	N	N	E	L	■	O	X	I	D	A	T	E
A	I	R	T	A	X	I	■	S	P	R	A	Y	E	R
L	T	S	■	G	U	M	S	H	O	E	■	A	M	O
D	U	E	T	■	S	O	L	O	S	■	T	W	I	X
E	N	R	O	N	■	N	O	W	■	G	R	A	Z	E
D	A	Y	L	I	L	Y	■	S	P	L	A	Y	E	D
■	■	K	E	Y	■	■	■	D	I	P	■	■	■	■
E	T	A	I	L	E	D	■	I	Q	T	E	S	T	S
N	O	T	E	S	■	I	N	C	■	Z	Z	T	O	P
C	O	E	N	■	I	V	I	E	S	■	E	U	R	E
A	S	I	■	A	M	O	E	B	A	S	■	N	N	E
M	O	N	S	T	E	R	■	A	M	I	S	T	A	D
P	O	T	O	M	A	C	■	T	O	R	P	E	D	O
S	N	O	C	O	N	E	■	H	A	I	R	D	O	S

132

A	C	T	F	I	V	E	■	O	F	F	C	A	S	T
F	A	I	R	B	A	N	K	S	A	L	A	S	K	A
F	R	E	E	A	S	S	O	C	I	A	T	I	O	N
A	L	G	O	R	E	■	M	A	N	X	■	M	P	G
B	E	A	N	S	■	P	O	R	T	■	M	O	J	O
L	A	M	S	■	B	U	D	S	■	L	O	V	E	S
E	S	E	■	B	R	N	O	■	R	O	O	■	■	■
■	E	S	P	R	I	T	D	E	C	O	R	P	S	■
■	■	A	I	M	■	R	A	M	P	■	L	I	D	
S	K	O	R	T	■	H	A	S	P	■	N	O	L	O
A	A	H	S	■	S	A	G	E	■	J	A	W	E	D
I	B	M	■	Z	E	R	O	■	D	U	P	I	N	G
D	O	Y	O	U	W	A	N	N	A	D	A	N	C	E
H	O	M	E	L	E	S	S	S	H	E	L	T	E	R
I	M	Y	O	U	R	S	■	C	L	A	M	O	R	S

133

F	A	W	N		A	B	B	A		T	A	S	K	S
E	C	H	O		H	E	A	R		I	R	E	N	E
M	E	A	T	T	H	E	R	M	O	M	E	T	E	R
A	S	T	A	R		T	R	Y	M	E		T	W	A
		H	R	A	P		S	A	G	A	L			
P	L	A	Y	M	E	O	R	T	R	A	D	E	M	E
S	A	P		S	O	X	E	R		P	I	S	A	N
E	S	P	O		N	Y	T	O	L		A	T	N	O
U	S	E	A	S		G	I	N	O	S		H	O	T
D	O	N	T	E	V	E	N	G	O	T	H	E	R	E
		S	H	E	E	N		P	I	E	S			
C	T	N		K	E	A	T	S		L	Y	C	E	E
W	H	E	R	E	S	T	H	E	R	E	M	O	T	E
T	A	X	E	R		E	U	R	O		A	R	A	L
S	I	T	E	S		D	R	E	W		N	E	T	S

134

N	A	S	T	Y	G	R	A	M		N	A	P	E	S
I	N	T	H	E	R	E	A	R		O	R	R	I	N
P	A	R	A	S	A	I	L	S		B	O	O	N	E
S	L	O	W		S	D	I		G	O	A	T	E	E
		S	T	P		Y	S	I	D	R	O			
S	R	O		U	S	U	A	L	L	Y		T	E	D
C	A	M	E	R	A	S	H	Y		S	T	Y	L	I
A	D	A	P	T	T	O		F	S	H	A	P	E	D
R	A	H	A	L		P	R	O	P	O	N	E	N	T
F	R	A		E	Y	E	E	X	A	M		S	A	O
		B	A	D	E	N	D		M	E	T			
S	T	E	P	I	N		Z	I	A		E	S	A	U
M	I	A	T	A		P	O	O	L	H	A	L	L	S
U	L	C	E	R		E	N	T	O	U	R	A	G	E
G	E	H	R	Y		D	E	A	T	H	S	T	A	R

135

S	T	I	L	L	D	R	E			A	L	B	A
C	O	N	E	H	E	A	D	S			M	E	A	N
A	R	C	T	A	N	G	E	N	T		O	A	T	S
R	E	L	I	S	T	S		O	R	I	E	N	T	E
F	A	U	N	A	S		T	W	I	N	B	I	L	L
A	D	D	O	N		J	E	T	P	L	A	N	E	
C	O	E	N		G	A	L	I	L	E	E		
E	R	S		D	E	S	E	R	E	T		L	O	B
	D	E	T	O	X	E	D		J	O	N	I
	S	T	E	A	R	N	E	S		T	A	M	E	S
T	H	E	O	R	E	M	S		L	I	M	B	I	C
Y	E	S	D	E	A	R		S	A	N	T	A	N	A
P	A	S	A		L	A	B	O	R	P	A	R	T	Y
E	T	A	T		Z	E	N	G	A	R	D	E	N
A	H	S	O			L	E	O	N	T	Y	N	E

136

W	H	I	P	I	T		S	P	A	C	E	J	A	M
H	A	M	E	L	S		C	O	C	A	C	O	L	A
A	M	P	S	U	P		H	I	T	S	O	N	G	S
T	R	U	T	V		O	M	N	I	S		K	O	S
S	A	D	O		N	A	U	T		P	Y	R	E
U	D	E		K	I	T	T	Y	K	E	L	L	E	Y
P	I	N	C	E	N	E	Z		R	D	A	
G	O	T	O	V	E	R		M	A	G	N	U	M	S
	R	I	T		T	A	K	E	O	N	M	E
J	O	H	N	N	Y	C	A	K	E	S		D	M	X
A	N	A	S		O	X	E	N		G	E	M	S
R	E	V		H	E	L	P	S		G	O	R	G	E
J	O	E	B	O	X	E	R		M	O	N	G	O	L
A	N	N	E	R	I	C	E		F	A	Z	O	O	L
R	E	S	T	S	T	O	P		A	T	O	D	D	S

137

M	A	D	E	M	I	N	C	E	M	E	A	T	O	F
E	C	O	N	O	M	I	C	W	A	R	F	A	R	E
L	O	S	A	N	G	E	L	E	S	T	I	M	E	S
S	P	E	C	I	A	L	I	N	T	E	R	E	S	T
█	█	S	T	E	M	S	█	█	I	S	S	█	█	█
█	█	O	D	E	█	F	F	F	█	T	R	E	E	█
S	T	U	R	M	█	B	E	E	F	S	█	A	X	L
M	O	R	S	E	C	O	D	E	S	I	G	N	A	L
O	J	S	█	N	I	L	E	S	█	L	A	K	M	E
G	O	A	L	█	M	A	X	█	T	V	S	█	█	█
█	█	U	G	A	█	█	P	I	E	R	O	█	█	█
C	O	M	M	E	R	C	I	A	L	R	A	D	I	O
F	R	E	E	T	R	A	N	S	L	A	T	I	O	N
C	H	A	N	S	O	N	S	D	E	G	E	S	T	E
S	E	T	S	O	N	A	P	E	D	E	S	T	A	L

138

P	I	Z	Z	A	C	R	U	S	T	█	B	L	A	B
A	R	I	O	N	A	S	S	I	S	█	F	O	R	A
C	I	P	H	E	R	T	E	X	T	█	F	O	R	T
A	S	S	A	M	█	█	D	A	R	K	█	K	I	T
█	█	N	O	G	O	█	M	A	N	C	A	V	E	█
P	S	A	█	N	O	O	N	█	P	E	L	T	E	R
H	O	C	K	E	Y	M	O	M	█	W	E	T	L	Y
O	L	E	N	█	A	P	L	U	S	█	A	H	A	B
N	A	T	A	L	█	H	O	T	P	O	T	A	T	O
E	R	I	C	A	S	█	S	E	C	T	█	T	E	X
B	A	C	K	L	I	T	█	D	A	T	A	█	█	█
O	R	A	█	A	N	O	N	█	█	O	L	D	I	E
O	R	C	A	█	B	R	O	O	D	M	A	R	E	S
T	A	I	L	█	I	T	A	L	I	A	N	A	R	T
H	Y	D	E	█	N	A	M	E	S	N	A	M	E	S

139

B	L	U	E	C	R	A	B	■	L	O	W	F	A	T
O	I	L	S	H	A	L	E	■	B	R	O	O	C	H
N	O	N	T	I	T	L	E	■	J	I	L	T	E	E
D	N	A	■	■	T	O	R	T	R	E	F	O	R	M
■	■	■	C	L	A	W	C	R	A	N	E	■	■	■
P	A	T	R	O	N	S	A	I	N	T	■	A	S	A
E	B	O	O	K	■	■	N	E	C	■	R	C	A	S
T	A	R	N	I	S	H	■	S	H	T	E	T	L	S
A	C	M	E	■	M	A	O	■	■	R	A	I	T	T
L	I	E	■	V	E	L	V	E	T	E	L	V	I	S
■	■	■	F	A	L	L	E	N	H	E	M	■	■	■
E	L	D	O	C	T	O	R	O	W	■	■	V	F	W
C	O	U	G	A	R	■	B	R	A	S	S	E	R	A
O	R	S	I	N	O	■	I	M	R	U	I	N	E	D
N	I	E	N	T	E	■	D	E	T	E	N	T	E	S

140

S	Q	U	A	B	B	L	E	■	J	A	M	C	A	M
E	U	P	H	O	R	I	A	■	O	R	I	O	L	E
T	I	P	S	H	E	E	T	■	K	I	D	U	L	T
B	B	S	■	M	A	L	I	C	E	■	E	L	S	E
A	B	A	S	■	K	O	T	O	■	H	A	D	T	O
I	L	L	I	N	■	W	U	N	D	E	R	B	A	R
L	E	A	N	O	N	■	P	I	E	R	■	E	R	S
■	■	■	S	O	U	P	■	C	L	O	P	■	■	■
S	E	A	■	G	T	O	S	■	L	I	T	O	U	T
E	X	Q	U	I	S	I	T	E	■	C	A	N	S	O
A	T	U	N	E	■	S	U	C	H	■	S	E	T	T
G	R	I	P	■	D	E	C	A	Y	S	■	M	I	A
R	E	V	I	S	E	■	K	R	A	T	I	O	N	S
A	M	E	L	I	E	■	U	T	T	E	R	R	O	T
M	E	R	E	S	T	■	P	E	T	P	E	E	V	E

141

		D	A	R	E	S	S	A	L	A	A	M	
	C	O	N	T	A	C	T	L	E	N	S	E	S
W	H	A	T	S	T	H	E	B	I	G	D	E	A	L
R	O	S	H		A	N	T	E			F	R	I	A
A	L	I	E	N	T	O		I	N	F		K	N	T
P	E	D	R	O		O	S	T	E	O	P	A	T	H
S	R	O		N	U	K	E		A	R	E	T	E	S
			T	O	P	S	E	C	R	E	T			
S	A	R	D	I	S		T	O	S	S		O	Y	E
P	R	E	S	S	E	S	O	N		E	R	T	E	S
E	F	S		E	T	O		C	H	E	E	T	O	S
N	A	T	E			B	R	E	A		T	A	M	A
T	R	Y	T	O	S	E	E	I	T	M	Y	W	A	Y
	F	L	A	S	H	I	N	T	H	E	P	A	N	
		E	S	T	A	T	E	S	A	L	E	S		

142

B	U	T	T	D	I	A	L	E	D		G	I	B	E
O	N	A	R	A	M	P	A	G	E		U	N	O	S
T	I	D	A	L	B	A	S	I	N		M	O	B	S
S	T	A	P	L	E	R		S	A	C		N	S	A
			P	A	C	T	S		L	O	V	E	L	Y
I	C	E		S	I	M	I		I	N	A	P	E	T
N	A	N	S		L	E	T	S		A	S	I	D	E
B	R	I	E	F	E	N	C	O	U	N	T	E	R	S
A	D	D	E	R		T	O	R	N		S	C	U	T
D	E	B	T	E	E		M	E	I	N		E	N	S
S	A	L	O	O	N		S	L	O	O	P			
O	L	Y		N	A	M		O	N	S	E	R	V	E
R	E	T	D		C	A	S	S	I	O	P	E	I	A
T	R	O	Y		T	A	K	E	S	A	S	E	A	T
S	S	N	S		S	M	A	R	T	P	I	L	L	S

143

C	A	S	H	B	A	R	S	■	K	A	R	S	T	S
O	S	C	A	R	W	A	O	■	N	I	I	H	A	U
N	O	I	F	S	A	N	D	S	O	R	B	U	T	S
G	N	A	T	■	I	D	I	O	C	Y	■	T	A	S
R	E	T	■	S	T	R	U	C	K	■	M	I	R	E
A	M	I	G	A	S	■	M	I	I	■	O	N	Y	X
T	A	C	O	S	■	O	P	E	N	E	D	■		
S	N	A	P	E	■	N	E	T	■	D	E	V	A	S
■			A	S	M	A	N	Y	■	G	R	A	C	E
H	A	P	S	■	A	B	T	■	P	A	N	G	E	A
O	N	I	T	■	N	O	O	N	E	R	■	A	D	O
O	Y	L	■	A	C	U	T	E	R	■	A	B	E	T
T	H	E	T	R	U	T	H	W	I	L	L	O	U	T
C	O	U	R	T	S	■	A	L	L	I	A	N	C	E
H	O	P	E	S	O	■	L	Y	S	A	N	D	E	R

144

A	P	P	L	E	C	A	R	E	■	R	A	N	C	H
D	O	U	B	L	E	B	E	D	■	O	M	A	H	A
I	M	T	O	O	S	E	X	Y	■	M	A	T	E	Y
D	E	T	■	N	A	Y	A	■	O	A	T	E	R	S
A	L	E	R	■	R	A	L	P	H	■	D	O	E	
S	O	R	O	S	■	N	L	R	B	■	P	O	K	E
■			S	T	E	T	■	S	A	V	A	G	E	D
Z	E	A	L	O	T	■		B	I	N	G	E	S	
A	L	E	Y	A	R	D	■	T	Y	N	E	■		
P	E	O	N	■	A	E	R	O	■	G	R	I	E	G
C	O	N	■	D	R	E	W	U	■	A	N	N	A	
O	N	F	I	R	E	■	L	A	N	D	■	T	R	I
M	O	L	D	Y	■	F	O	R	C	E	Q	U	I	T
I	R	U	L	E	■	B	A	D	A	D	V	I	C	E
X	A	X	E	S	■	I	N	S	P	E	C	T	O	R

145

B	O	S	C	O			J	A	C	K	L	O	R	D
A	X	T	O	N		R	E	T	R	I	E	V	E	R
S	N	A	R	E		A	B	O	U	T	F	A	C	E
Q	A	D	D	A	F	I		N	E	S	T	L	E	S
U	R	I		M	E	N	D	E	L			T	I	S
E	D	A	M		L	I	E	S		C	H	I	V	E
		A	L	I	E	N		P	A	I	N	E	D	
	L	I	F	E	P	R	E	S	E	R	V	E	R	
C	E	L	I	N	E		U	L	N	A	E			
A	T	L	A	S		O	V	U	M		S	O	A	P
T	A	G			P	R	E	M	E	D		R	U	E
C	L	E	A	R	E	D		D	N	A	T	E	S	T
H	O	T	P	O	T	A	T	O		W	H	I	T	E
O	N	I	O	N	R	I	N	G		N	A	D	E	R
W	E	T	P	A	I	N	T			S	W	A	N	S

146

J	U	J	I	T	S	U		J	A	Z	Z	A	G	E
E	L	A	T	I	O	N		S	H	O	O	T	U	P
T	A	K	E	A	I	M		B	O	O	T	E	E	S
S	L	A	M	S		A	L	A	R	M		D	S	T
F	U	R	S		S	P	I	C	A		V	I	S	E
A	M	T		D	E	P	T	H		F	A	R	S	I
N	E	A	T	I	D	E	A		S	A	L	T	O	N
		A	C	E	D		Z	A	N	E				
F	I	B	B	E	R		H	A	N	G	T	I	M	E
A	P	L	U	S		P	A	N	T	S		C	O	X
S	A	I	S		L	A	N	Z	A		B	A	R	T
T	N	T		A	U	S	S	I		P	E	N	T	E
C	E	Z	A	N	N	E		B	U	I	L	T	I	N
A	M	E	R	I	G	O		A	T	A	C	O	S	T
R	A	N	K	L	E	S		R	E	S	H	O	E	S

147

P	U	D	D	Y	T	A	T			P	L	A	S	M
I	N	I	T	I	A	T	E			C	L	I	C	H	E
L	I	E	S	D	O	W	N			H	U	N	T	E	R
E	T	D			D	I	A	N			A	R	C	A	D	E
				I	S	R			N	R	A				
A	F	I	R	S	T			K	E	L	L	O	G	G	S
N	O	D	U	H			J	E	W	I	S	H	R	Y	E
I	R	O	N			P	U	L	S	E			B	A	R	N
M	I	N	T	J	E	L	L	Y			C	O	C	O	A
A	T	T	O	R	N	E	Y			C	O	Y	E	S	T
			E	A	P			B	A	R				
S	P	R	A	W	L			T	E	R	N			A	S	U
C	O	O	L	I	T			H	E	R	C	U	L	E	S
A	L	B	A	N	Y			O	N	E	O	R	T	W	O
R	E	O	R	G			M	E	L	B	L	A	N	C

148

S	G	T	S	C	H	U	L	T	Z			C	R	A	B
U	R	A	N	I	U	M	O	R	E			L	I	L	O
D	A	T	I	N	G	P	O	O	L			U	G	L	Y
S	P	I	T	E			I	K	I	D			S	H	O	W
Y	E	N	S			O	R	S			A	C	T	T	W	O
				P	A	E	A	N			H	E	M	A	N
B	I	O	G	A	S			T	A	M	A	R	I	N	D
U	N	M	A	T	E	D			S	I	L	E	N	C	E
S	T	E	V	E	S	A	X			R	E	D	D	E	R
H	E	L	E	N			M	R	M	E	T				
W	R	E	A	T	H			A	I	D			S	E	T	I
H	A	T	H			A	P	T	S			P	I	C	O	T
A	L	P	O			N	A	I	L	S	A	L	O	N	S
C	I	A	O			S	A	N	A	N	T	O	N	I	O
K	A	N	T			A	R	G	Y	L	E	S	O	C	K

149

B	A	M	B	I		M	I	N	I			T	S	K	S
O	P	A	R	T		U	P	O	N			U	T	A	H
S	A	L	E	S	R	O	O	M	S			N	O	L	O
C	R	E	A	M	A	N	D	S	U	G	A	R			
			S	E	M			G	L	O	R	Y	B	E	
R	I	T	T		R	A	H		T	O	O	B	A	D	
I	C	I		B	O	R	O	N		F	L	O	S	S	
M	E	L	T	E	D	C	H	O	C	O	L	A	T	E	
M	A	T	E	S		S	U	D	A	N		R	E	L	
E	X	A	L	T	S		M	E	N		A	D	D	S	
D	E	W	L	I	N	E		C	A	B					
		H	A	R	A	J	U	K	U	G	I	R	L	S	
P	A	I	L		C	E	L	I	N	E	D	I	O	N	
S	I	R	I		K	C	A	R		N	E	L	L	E	
I	S	L	E		S	T	N	S		A	D	E	L	E	

150

P	R	O	A	C	T	I	V			B	B	G	U	N
H	A	S	N	O	I	D	E	A		P	U	L	S	E
E	M	M	A	S	T	O	N	E		O	G	E	E	S
L	E	O	I		O	L	D	G	E	E	Z	E	R	
P	A	N	S	Y		O	I	L		A	C	N	E	
S	U	D		E	V	E	R	S	O		P	L	A	T
		E	T	A	T	S			P	U	M	A		
O	B	T	A	I	N	S		J	E	Z	E	B	E	L
B	A	A	S			A	I	R	E	R				
I	C	K	Y		D	I	S	B	A	R		S	T	U
S	K	E	G		O	A	F		O	C	E	A	N	
	B	O	O	K	S	M	A	R	T		H	E	R	D
M	O	V	I	E		B	R	E	A	K	I	N	T	O
O	N	E	N	D		S	A	N	D	A	L	T	A	N
B	E	R	G	S			S	T	A	L	L	O	N	E

The New York Times

Crossword Puzzles

The #1 Name in Crosswords

Available at your local bookstore or online at nytimes.com/nytstore

Coming Soon!

'Tis the Season Crosswords	978-1-250-05589-7
Best of Friday Crosswords	978-1-250-05590-3
Best of Saturday Crosswords	978-1-250-05591-0
Easy as Pie Crosswords	978-1-250-05592-7
Large-Print Extra Easy Crossword Puzzle Omnibus	978-1-250-05593-4
Piece of Cake Puzzles	978-1-250-05594-1
Snowed-In Sunday Crosswords	978-1-250-05595-8
Sunday Crossword Puzzles Volume 40	978-1-250-05596-5
Coffee Shop Crosswords	978-1-250-06336-6
Cup of Tea and Crosswords	978-1-250-06333-5
Easy Crossword Puzzles Volume 16	978-1-250-06337-3
Extra Easy Crosswords	978-1-250-06338-0
Marvelous Monday Crosswords	978-1-250-06339-7
Smart Sunday Crosswords Volume 1	978-1-250-06341-0
Sweetheart Sunday Crosswords	978-1-250-06334-2
Terrific Tuesday Crosswords	978-1-250-06340-3
Will Shortz Presents The Crossword Bible	978-1-250-06335-9

Special Editions

Winter Wonderland Crosswords	978-1-250-03919-4
Pocket-Size Puzzles: Crosswords	978-1-250-03915-6
Will Shortz Picks His Favorite Puzzles	978-0-312-64550-2
Crosswords for the Holidays	978-0-312-64544-1
Crossword Lovers Only: Easy Puzzles	978-0-312-54619-9
Crossword Lovers Only: Easy to Hard Puzzles	978-0-312-68139-5
Little Black & White Book of Holiday Crosswords	978-0-312-65424-5
Little Black (and White) Book of Sunday Crosswords	978-0-312-59003-1
Will Shortz's Wittiest, Wackiest Crosswords	978-0-312-59034-5
Crosswords to Keep Your Brain Young	978-0-312-37658-8
Little Black (and White) Book of Crosswords	978-0-312-36105-1
Will Shortz's Favorite Crossword Puzzles	978-0-312-30613-7
Will Shortz Presents Crosswords for 365 Days	978-0-312-36121-1

Easy Crosswords

Easy Crossword Puzzles Volume 15	978-1-250-04486-0
Easy Crossword Puzzles Volume 14	978-1-250-02520-3
Volumes 2–12 also available	

Tough Crosswords

Tough Crossword Puzzles Vol. 13	978-0-312-34240-3
Tough Crossword Puzzles Vol. 12	978-0-312-32442-1
Volumes 9–11 also available	

Sunday Crosswords

Sweet Sunday Crosswords	978-1-250-01592-6
Sunday Crossword Puzzles Volume 38	978-1-250-01544-0
Sunday in the Surf Crosswords	978-1-250-00924-1
Simply Sundays	978-1-250-00390-4
Fireside Sunday Crosswords	978-0-312-64546-5
Snuggle Up Sunday Crosswords	978-0-312-59057-4

Stay in Bed Sunday Crosswords	978-0-312-68144-9
Relaxing Sunday Crosswords	978-0-312-65429-0
Finally Sunday Crosswords	978-0-312-64113-9
Crosswords for a Lazy Sunday	978-0-312-60820-0
Sunday's Best	978-0-312-37637-5
Sunday at Home Crosswords	978-0-312-37834-3

Omnibus

More Monday Crossword Puzzles Omnibus Vol. 2	978-1-250-04493-8
More Tuesday Crossword Puzzles Omnibus Vol. 2	978-1-250-04494-5
Monday Crossword Puzzle Omnibus	978-1-250-02523-4
Tuesday Crossword Puzzle Omnibus	978-1-250-02526-5
Crossword Puzzle Omnibus Vol. 16	978-0-312-36104-1
Sunday Crossword Omnibus Vol. 10	978-0-312-59006-2
Easy Crossword Puzzles Omnibus Volume 10	978-1-250-04924-7
Previous volumes also available	

Portable Size Format

Will Shortz Presents A Year of Crosswords	978-1-250-04487-7
Curious Crosswords	978-1-250-04488-4
Bedside Crosswords	978-1-250-04490-7
Crosswords to Supercharge Your Brainpower	978-1-250-04491-4
Best of Sunday Crosswords	978-1-250-04492-1
Teatime Crosswords	978-1-250-04489-1
Soothing Sunday Crosswords	978-1-250-03917-0
Best of Wednesday Crosswords	978-1-250-03913-2
Best of Thursday Crosswords	978-1-250-03912-5
Sunday Crossword Puzzles Volume 39	978-1-250-03918-7
Stress-Free Solving Crosswords	978-1-250-04921-6
Will Shortz Wants You to Solve Crosswords!	978-1-250-04918-6
Crosswords to Start Your Day	978-1-250-04919-3
Will Shortz Presents Good Times Crosswords	978-1-250-04941-4
Crosswords For Your Commute	978-1-250-04923-0
Super Sundays	978-1-250-04922-3
Easy Does It Crosswords	978-1-250-04920-9
Relax and Unwind Crosswords	978-1-250-03254-6
Smart Sunday Crosswords	978-1-250-03253-9
Vacation for Your Mind Crosswords	978-1-250-03259-1
Crossword Diet	978-1-250-03252-2
Grab & Go Crosswords	978-1-250-03251-5
Colossal Crossword Challenge	978-1-250-03256-0
Holiday Crosswords	978-1-250-01539-6
Crafty Crosswords	978-1-250-01541-9
Homestyle Crosswords	978-1-250-01543-3
Picnic Blanket Crosswords	978-1-250-00391-1
Huge Book of Easy Crosswords	978-1-250-00399-7
Keep Calm and Crossword On	978-0-312-68141-8
Best of Monday Crosswords	978-1-250-00926-5
Best of Tuesday Crosswords	978-1-250-00927-2
Mad About Crosswords	978-1-250-00923-4
All the Crosswords That Are Fit to Print	978-1-250-00925-8
For the Love of Crosswords	978-1-250-02522-7
Sweet and Simple Crosswords	978-1-250-02525-8
Surrender to Sunday Crosswords	978-1-250-02524-1
Easiest Crosswords	978-1-250-02519-7
Will's Best	978-1-250-02531-9
Other volumes also available	

St. Martin's Griffin